# Start with a Hull

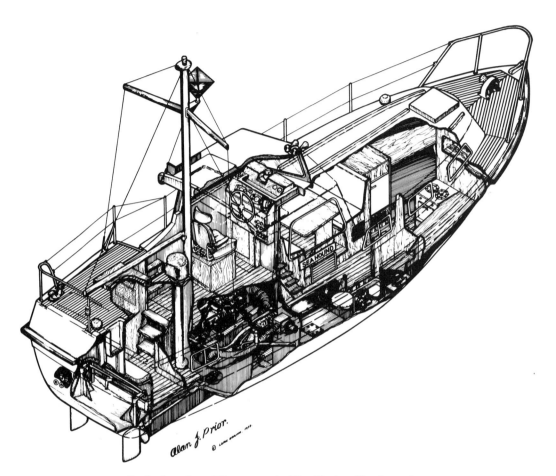

Early drawing of the concept of the Goring-Hardy cruiser

# Start with a Hull

## Fitting out a GRP hull from start to finish

Second edition

## Loris Goring

ADLARD COLES NAUTICAL
London

*To Wellington, the late but very original Sea Hound,
and his walking deck-hand Anne*

Published by Adlard Coles Nautical
an imprint of A & C Black (Publishers) Ltd
35 Bedford Row, London WC1R 4JH

Copyright © Loris Goring 1986, 1992

First published in hardback in Great Britain by
David & Charles (Publishers) Limited 1986
Second edition published in paperback by
Adlard Coles Nautical 1992

ISBN 0 7136-3563-0

A CIP catalogue record for this book is available
from the British Library.

Printed and bound in Great Britain by
J W Arrowsmith Ltd, Bristol

# CONTENTS

# LIST OF ILLUSTRATIONS

# FOREWORD TO THE FIRST EDITION

Although this book is based on, and illustrated with, many drawings and photographs of *Sea Hound of Dart* and therefore biased towards motor cruisers, l hope to have created a balance, so that the book will be of interest and value to both motor boat and sailing enthusiasts who are thinking of completing a glass-reinforced plastic hull. Above all, I hope the book will help readers to organise their ideas for design, materials and construction and give them confidence to undertake their own boatbuilding project.

Perhaps the motto of the SAS will be a spur: 'He who dares, wins.'

# FOREWORD TO THE SECOND EDITION

In this, the second edition of *Start with a hull,* the technical information has been updated and the names of products and suppliers revised so that those interested may be able to go directly to a source for advice and materials.

It says a great deal for the quality of products originally built on to the boat that they have lasted extremely well. However, even the best products wear out, become obsolete and need replacing; I have therefore added an additional chapter giving details of modifications that have been made to the boat to replace the original products and systems.

*Loris Goring*
Brixham, Devon

# 1 FIRST STEPS

If money were unlimited there would be no problem. We would all have the boat of our dreams, built to order by experts. But most yachtsmen are not in that happy state and have to become experts themselves, or at least know when and why to consult the professionals, if they are to make a good job of fitting out a hull.

Safety is of prime importance. In the following chapters I will try to deal with every aspect of amateur construction to ensure that you avoid the pitfalls and make your boat as safe as possible.

The hull, for example, must be suitable for the particular type of water on which it will be used. In the past boats evolved slowly. The hull form was adapted to suit local sea, river or estuary conditions and was made of a material readily available in the area. The result was working boats of remarkable efficiency.

Pleasure yachts have a comparatively short history and it is only in recent years that they have come within reach of ordinary people. The boom in boating — particularly as new techniques were developed and mass-produced glass-reinforced plastic hulls came on to the market — has meant too much careless design and construction. Experimental hull forms have come forth like a rash, often with little thought given to the conditions they will have to endure.

The cost of a master mould can run into many thousands of pounds; even so, it is much less than the cost of producing a prototype motor car. No wonder that the yachtsman has a baffling array of hull forms to choose from.

In the simplest terms, a boat has two basic functions. First, it must operate efficiently in the appropriate sea and river conditions. Second, it must provide shelter and reasonable comfort for the crew.

A canal boat designed for inland waterways with shallow draught, low power and a beam of 6ft 10in (2.08m) is not going to be safe or navigable in a Force 8 gale off Ushant; nor is the blue-water yacht with a 10ft (3m) draught going to proceed too well up a 2ft (0.6m) deep canal. But there are yachtsmen who believe they can find a hull that will perform well in any operational area. It might be pertinent to visit a maritime museum and study the way efficient boats have evolved, then look carefully at the hull form you are considering. True, most old hull forms were designed for carrying cargo, with the comfort and pleasure of the crew of minor importance; but they were designed to carry cargo as quickly and safely as possible. This is not a bad object to keep in mind. I am not saying that all sailing yachtsmen should end up with a Thames barge or a tea clipper but some idea of design and practicability is an advantage when choosing a hull.

For anyone wishing to delve deeper into the intricacies of design and hull form, Appendix B lists books that could be usefully consulted.

## Sailing Boats

Long before Charles II brought the word 'yacht' into the language in 1660, great personages and kings used fast boats to take them around the limited world they knew. The first English yacht was well equipped to deal with awkward harbour masters, as she carried eight guns. In time, sailing yachts were refined (the eight guns being dispensed with to increase speed and comfort). Paid hands did not get the comfort, only the owners, but as paid hands have faded into the past and relatives and friends have taken their place, priorities for comfort had to be evenly distributed.

## Cruising Yachts

These are the direct descendants of the fast, upper-crust passage-makers.

Dr E. A. Pye, a past master at the game of cruising, chose a West Country fishing smack. *Moonraker* was converted for a cruise across the Atlantic, through the Panama Canal, up to British Columbia. E. G. Martin's *Jolie Brise* started life as a Havre pilot cutter and saw him safely through 10,000 miles of cruising across the Atlantic and back. Fishing boats like the famous Brixham sailing trawlers were popular. They had to have a kindly motion so that the crews could work on deck comfortably and the boats would often go on

sailing themselves while the catch was being gutted. A safe and comfortable motion is just as important for a sailing cruiser so that the crew does not get exhausted by violent antics or difficulty in trimming, sail changing and steering.

In the years following World War II when ocean cruising again became possible, a new generation of these working-boat-derived cruisers was built with cut-away forefoot leading into a shorter keel and terminating in a well-raked rudder.

Eric Hiscock's *Wanderer III* designed in 1952 by Laurent Giles & Partners, which is featured in his book *Cruising Under Sail*

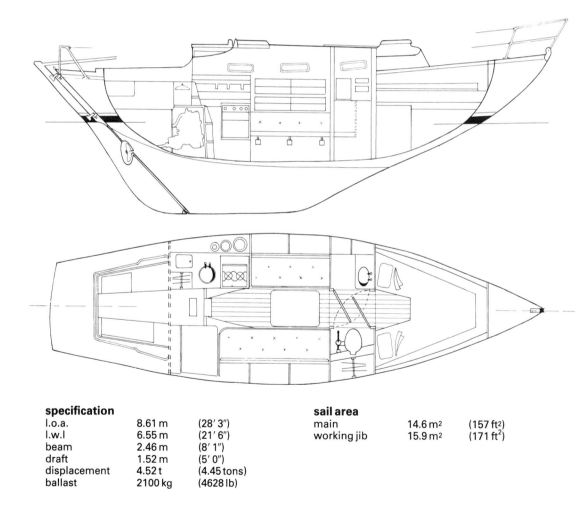

| specification | | | sail area | | |
|---|---|---|---|---|---|
| l.o.a. | 8.61 m | (28' 3") | main | 14.6 m² | (157 ft²) |
| l.w.l | 6.55 m | (21' 6") | working jib | 15.9 m² | (171 ft²) |
| beam | 2.46 m | (8' 1") | | | |
| draft | 1.52 m | (5' 0") | | | |
| displacement | 4.52 t | (4.45 tons) | | | |
| ballast | 2100 kg | (4628 lb) | | | |

**Fig 1** Tyler 28

should be compared to some of the later generation pure cruising boats which are available as complete mouldings from Tylers (Fig 1) the Tyler 28 or the 1979 design by John Sharp, (Fig 2) the Halmatic 30. The Halmatic 30 Mk II is fast and close winded and would probably be much happier than the average crew out in a blow. With a displacement of 4.5 tons unladen and a ballast ratio of 50 per cent, you have a yacht which has the reasonably comfortable motion essential for a cruising boat.

The low profile of the cabin top is typical in both the Tyler and Halmatic yachts and the rest of the deck area is uncluttered for working. The low profile could be a safety factor when decks are swept by rogue waves.

The Volvo MD78 17hp diesel engine would be more than ample to drive this hull at its best speed of about 6.3 knots. For the home builder, one attractive feature of the Halmatic 30 Mk II is the availability of an accommodation module moulded in GRP. Although too much GRP inside a boat can give the feeling that you are living in a refrigerator, with cushioning and relieved by plenty of teak woodwork, there are distinct advantages. The hull will have much greater strength, eliminating the need for extra structural framing and it gives a good foundation to build on and finish. This saves the most valuable commodity after money — time.

When selecting a sailing-boat hull, bear in mind that any boat that sails sluggishly on an inefficient hull is not going to be fun to own. In fact, you will regret the time you spent building it. Take time to compare performance and study the yachting press for reports and comments by journalists and readers. Digging out every bit of information is time well spent.

## Cruiser Racers

This is the generic term for sailing yachts descended from pure racing craft. They are more extreme in concept, often with so much bias towards racing design as to be occasionally suspect as cruisers.

To obtain speed, wetted area is cut down to a minimum, a deep fin keel being separated from the rudder which is hung on its own skeg. Light displacement and huge sail areas often lead to conditions of stability that can only be handled by a large crew of beefy young men. The hull form dates to the 1950s when yachts like John Guzwell's *Trekka*, a development of Laurent Giles & Partners' earlier tiny ocean-racer *Sopranino*, made long ocean passages. As the racing-boat hull forms have been refined by the fire of competition, so the much needed characteristics of the cruising boat go overboard. Many, for example, will not lie quiet while the helmsman leaves the tiller and many of these boats cannot be allowed to dry out alongside a wall without the risk of the forward end dropping.

Most of us sail short-handed with an amateur crew who do not know the ropes as well as they might. If you choose a boat that is too biased towards a racing machine you won't be happy at the way an inexperienced crew is able to cope. In certain circumstances, this could lead to not being able to cope at all.

## Bilge-keel Designs

These are thought by some to be the answer when a boat has to dry out on a mud berth or which will be used in both shallow and deep cruising areas. They do not go to windward as well as the deep-keeled yacht but serve the first purpose admirably, provided the keels are adequate in strength and joined to the hull in such a way that the enormous strain sometimes imposed does not result in fatigue or structural damage. Many hulls are offered with alternative keel forms and you choose the one best suited to your own cruising area.

## Centre-plate or Drop-keel Yachts

These have the advantage of good performance from low wetted areas and, with the ability to reduce draught by keel retraction, can be used for pottering in shallow waters. On large boats the keel lifting mechanism can become quite complex, with hydraulic gear needed to lift several tons up and down via a small operating lever on the pump. Smaller yachts have much simpler mechanisms with winding gear and wire rope for the operation.

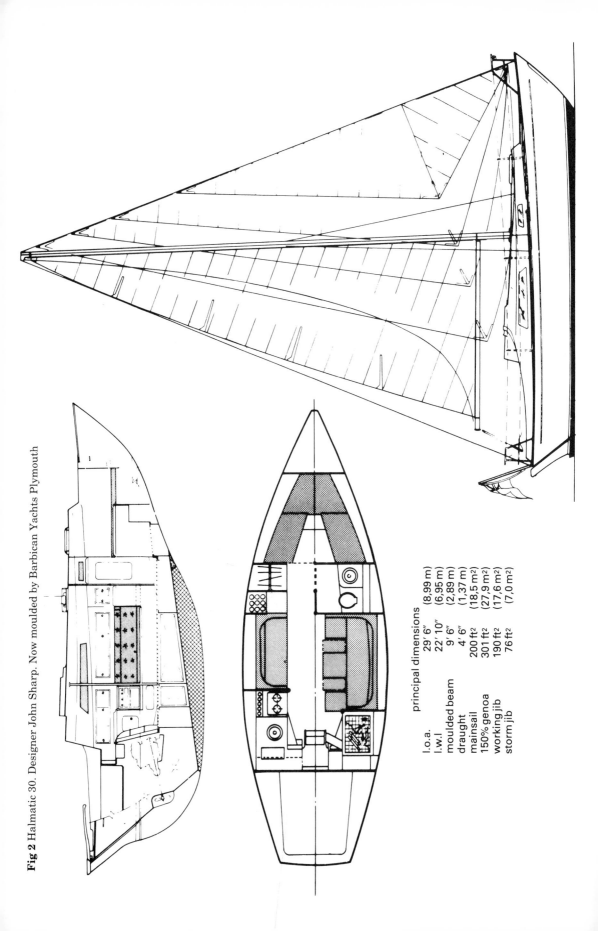

**Fig 2** Halmatic 30. Designer John Sharp. Now moulded by Barbican Yachts Plymouth

principal dimensions

| | | |
|---|---|---|
| l.o.a. | 29′ 6″ | (8,99 m) |
| l.w.l | 22′ 10″ | (6,95 m) |
| moulded beam | 9′ 6″ | (2,89 m) |
| draught | 4′ 6″ | (1,37 m) |
| mainsail | 200 ft² | (18,5 m²) |
| 150% genoa | 301 ft² | (27,9 m²) |
| working jib | 190 ft² | (17,6 m²) |
| storm jib | 76 ft² | (7,0 m²) |

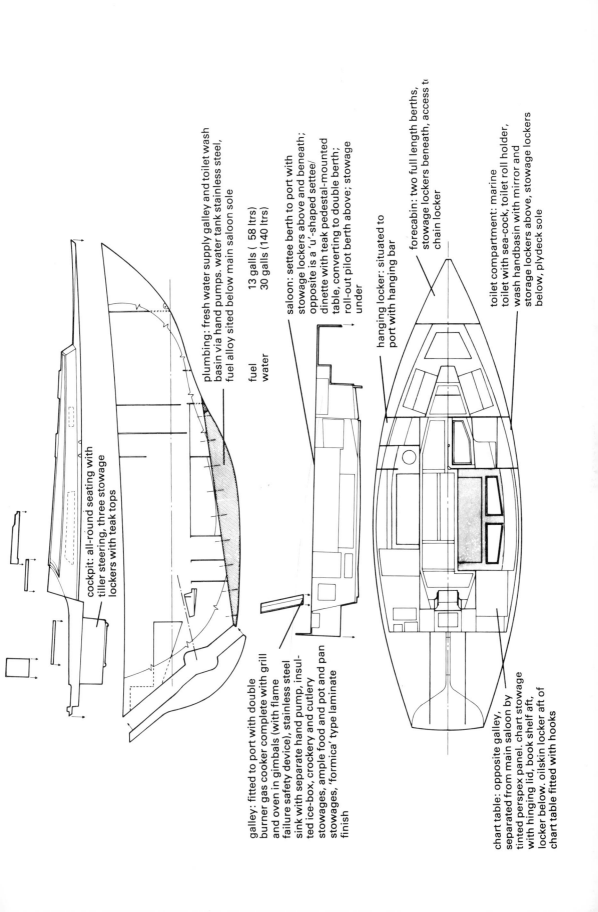

cockpit: all-round seating with tiller steering, three stowage lockers with teak tops

plumbing: fresh water supply galley and toilet wash basin via hand pumps. water tank stainless steel, fuel alloy sited below main saloon sole

fuel      13 galls ( 58 ltrs)
water     30 galls (140 ltrs)

saloon: settee berth to port with stowage lockers above and beneath; opposite is a 'u'-shaped settee/dinette with teak pedestal-mounted table, converting to double berth; roll-out pilot berth above; stowage under

hanging locker: situated to port with hanging bar

forecabin: two full length berths, stowage lockers beneath, access to chain locker

toilet compartment: marine toilet with sea-cock, toilet roll holder, wash handbasin with mirror and storage lockers above, stowage lockers below, plydeck sole

galley: fitted to port with double burner gas cooker complete with grill and oven in gimbals (with flame failure safety device), stainless steel sink with separate hand pump, insulted ice-box, crockery and cutlery stowages, ample food and pot and pan stowages, 'formica' type laminate finish

chart table: opposite galley, separated from main saloon by tinted perspex panel. chart stowage with hinging lid, book shelf aft, locker below. oilskin locker aft of chart table fitted with hooks

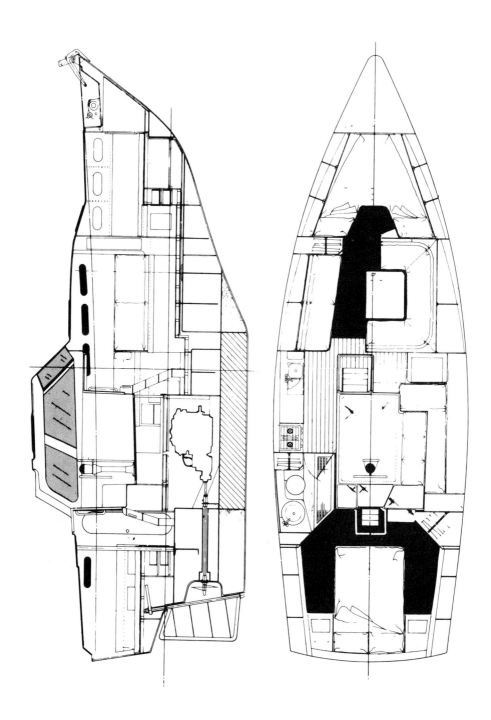

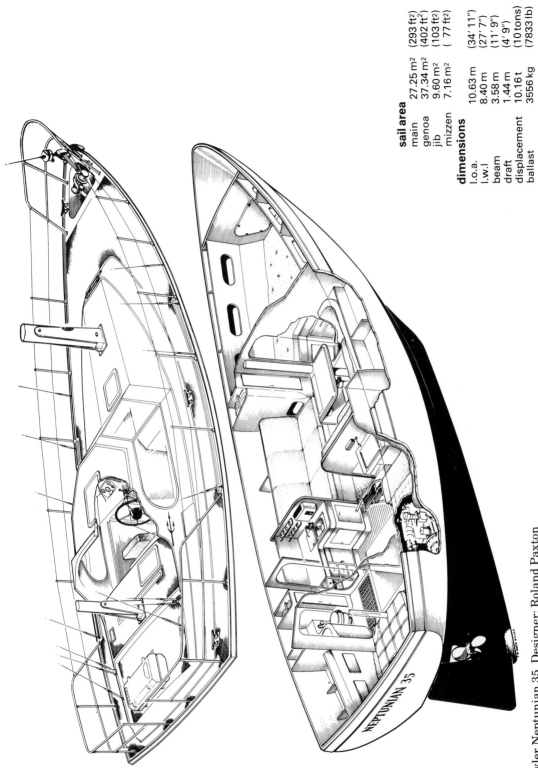

| sail area | | |
|---|---|---|
| main | 27.25 m² | (293 ft²) |
| genoa | 37.34 m² | (402 ft²) |
| jib | 9.60 m² | (103 ft²) |
| mizzen | 7.16 m² | ( 77 ft²) |
| **dimensions** | | |
| l.o.a. | 10.63 m | (34′ 11″) |
| l.w.l | 8.40 m | (27′ 7″) |
| beam | 3.58 m | (11′ 9″) |
| draft | 1.44 m | (4′ 9″) |
| displacement | 10.16 t | (10 tons) |
| ballast | 3556 kg | (7833 lb) |

**Fig 3** Tyler Neptunian 35. Designer: Roland Paxton

For the owner wishing to change cruising grounds by towing the boat on a trailer, the shallow draught and retractable keel make it easy to design a road trailer for towing behind the family car.

You do lose some cabin space where the keel and lifting gear intrude, but the boat that does everything without some sacrifice has yet to be invented.

All sailing boats appear to have one fault in common: a total lack of consideration in the position of the auxiliary engine. It is usually placed in the region of the main bulkhead or under the centre of the cockpit floor where it is almost totally inaccessible.

I have seen engines that cannot be reached around the sides, where access is through a minute hatch in the cockpit locker and where gear-boxes are canted down so as to make oil changing practically impossible. I get incensed with this aspect of design and make no apology for emphasising these points again in the engine installation section.

Before you buy any hull, especially a sailing-boat hull, examine the space intended for the engine and look at a completed installation. When all design points in a hull seem to be equal, give your cheque to the moulder with the best engine access. It should not be necessary to tear the boat apart to remove an engine needing serious attention.

## Motor Sailers

These have gained great popularity in recent years and there are a fair number of moulded hulls and superstructures to choose from. While the purist insists that the motor sailer neither sails nor motors well, for many yachtsmen its attractiveness is the sheer practicality of the features offered. It will go in any direction — and in rough weather. Hull forms, perhaps more full than the ideal blue-water cruising boat, nevertheless usually have good keels and well-protected rudders and screws: a seaworthy craft. Fig 3 shows the Tyler-moulded Neptunian 35 designed by Roland Paxton. This one is at the ambitious end of the self-build market but offers the craftsman a worthwhile oppor-

tunity to try his skills. There are hulls on the market of poor form and quality which would not be worth spending any time or money on.

The Neptunian has a large sheltered wheel-house, comfortable in bad weather yet giving the helmsman a good view of sails and set of the wind. Too much windage or top hamper is bad on any type of boat. This wheel-house does not destroy the fine form of the superstructure.

In this category you will find boats designed with greater emphasis on one or other of the features. Some with a bias to sailing will have finer lines for performance; others with more powerful engines to drive a fuller displacement form. Decide carefully where you want the emphasis to be.

## Motor Boats: Displacement Types

Displacement types are slow and steady. Canal narrow boats, for instance, are restricted in speed so that they do not wash away the banks. These and the displacement type of sea-going boat are designed to push the water out of the way as they proceed at a sedate pace. Hull forms vary to cope with specific areas of use.

*Sea Hound of Dart* (Fig 4) has a sea-going displacement hull. Like other displacement boats it is not for the nervous yachtsman who feels that at the first sign of a cloud he must make a speedy dash to harbour.

A well-designed displacement hull is economical to operate and gives a feeling of confidence in normal weather conditions. When the going gets tough they plod on in a more seaworthy manner than the crew. Again, a nice deep keel gives excellent directional stability and a full hull form makes for plenty of accommodation space.

## Motor Boats: Semi-displacement Types

Although these are designed as a compromise — the rounded sections of a displacement boat are retained but fined down aft to derive dynamic lift when plenty of power is applied — they have tremendous seaworthiness and speed.

Cost is a major factor. Two hefty engines are needed for convenience and safety. These are costly to buy and high fuel consumption makes for high fuel running costs. However, professionals like the police, pilots and coastguards find them admirable for even the most hazardous duties. The fine lines mean limited accommodation space but they can maintain speed at sea in conditions that would make a fast maritime pancake-bottomed boat slow down and become unseaworthy.

For more years than I care to remember I have been writing about the virtues of the Nelson 34 hull as a supreme example of a seaworthy fast motor boat. Similar in concept is the John Askham-designed Weymouth 34 moulded by Halmatic and available as a part-assembly for home completion. Fig 5 shows the general arrangement and, like Tylers, the Halmatic mouldings are first class. Both designs make excellent fast cruising boats where speedy passages make sure you are seldom caught out and, if you are unlucky, they keep going through quite nasty seas.

## Planing Craft

All sorts of hull configuration have been developed to move boats fast over water with minimum power. The Ray Hunt deep 'V' hulls were, in their racing days, classic shapes that, under power, were seaworthy craft able to maintain high cruising speeds in quite difficult conditions. On the other hand, there are maritime pancakes which gain their speed with a very flat run aft at the expense of seaworthiness. They are fine on inland waterways and a calm sea but are blown about like paper bags when the sea gets up. They suffer badly from directional instability, especially when running before the wind and sea when the stern gets pushed round to the point of broaching. They can be decidedly uncomfortable as they fall off quartering waves on the bow not knowing quite which way to fall and so keeping the helmsman on tenterhooks. In bad seas, the only way to cope is to slow them right down when their light displacement makes them decidedly uncomfortable for the crew. Accepting their limitations, they can give excellent accommodation space and make a good boat for calm waters.

Large topsides and broad transoms make for excellent accommodation and those of us cramped in less spacious craft might gaze on these gin palaces with envy. If your priority is for living aboard and entertaining on the marina, fine. If you wish to go to sea and make passages in unpredictable weather, the temptation to fit out this kind of hull should be resisted.

## Trawler Yachts

This type of motor boat has its enthusiasts and, like the cruiser/racer yacht sometimes ends up being neither one thing nor another. Above the water-line it is made to look like a tough working boat with lantern wheel-house jutting forward in an aggressive way with much windage aft to give deck accommodation. This makes for a lot of top hamper, especially when an outside steering position is plonked on the top. Below the water-line there is seldom a true trawler displacement hull. What you will probably find is either a semi-displacement form with rounded bilges and flat run aft or a shallow 'V' that generates enough dynamic lift to give the boat mid-range speeds economically.

As I write I can see through the window our fleet of Brixham fishing trawlers. Not one has a hull shape of a trawler yacht. The professionals still favour slow boats, even with the pressure of getting their fish fresh to market.

If you do decide on a thoroughbred trawler-type hull you can find them for home completion and a very seaworthy boat they will make, too. You won't need the heavy displacement of a loaded fishing boat and medium displacement forms are inexpensively driven and seaworthy, well able to take the smaller weights associated with the interior fitting of a pleasure boat.

Whichever type of hull you eventually choose, do not get carried away with enthusiasm, so that the drawbacks of a particular hull form or its accommodation are overlooked. Love is blind and I would suggest that the prospective amateur boatbuilder is, too. A little cautionary thinking will do no harm. In fact, you

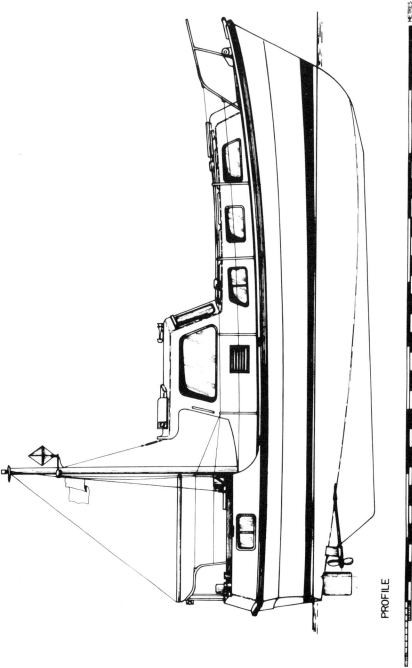

PROFILE

METRES
FEET.

SCALE 1:25

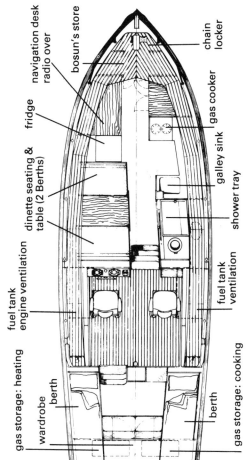

**Section through midship looking aft**

heater
services
dinette/2 berths
wine locker
soil tank
lockers
wc
shower tray
tank access

navigation desk
radio over
bosun's store
fridge
chain locker
gas cooker
galley sink
dinette seating &
table (2 Berths)
shower tray
fuel tank
engine ventilation
fuel tank
ventilation
gas storage: heating
wardrobe
berth
berth
gas storage: cooking

**Plan**

GORING-HARDY 940 CLASS

scale 1:25

round bilge displacement hull

| | | |
|---|---|---|
| loa | 30' 9" | 9.40m |
| beam | 10' 7" | 3.25m |
| draft | 3' 3" | 1.00m |
| power | 2 Perkins 4.108m diesels | |
| range | 260nm | |

**Fig 4** *Sea Hound of Dart*

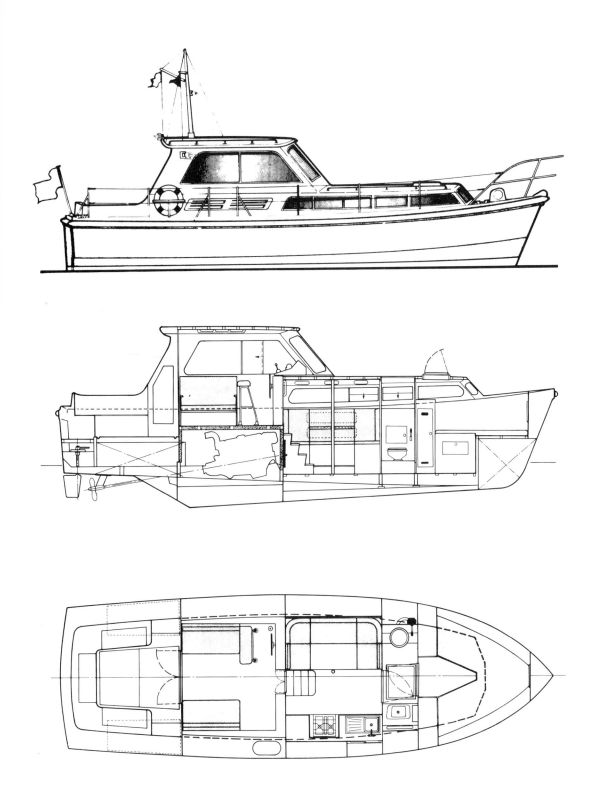

**Fig 5** Weymouth 34. Designer: John Askham

should really go out in a finished boat on an expedition which will give you plenty of time to assess its true potential. Who would buy a car without first going out for a test drive? Talk to owners of boats similar to the one you are contemplating. There are a few owners' associations, but with a bit of detective work you should be able to find professionally built boats with the same hull. The superstructure might be different and interior detail altered, but the basic qualities should be apparent.

## Hull Size and Running Costs

An important factor is the relative cost of completing different sizes and types of boat. For example, the cost of engining a canal narrow boat of 30ft (9.1m) is quite small and would be little different for a boat of 40ft (12.1m). On the other hand, the difference in price between engining a fast-planing hull of 30ft (9.1m) and one of 40ft (12.1m) would be enormous. A twin-engined installation is often more than double the price of a single-engine install-ation. Not only are components duplicated but wiring and fuel systems have to be-come more complex. In Chapter 5 I will deal with this in more detail, but both building and future running costs should come into the initial planning. Even the overall length will affect running costs as marinas charge on boat length. A 32ft (9.7m) hull might well cost less in berthing charges than a 29ft (8.8m) hull that has overhanging davits to carry the tender, so putting up its overall length to 33ft (10m). Most marinas charge on the overhangs so it might well be better to do without, unless perhaps you go for a handsome yacht that carries a bowsprit.

Future running expenses must be borne in mind if you are eventually to enjoy boating and not be inhibited by cost. Even an extra can of anti-fouling might stretch the budget when it comes to fitting out.

I tried to be realistic about how big a boat I could build and maintain comfortably, bearing in mind the small motor boat that I had cruised for a number of years previously. I decided on a sea-going displacement motor cruiser, although this type of craft has not found much favour in recent years, the planing and semi-displacement types being very much more prominent.

As luck would have it, I found that Tylers of Tonbridge had just purchased the rights to mould a displacement hull designed by D. D. H. Lefeber of Eista Werf NV in Holland. Fig 6 shows the original which I felt was pretty well what I was looking for, although it did seem to need a better superstructure at the aft end. I was delighted when John Tyler agreed to a stern cabin modification and the new design would be known as the Goring-Hardy.

For the prospective amateur builder it is interesting to know what goes on in the professional designer's mind. Lefeber's idea was to create a 'sturdy and workman-like boat with easy handling, good fendering all round: let's say a nicer kind of work launch'. It may well be a coincidence that some of the Nelson 34 boats were finished off in Holland, but the Nelson and Eista Werf boats have strikingly similar sheerlines.

The Hardy 9.40 has a relatively fine entrance with well-veed sections and deep forefoot for better directional stability. For any type of sea-going craft the possibility of broaching has to be taken into account. The long keel of this design ends in a hefty deadwood which is a prime contributor to directional stability. As Sea Hound of Dart was to have twin engines we decided to modify the deadwood so that it ended in an angled skeg, but plenty of area was retained in the deep keel to take care of directional stability.

Aft of the midsection, which still has a good deadrise of 23°, the sections and buttocks flatten and straighten to give a long clean run, helping speed potential and minimising squatting. Squat occurs in displacement hulls when they are driven faster than their ideal speed/length ratio. This ratio has such an important bearing on seaworthiness that it is worth examining in greater detail.

The speed/length ratio of a displacement hull is given by the formula:

$$\frac{V}{\sqrt{L}} = \frac{\text{Speed in Knots}}{\text{Square root of water-line length in feet}}$$

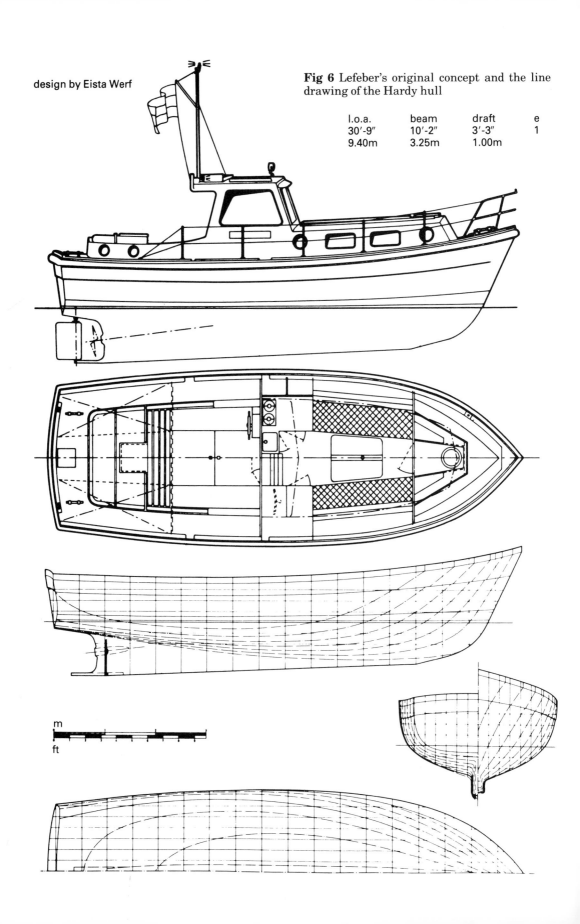

design by Eista Werf

**Fig 6** Lefeber's original concept and the line drawing of the Hardy hull

| l.o.a. | beam | draft | e |
|--------|-------|-------|---|
| 30'-9" | 10'-2" | 3'-3" | 1 |
| 9.40m | 3.25m | 1.00m | |

m

ft

This simple formula has a vital bearing on the powering of the craft and her best cruising speed. The speed also has a crucial bearing on how the boat performs in a nasty sea. When the ratio is at unity, any displacement hull has minimum resistance to the water. In theory, *Sea Hound* needs a minimum amount of engine power when she is being driven through the water at a speed of the square root of her water-line length, ie approximately 5.3 knots. As the speed/length ratio increases so do the power requirements — quite dramatically, too. At a speed/length ratio of 1.4, the resistance has increased about five times and at a ratio of 1.6 about seven times.

Although a speed/length ratio at unity might seem the best cruising speed because minimum power is used, this is not so. Sea-going craft and even those in rivers are likely to meet steep waves or strong currents of up to 8 knots. No yachtsman is going to be happy going X knots backwards. The kind of craft most of us are able to afford are short of water-line length needed to attain higher speeds easily. Therefore, they have to be designed with speed/length ratios above unity.

The wave-making characteristics of the displacement hull at these greater than unity speed/length ratios must also be taken into account. The increase in resistance as speed builds up is because power is being used to create waves. These waves are as shown in Fig 7A. Kenneth Barnaby in his classic work *Basic Naval Architecture* (Hutchinson) gives the formula that states that the number of waves in a boat's length is:

$$\frac{1.795}{(V/\sqrt{L})^2}$$

This means that for a given length of hull at a certain speed/length ratio there will be one wave at the bow and another exactly at the stern precisely one wave length from crest to crest. This speed/length ratio works out at 1.34. The boat will trim level on these two crests. This applies to any boat of the displacement type. If you apply more power by opening up the engine, the aft transverse wave moves away from the stern and the aft end begins to squat in the water of the trough. Fig 7B shows how you can waste a lot of power making a big hole in the water. *Sea Hound*'s water-line length is 27.5ft (8.3m) and the anticipated ideal speed was expected to be:

$$1.34 \times \sqrt{27.50} = 7.02 \text{ knots}$$

With the excellent flat run aft I anticipated a comfortable cruising speed slightly above this at 7.5 knots and a top speed in the region of 8.8 knots. This latter figure would enable the boat to keep going in the Alderney race!

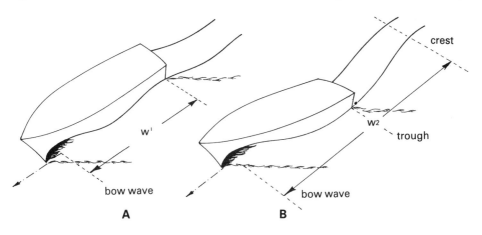

**Fig 7** Wave making

Another important fact about a displacement hull in a following sea is that if you can keep the boat's speed down to a speed/length ratio of 1.34 or so, you stand less chance of getting pooped. The propeller stream of a squatting boat stands a good chance of producing instability in a following wave, allowing it to break over the transom.

While thinking about the worst conditions one can be caught out in, I decided that, when designing the new aft cabin, it should provide space for the tender. I was thinking of the tremendous leverage davits would have on the transom if a wave crashed over the tender hanging there.

On discussing the hull form with Mr Lefeber I learned that he had designed for a speed/length ratio of 1.45 so the designed speed was expected to be:

$$1.45 \times \sqrt{27.5} = 7.6 \text{ knots cruising speed}$$

It is well worth while finding out these figures for the hull you intend to complete. Performance or seakindliness that falls short of your expectations when you have put hundreds of hours into finishing a hull would be a big disappointment.

When talking to the professional, write questions down beforehand and be specific. This may sound obvious, but time costs the professional money and he is not going to be pleased if you ask a lot of silly questions. But he will be helpful if he knows you have given every aspect careful thought.

## Involvement in Design

If you are content to finish one of the boats available in kit form and don't intend to make any deviation from the plans, your information-seeking will be minimal. If you are to design the complete interior and alter the superstructure and engining, as I did, the demands are very much greater.

In altering any design you must understand something of naval architecture yourself or employ a professional designer to work through the new concept. Members of the United Kingdom Yacht Brokers, Designers and Surveyors Association have the necessary skills and qualifications.

I knew of someone finishing a cruiser/racer sailing yacht who, without consulting the designer, put into the boat a much heavier engine than specified. The consequence was that the excellent sailing performance was completely ruined because the sailing dynamics were upset by the extra weight aft.

Weight alterations in any craft mean that stability calculations have to be recalculated. Capsizing moments must be kept within safe limits. With planing or semi-displacement craft, too much extra weight over the designed limit means difficulty in getting on to the plane or finding that designed speed is impossible to achieve. In trying to drive an underpowered hull 'over the hump' extra fuel will be gobbled up.

There are no short cuts if modifications are made. The amateur home constructor should seek professional advice.

## People on Boats

Any boat must be comfortable to live and work aboard.

A narrow fast motor-boat hull with priority given to space for the engines can only give cramped living space for the crew. A nice fat boat with spacious accommodation may well behave in a disgraceful fashion at the first sign of a heaving wave. Bear these points in mind when choosing your hull.

Professional builders seem to delight in putting the maximum number of berths into the smallest hull they can market and appear to think that if not on deck, crews are lying horizontally below. A 26ft (7.9m) boat with six berths will hardly be comfortable on a wet day when no one wants to go ashore and all have to be fed and watered. While it is pleasant to take friends cruising, there is nothing like the confines of a boat for bringing out the worst in human nature!

Work on board must be made as easy and pleasant as possible. Small design faults can become a source of major irritation: inadequate side decks that jam feet between coaming and cabin top; deck areas so full of rigging that the crew must be contortionists in order to make a sail change, and so on. Remember that adequate working space could have a direct effect on the safety of the craft.

I shall go into more detail about these points later, but there is more to consider before you buy the hull.

### Yourself

Your enthusiasm can be taken for granted. If you are a family man, you need to canvass family opinion.

When I was building *Sea Hound of Dart* I originally anticipated about eighteen months of spare-time work to finish her. The project actually took two years and three months. Fortunately, I have a tolerant wife! During the construction I had just eleven non-working days. Holidays were spent at boat shows and suppliers, ordering and selecting the equipment to put aboard. Make no mistake, it is a big commitment. However, if you, and those around you, understand this, all should be well. And if you have young children they can be a great asset for squeezing into otherwise inaccessible parts of the hull to put nuts on bolts or hold items while you fix them from the outside!

Being aware of your own skills and limitations is important. You do need a good degree of woodworking skill to fit out the interior of a boat but, even so, there are some boat kits which need little more than screwdriver, hammer and common sense to achieve good results.

Recognising your own limitations is the first step to overcoming them. In my own case, plumbing is not my scene. I can fix a water-pipe compression joint exactly as described by the maker and when the water is turned on I get soaked. Anything you can't safely tackle should be subcontracted. I found many experts willing to help out, sometimes in their spare time. Some tasks are impossible to carry out alone, anyway — for example, when the rubber fender was fitted on *Sea Hound*. Each section weighed about 110lb (50kg) and measured 11ft (3.36m); it took three of us to get each one into position, drill and bolt them up.

Professional help does put up the cost but it shortens building time. Always ask for estimates and don't distract the man on the job as his time costs you money.

Try to appreciate the business people who will be supplying the necessities for your boat. A friendly working relationship is worth its weight in gold. A considerate customer will be appreciated. Make out your orders accurately and allow plenty of time for processing and delivery.

### The Cost of Construction

This is where we sink the myth that if you have to ask the price you cannot afford it. It's a big mistake not to work out the price of the finished boat before you start. You may find that home construction will not save you quite as much as you think.

The cost of a bare hull can be a temptation for the unwary. The add-on costs will be much greater than the cost of the moulding. A kit boat will be cost itemised; the final price of a completed boat, bought as a bare hull, can vary enormously, depending on the degree of sophistication you want. A basic estimate might be about three times the price of the bare hull.

There is no short cut to a sensible estimate: you price the full specification.

In Appendix A I have listed the materials and equipment that I costed out on my own boat. As prices date I have left the space for your own estimated prices for individual items. Your own list is bound to vary, depending on your budget and the equipment and finish you want. If you are aghast at the total and need to pare down specifications to keep within the budget, cut out only the fancy stuff and not the items that will guarantee a safe, seaworthy vessel. Bollards before barometers!

If you are lucky, you may be able to buy items at trade prices, on special offer or from bankrupt stock. The amateur cannot expect the chandler to fall over himself to give discount. Although three gross screws might seem a large order to you, to the chandler this is still small beer. If you can get agreement for the whole list of items from one supplier you might be in a position to get better terms. Often you can cut out the middle-man by buying direct from manufacturers. For example, I found a local firm, experts in stainless-steel welding, who turned out to be suppliers to one of the biggest chandler's. They were happy to supply me direct and, better still, were able to make up special fittings to my own design at much lower cost than production items. Some moulding suppliers run their own chandlery stores stocking all the items you need to finish their hull. They can be competitive, but prices should be checked. You can ask for pro forma invoices — that is, invoices giving the price of goods delivered to you, before confirmation of the actual order. The actual price is then known before commitment is made.

A big temptation is to buy cheap products. Beware of false economy. A cheap sea-cock that corrodes away in a couple of years and sinks your boat is hardly inexpensive. A boat that is to operate in fresh water can, perhaps, be built to a less demanding specification than a sea-going boat where the corrosive environment can, literally, be lethal. Looking to long-term maintenance, I have always found that products of quality give lasting satisfaction. They offer greater safety and the manufacturers are likely to be still around if things do go wrong and you need service or repairs.

By opting for simplicity of design one can safely cut down cost. A hand-operated sea toilet will be much less expensive than an electrically operated one. Pumping sewage overboard through a sea-cock will be less expensive, if environmental laws allow, than pumping into a holding tank.

Another acceptable way to cut down costs is to scour the market for special offers, unwanted stock, bankrupt stock and marine auctions. Be cautious over second-hand goods, especially used ones, and out-of-date items. Some excellent firms in the marine trade can service items they produced in the year dot, but, generally speaking, modern design has made great strides in quality and fitness for purpose.

## Outside Financing

It is possible to finance the self-built boat and some companies will make an advance for the purchase of the hull, engines, etc. Naturally, they have to protect their investment so will usually insist on a regular survey of work in progress to ensure that standards are being maintained.

If you fail to keep up the payments they want a marketable property for resale. Interest rates are high. If you are temporarily financially embarrassed but foresee a sharp rise in future income, then this form of finance for your project might be worth considering. Once the boat is built and registered a loan can often be converted to a full marine mortgage. Up to that time the agreement will be a straightforward hire-purchase agreement with all the small print strictures this entails.

## Cash Flow and Ordering

Unless you are fortunate with storage space, you must give consideration to storage of materials and cash flow before the project starts. I built my boat in the open, but I did meet someone who was fitting out his Nelson 34 in the ballroom attached to his elegant house. I don't know if the sprung floor created difficulties in getting levels, but the space was a treat.

Suppliers should be given exact specifications of the goods you want, plus expected delivery dates. Manufacturers' and chandlers' catalogues vary considerably in the technical information they offer, so a letter or telephone call might also be necessary. It is cheaper to do this beforehand than parcel and post back an incorrect item. Not all firms will accept back unsuitable goods. Read the small print for terms and conditions. Even in these days of consumer protection there may be clauses that incur penalties. Minimum order values are a case in point. While it is accepted that processing a small order can be time-consuming and therefore costly, some charges are ridiculous. For example, one manufacturer of fasteners has a minimum order charge of £80 — an embarrassment to a customer needing a few bolts or screws.

When taking delivery, read the conditions regarding damage to goods before you sign for them. As the print is usually so small and you might not wish to delay the delivery man, all you can do is sign 'Accepted Unseen'. Claims have to be registered within a stated period if there are shortages or damage. It is irritating to have to read all this when you could be getting on with something more positive, but it is in your own interests should things go wrong.

**Paper-work**
This must be included in your estimate of the time you will spend building your boat. Making out orders, receiving invoices, writing letters and paying bills are all part of the project. If you can minimise the number of firms you deal with, so much the better. If you can arrange monthly accounts this saves time. Some firms give an extra discount for promptly settled bills.

**Storage**
Even if you could afford to have all the building materials, timber, chandlery, etc delivered at the same time, unless you have an empty barn or outbuilding at your disposal, storage is going to be a problem. Certain materials deteriorate in damp conditions and others have a limited shelf life. Adhesives and sealants 'go off' if stored too long and it is economical to purchase them in small quantities to fit in with the building programme.

Storage also brings in the question of safety. Small quantities of resin, thinners and paint cleaners will not infringe the laws relating to the storage of dangerous chemicals. Even so, they are highly inflammable. You must take precautions. If in doubt, the local fire service will advise, but if you are sensible and make sure that storage instructions given on labels are followed, you should have no trouble.

I was fortunate in that I have a large workshop and I was able to utilise space under the house. I was able to buy and store all the teak planks, rough sawn, and 8 × 4ft (2,440 × 1,220mm) marine plywood, at the start of the project. As it was just before inflation took off, by the time I had finished building costs had risen by 150 per cent. It is worth while keeping an eye on inflation trends.

**Arranging the Building Site**
If you have room, building a boat at home has many advantages. One, naturally, is cost. Boat-yard space is quite expensive. This can be a heavy financial drain, espe-

cially if building time has to be extended. If you have to use a boat-yard you will most likely have to sign a special agreement which may limit the professional help you can bring into the yard. This is understandable. The owner of the yard, if work is slack, will not want outsiders taking over jobs his own workmen could do. However, this will be very limiting for you if you need specialist advice and labour, or if you have friends who are experienced craftsmen. Time taken travelling to the site must be taken into account. Scout out all possibilities of building close to home, if your own garden is not suitable. My own garden was too small and steep, but I had a good neighbour who let me use part of his lawn. The fact that he is Captain Adrian Small who has captained *The Golden Hind* and *Nonsuch* replicas might have had something to do with it!

Site security is important. Most marine insurers have a policy to cover risks while building. Making the hull secure against theft of tools or equipment is difficult in the first stages of construction. Any access ladder should be removed, chained and locked and, if necessary, temporary doors with locks should be fitted.

**The Building Cradle**
The moulding shop will probably want to remove the hull from the mould fairly quickly after certain reinforcing has been put in. The mould is an expensive item to keep out of use. There will usually be some form of standard cradle for each type of hull and you should find out if one is available. You must have some form of cradle to hold the boat level so that all later fittings are plumb with the water-line.

The choice will be between buying, hiring or making your own cradle. It may be made of wood or steel. Which of these choices and materials you make will depend on your circumstances. The steel cradle, even for a 30ft (9.1m) boat, is a heavy item and not tucked away easily during the sailing season. It does, however, give excellent support during transportation of the hull to and from your building site and, when winter gales blow, you should have no fears about the boat blowing over.

The moulders should be prepared either to offer to get the cradle made or to let you have suitably dimensioned plans so that you can make one yourself or have it made locally. Your telephone directory is the shortest route to a steel fabricator. Small firms often do an excellent job at reasonable cost.

A wooden cradle can be made from second-hand timber bolted together, but don't be fooled into thinking that timber and bolts are less expensive than steel. Long bolts and steel reinforcing plates to stop the wood splitting are quite pricey and 4 × 4in (102 × 102mm) and 4 × 2in (102 × 51mm) second-hand timber hardly less so. Either type of cradle is best bolted together. It's easy then to take it apart later for storage.

I first hired, then eventually bought, a steel cradle which has proved an excellent investment.

The design of the cradle is important. It is not meant solely to keep the boat somewhere near upright for winter storage. It has to keep the boat perfectly upright and provide sufficient support so that the keel is supported at about 3ft (914mm) intervals throughout the midsection of the hull and the underpart of the hull is held firmly so that distortion does not occur on severe pressure points. In any case, the keel should have extra support at either end of the cradle to prevent distortion when work is being done on the forward and after ends of the deck. Fig 8 shows points to be considered in a good boatbuilding cradle design, and its siting.

A   No matter what material the cradle is made of, unless put on a perfectly level surface, it can suffer torsion. It will transmit this so that the hull becomes twisted. Railway sleepers are useful on soft ground as their area of contact with both cradle and ground is such that the load is well spread. As well as the main cross-pieces on the cradle ends, there should be several cross-members to add to stiffness and to give support at several places on the keel.

B   You should also have loose cross-members, made from blocks of wood, and wedges to give support outside the cradle towards the extremities.

C   With a steel cradle, blocks of marine-grade plywood are secured at each cross-member to prevent contact between steel and GRP, since the GRP could suffer compression damage.

D   The weight of the boat must be taken on the length of the keel and the corner supports of the cradle only serve to keep the boat upright. The corners of any cradle should be made so that the boat just rests comfortably on the supports. Wedging can be used on wooden cradles. On this cradle, 'D'-section rubber fendering takes the chafe. The fendering is fitted to wooden blocks which are coach-bolted to the steel legs.

E   Grass and weeds should be removed from under the boat as they can be a fire hazard in dry weather.

F   Well before the hull is due for delivery, check the access road to the building site. For a substantial boat there will be the weight consideration. The local authority road-works department will advise. Certain sized loads will require police permission and possibly an escort. The moulder will arrange this for delivery but at launching time it is your responsibility.

G   Trees that obstruct highway access may have to be lopped. Certain rules govern the overhang of trees on public roads. Your local authority will advise. If the access road is private you must approach the owner of the tree.

H   Overhead power cables and telephone wires are a hazard. At a cost you might be able to have a line temporarily disconnected.

Check with the appropriate authority if there is the slightest doubt that an obstruction will occur. If possible, arrange a working supply of electricity which can be by cable from a domestic supply nearby. My supply came by a portable cable drum from the house. Check the cable rating if there is a long run as voltage drop can reduce power so that power tools will not give of their best.

I   Spreaders and lifting strops are usually considered part of the next section (Crane Hire), but not necessarily so. They are an extra that you might have to hire separ-

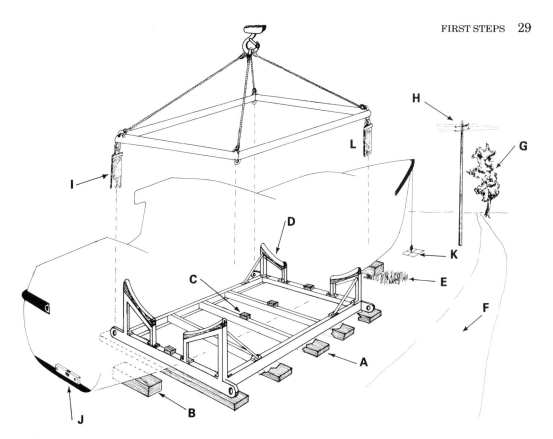

**Fig 8** Cradle design and building site

ately, although the bigger crane-hire firms can normally meet your needs. The spreader is to keep the lifted weight of your boat from crushing it. Ideally, there will be lifting eyes at the bottom corners of the steel cradle. By providing these no weight comes on to the hull and, better still, the strops are kept almost clear. The strops are enormously expensive but, with some give, they fit comfortably around the hull and, provided they are kept clean, do no damage to the gel coat. When you get the strops to the site spend a a few minutes cleaning them.

**J**   It is very important to get the boat level on the water-line. Do this as soon as the boat is delivered. I have a 6 ton hydraulic jack from early boating days which made it easy to do small adjustments, but it is a job much better done when the boat is suspended so that slivers of timber can be inserted easily. You'll need a long level and several readings should be taken round the water-line and across the transom. A good hull moulder will have put raised dots on the hull so that you can recognise the true designed water-line. If there is no marking you can hardly keep the crane waiting while you mark the hull. In any case, if you are building on soft ground, even if you have spread the load over many railway sleepers, you will get some slight sinkage and the fine adjustments will have to be redone at a later date.

**K**   There are plenty of jobs you can do before starting on the work that requires the boat to be absolutely level and plumb, but before any work is commenced check out with a plumb bob at bow and stern. A flat stone set into the ground makes a permanent reference mark once the perfect alignment is achieved. A good way to check levels once you have drawn in the water-line with a chinagraph pencil or used the moulded marks, is to fill a length of transparent hose with water and, taking it under the keel, put the menisci against the marks. The menisci are always level but your hull might need tilting so that the water-line matches them.

**L** The boat will get heavier as construction proceeds. Mine started out weighing a couple of tons and ended up at 6 tons dead weight. Throughout the building occasional checks should be made to see that the hull has not shifted.

### Crane Hire

This will be necessary when the hull is delivered and when the finished boat is ready to be taken to its launching site. Local addresses are listed in *Yellow Pages* and it is sensible to ask for quotations. Prepare a list to specify exactly what lift you want, date, time, site approach and condition, the weight to be lifted and distance. It is possible to hire huge cranes that will swing a boat into the back garden over the house, but you won't need to go to such expense if it's only a matter of a lift into the front drive. Reputable crane-hire companies will send a sales representative to advise. He will cast an expert eye over the lifting site to check the soundness of the ground, the proximity of telegraph poles, overhead cables, etc. He will base his quotation on these facts. Ask him for a Hire Agreement form so that you can study the small print before you receive the quotation. You are about to sign a legal contract and the conditions must be understood. For example, it is by far the best if you can hire 'Lump Sum', which is a single fee to cover the travelling time of crane and driver, a set number of hours' hire while travelling and working, and slings and spreader suited to the lift. Note exactly what is and isn't included in the lump sum.

'Site Condition' usually appears as a clause in the contract. The hirer is usually responsible for providing a hard standing and access to the site of the lift. I had taken note of this clause when *Sea Hound* was launched and had arranged for extra sleepers for the crane to stand on. The crane driver said these were not needed but I got him to put this in writing and I had a witness. It was lucky that I did. Although we had a safe lift off, all 10 tons of the crane sank axle-deep in the lawn. Instead of following us down to the harbour

to launch the boat into the water, it had to stay put until another 12-ton crane came 30 miles (48km) to pull it out. The cost of retrieving the crane was heavy but it wasn't my expense.

The crane owner might limit insurance liability. Any insurance you take out on the boat should be extended to cover any excess of the limited liability on the contract. You may be liable for damage to property, underground pipes and cables, overhead wires and poles carrying them. The insurance fee is small compared to the cost you could incur if anything went wrong. Despite having a large hole in my neighbour's lawn, the only extra bill I had was for 10 tons of earth and a bag of grass-seed.

### The Moulder's Deal

Starting with a hull can mean precisely that. A decent moulder will put a few battens across the bulwarks to prevent the hull going out of shape before it is delivered to you and you are able to reinforce it with bulkheads and the like. In recent years, though, the business of the amateur fitting out boats has grown so much that today many moulders offer a comprehensive package of mouldings, equipment, engines — in fact, everything to fit out the hull to a good standard.

In 1981 the Ship & Boat Builders National Federation introduced a form which gave the customer for a kit boat sound guidance for his acceptance of a boat which, if completed according to plans and the designer's specification, would meet the strength and integrity standards intended by the designer. The Minimum Structural Kit Acceptance Certificate does not affect the customer's statutory rights in law but is, I believe, a well worth-while certificate as a foundation for the building of a sound boat. On this form Part A lists eleven structural items which are best completed by the moulder prior to a kit leaving his works. They are: hull laminate, basic bottom framing, basic side framing, main bulkheads, interior mouldings supplied and bonded in if required by the designer, deck and coach-roof, connection of deck to hull, fitting of keel bolts and internal ballast (as applicable), rudder skeg, rudder and mast support foundation (if needed).

Part B covers items the customer must agree to complete to specification and drawings to achieve the strength and integrity intended by the designer. These include: partial or secondary bulkheads, items of furnishings contributing to hull strength, chain- or stay-plate reinforcements, fitting of chain plate, shaft brackets, engine girders, windows, hatches and inlet and discharge openings in the hull. These items must be regarded by any home finisher as the areas of importance and in later chapters they will be dealt with in greater depth.

It is essential to know precisely what you get for your money. This is a typical Tyler Mouldings option scheme for a 31ft (9.5m) sailing yacht:

*Option 1* GRP hull with white pigmented gel coat above the water-line and clear gel coat below the water-line. Mouldings fitted with transverse panting frame. Flash-lines ground off, taped and gelled, otherwise hull is supplied in ex-mould condition needing final cosmetic finishing by owner or yard. Spreader timbers are fitted to open hulls to retain the correct shape during transport.

*Option 2* As Option 1, but with white GRP deck, coach-roof and cockpit mouldings tagged to the hull for transport purposes. The deck, cockpit and coach-roof mouldings incorporate an anchor well, hatch, general stiffening, mast step pad and reinforcement for genoa track, main sheet track and four winches. Copper cockpit drain spigots are fitted. Flash-lines on the hull are ground off, gelled, rubbed down, polished and surface cosmetic work is carried out.

*Option 3* GRP hull, deck, coach-roof and cockpit mouldings as Option 2, but securely bonded together. The bonding incorporates additional reinforcement for chain plates. In addition, the mouldings include four half bulkheads of Lloyd's-approved marine ply securely bonded to hull and deck. Approximately 3,350lb (1,520kg) cast-iron ballast is fully encapsulated within the hull.

When faced with such an option choice, the prospective owner has to decide if the increased specification offers better value for money when balanced against his own ability to bring the simpler specification up to the higher one.

With *Sea Hound* I knew I was to finish her in the open. I also realised that a heavy hull needed the maximum support for the long journey on a low loader to my home. I took into account the difficulty in handling large heavy lumps of ¾in (19mm) marine plywood for bulkheads and, after this, had no hesitation in letting Tylers mould in the bulkheads, engine beds and drop the engines on to them. I also had tankage for fuel, water and sewage moulded in as I believe they have additional benefits beside holding liquids. They give extra stiffness to a hull and, in my boat, the top of the water-tank makes virtually the whole of the forward end double bottomed.

As well as basic hull and superstructure options you will find a list of extras available: special colours, additional part bulkheads, hatch covers, rudder assemblies, locker covers, sole bearers and even part and complete engine and stern gear packages. With moulded items such as locker covers, rudders and hatch covers, there is much to be said for having these extras as they match the hull and are designed for the job. As for the engines, the choice is perhaps more open. Although the designer usually offers the engine package that has been worked out for the boat, you will find that you can choose other engines of similar size, weight and price. Discussion with the moulding manufacturer will satisfy you as to the suitability of your choice and the cost of moulding in engine beds to suit the alternative specification. However, bear in mind what I said about overweight engines ruining performance and take heed of any advice you are given.

Some of the smaller boats come from the factory as complete kits with everything provided: woodwork cut to shape and everything to finish the boat with the minimum of fuss.

Know what you are getting for your

money and make sure that it is within your capabilities to bridge the gap between what you buy to start off with and the finished boat.

Before the moulding contract is signed you still need to study a little more about the product.

A winter walk round a yard where boats are laid up can tell you a lot about how a particular moulder's work is standing up to weathering and osmosis. Sometimes a chat with a YBDSA surveyor will reveal if a particular manufacturer is becoming known for producing problem mouldings.

# 2 PLANS AND MOULDINGS

**The Design**

Having sorted out some of the basic items, you now need to put the boat of your choice — and the company who are to mould her — under a more careful scrutiny.

In your initial enthusiasm you may have overlooked a number of design problems. While the interior of a boat can look immensely appealing under the warm lights of the boat show, that same interior might prove uncomfortable, smelly or even unsafe in actual use. Designers and commercial builders often have little idea of the problems they create for future owners when they produce boats with serious design shortcomings. They expect people to adapt to their design and make the owner the victim of their whims. They make no allowances for the disgruntled cook coping with an inconvenient galley, a crew cursing the hazards of a cluttered foredeck and an owner who dreads the servicing of an inaccessible engine. Some interesting pointers about engine design and installation can be noted from data provided by the Royal National Lifeboat Institution for the period 1975–82 in Table 1.

Before sailing yachtsmen get too smug about the high rate of rescues of power-driven vessels, this category does unfortunately include every type of power-driven runabout, fishing launch and the like that has ventured offshore into waters for which they were not designed. Nevertheless, machinery failure at such rates for both sailing and motor boats does suggest that, in many installations, even the professionals adopt substandard practices which contribute to rescue statistics.

The sailing yacht is not disabled if the engine fails as she can usually return to port under sail. It is possible that this factor accounts for the smaller number of sailing yachts suffering machinery failure and calling for rescue. However, machinery failure still contributes to too many emergencies. When you build your own boat you can see that the engine has the best possible installation to minimise this risk.

Steering failure is the next highest statistic. Make sure that the steering is engineered in the strongest possible way so that it will stand up to really heavy duty. The danger of being out of fuel can be

*Table 1:* RNLI RESCUES 1975–82, WITH CAUSES

| Cause of need for rescue | Services Rendered to Yachts and Multi-hulls with Auxiliary Engine | Services Rendered to Power-driven Pleasure Craft |
| --- | --- | --- |
| Machinery failure | 343 | 1,602 |
| Out of fuel | 37 | 107 |
| Fouled propeller | 56 | 82 |
| Fire | 20 | 53 |
| Steering failure | 152 | 40 |

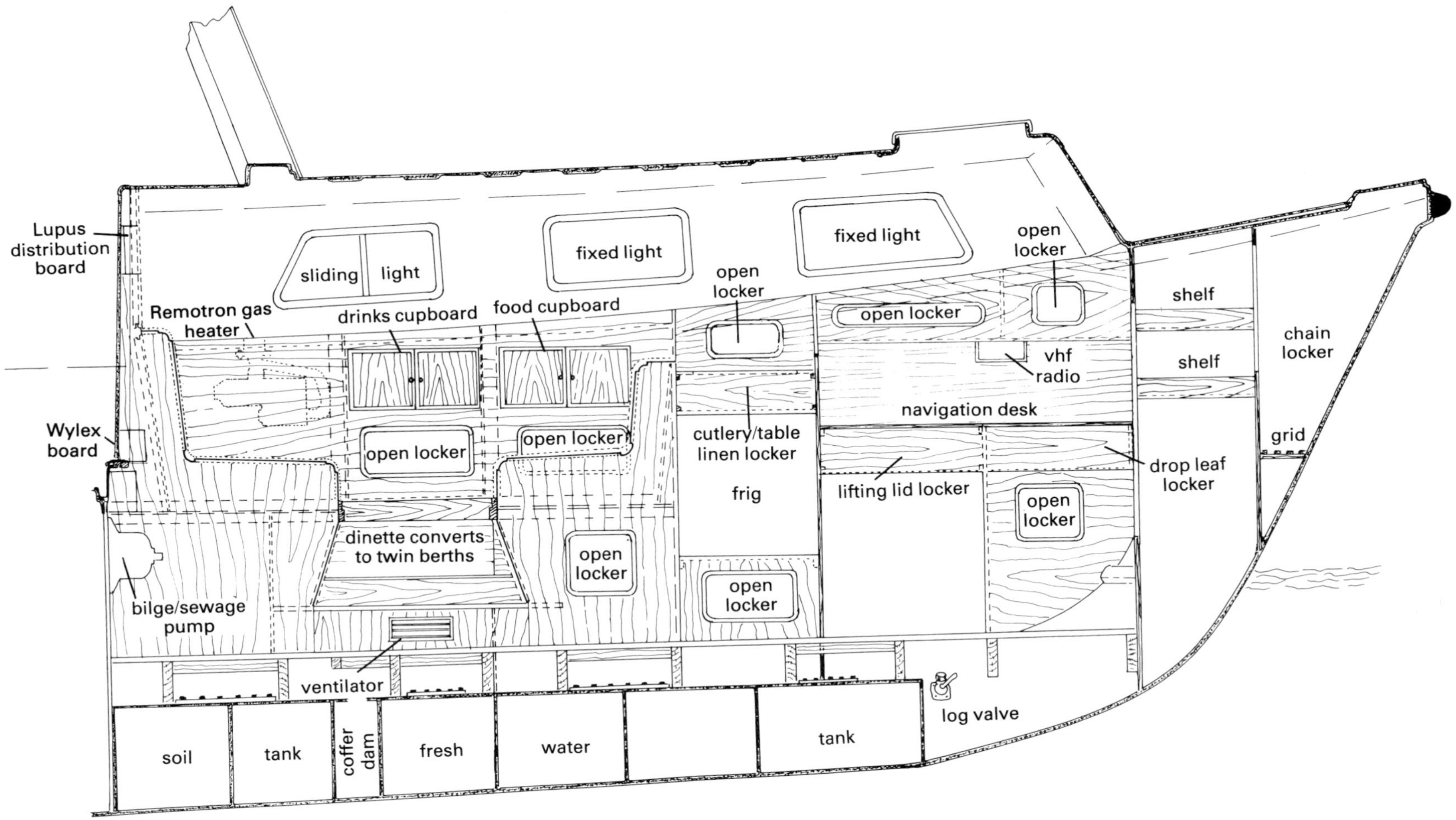

**Fig 9a** Port forward accommodation of *Sea Hound of Dart*

chain locker

grid

shelf

shelf

drop leaf locker

open locker

vhf radio

open locker

navigation desk

lifting lid locker

log valve

tank

fixed light

open locker

open locker

cutlery/table linen locker

frig

open locker

fixed light

food cupboard

open locker

open locker

water

sliding light

drinks cupboard

open locker

dinette converts to twin berths

fresh

coffer dam

ventilator

tank

Remotron gas heater

bilge/sewage pump

soil

Lupus distribution board

Wylex board

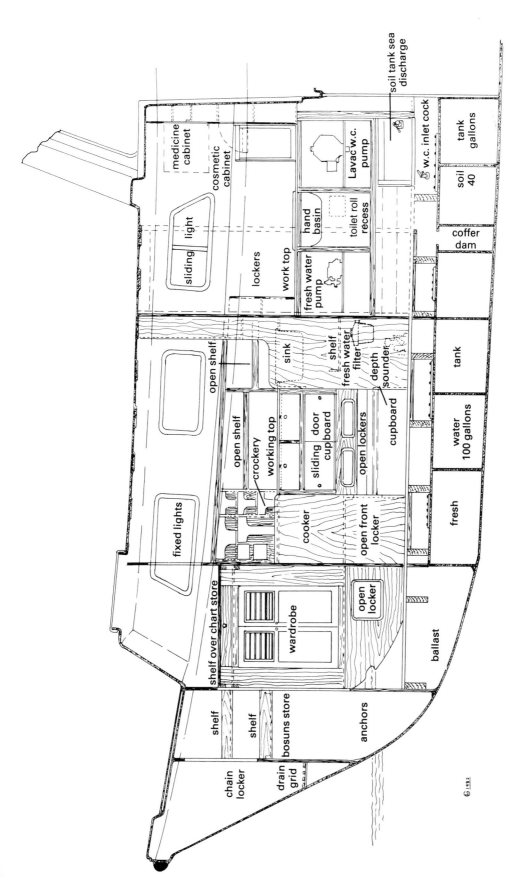

**Fig 9b** *Sea Hound's* starboard forward accommodation

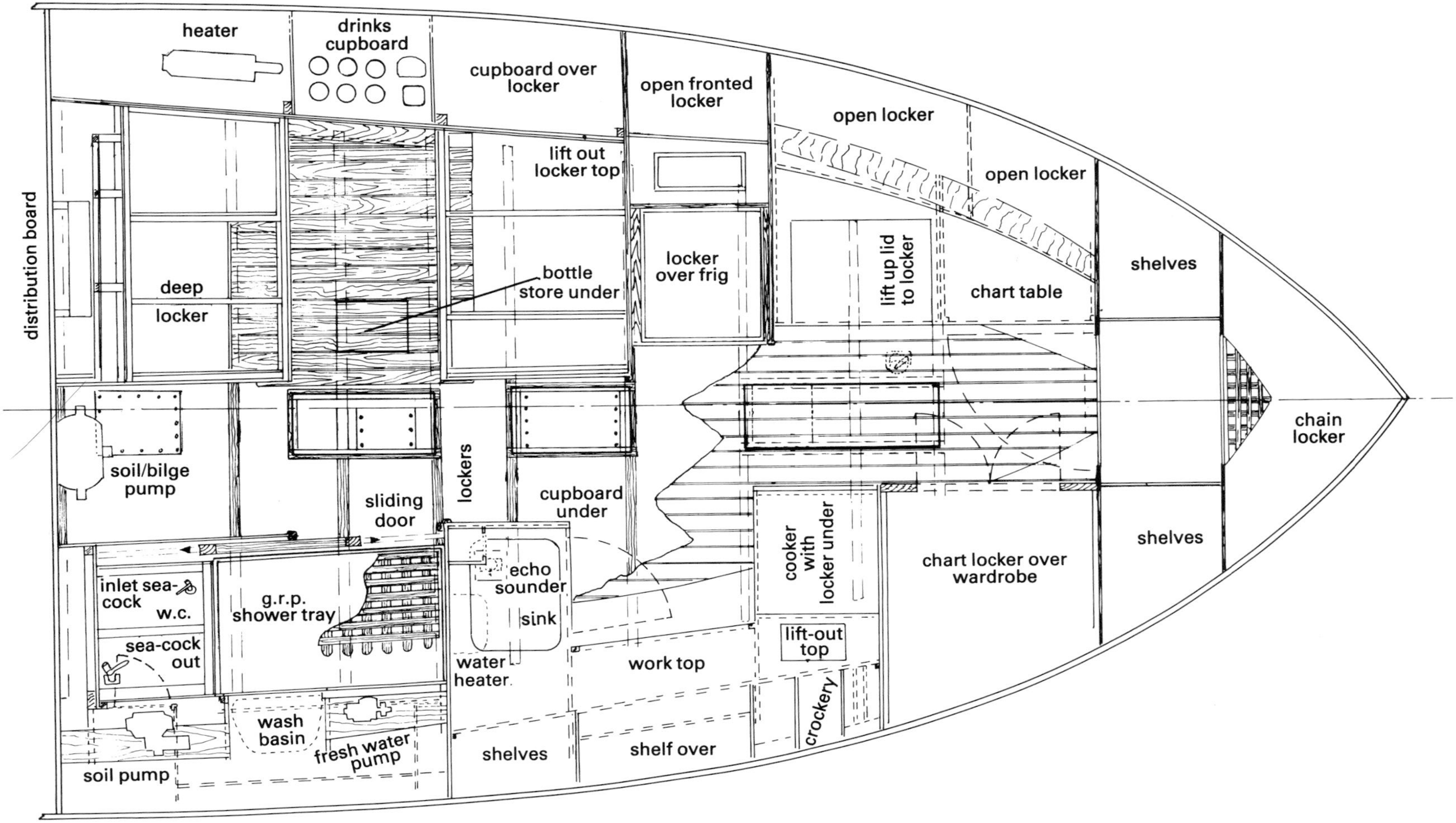

**Fig 9c** Plan of *Sea Hound of Dart's* forward accommodation

Labels on plan:

chain locker

shelves

shelves

open locker

chart table

chart locker over wardrobe

open locker

lift up lid to locker

cooker with locker under

lift-out top

crockery

open fronted locker

locker over frig

work top

shelf over

cupboard over locker

lift out locker top

bottle store under

cupboard under

echo sounder

sink

water heater.

shelves

drinks cupboard

lockers

sliding door

g.r.p. shower tray

wash basin

fresh water pump

heater

deep locker

soil/bilge pump

inlet sea-cock

w.c.

sea-cock out

soil pump

distribution board

minimised with fuel tank design and running trials to determine consumption. The risk from fire should be tackled at source — selecting design and materials that will reduce the risk and providing a good fire-fighting system.

Although RNLI lifeboats have access hatches to propellers in order to clear fouling by ropes, it is, perhaps, asking too much for a pleasure yacht to incorporate them. True, inland waterways craft often have a weed and debris clearing trap, but the best most of us can do is to keep a wary eye open for the ever-increasing dangers from crab pots and plastic rope.

By looking at the basic general arrangement of the boat and the kind of primary installations — engine, steering, underwater outlets and inlets — you can do a lot to ensure that your new boat does not end up as another rescue statistic. You may have to pay for a General Arrangement drawing, but the cost may be refunded if you purchase the hull. As you pore over this plan, imagine how easy it would be to work the boat and how comfortable to live on board.

Occasionally, you can find a moulder who has had a full set of construction plans made, complete with dated modification sheets. These simplify your work enormously. Some of the detailed drawings I had prepared for my own boat are shown in Fig 9. Studying such drawings will give you confidence in the jittery moments before you place the actual order.

Many hull moulders have a special design service with a naval architect able to produce an interior design to the individual's taste. He will ensure that the initial design is not jeopardised. This is a good safeguard in the long term, but it does have to be paid for. You could, of course, retain your own naval architect to oversee the moulding and to complete the design. It is a matter of what you can afford and how deeply you want to become involved.

## Ergonomics
This is the study of man in relation to his working environment.

Large sums of money are spent on aircraft cockpits to ensure that the pilot is seated comfortably, that all the instruments are visible and that he can reach all the controls. Failure to make proper provision in all these aspects might contribute towards a crash. We hope nothing quite so dramatic will happen in a yacht, but ergonomic design is just as essential for a boat. Research does cost money, of course, and production runs might not be sufficient to warrant the outlay. However, you can do a great deal yourself in this direction without spending any money. For example, to move a valve skin fitting a couple of inches so that it is easily reached is not going to upset the design or cost a fortune. It may well be more expensive to construct a greaser in a convenient place — but much cheaper than a wrecked propeller shaft later on because the greaser is inaccessible.

Life aboard is supposed to be a pleasure. Working the boat and looking after it should also be a pleasure. Poor ergonomic design takes much of this sparkle away.

Making a boat fit us rather than the other way round has its dangers. People do not come in standard sizes and if a person builds berths of, say, 5ft 2in (1.57m) to suit his own frame, he will have a sales problem in the future. Wild deviations from norms must be carefully considered; but first you need to know about norms and how they can be applied to the design.

Provided you are close to average size you can make use of data presently available from ergonomic research. This gives seating dimensions, galley working-top heights, seating angles, berth lengths, etc, based on average body data sizes. If you build in furniture to these norms you will produce a boat that will be saleable to a future customer.

If you look at Fig 10 you will see some basic dimensions that might be of value.

**A**   Body height sitting is the vertical distance from the sitting surface to the top of the head. For men, about 38in (965mm) is sufficient. Add this on to a clearance above the helm position or for sitting in the cabin to get a figure for vertical distance between the seat surface and the cabin or wheel-house roof.

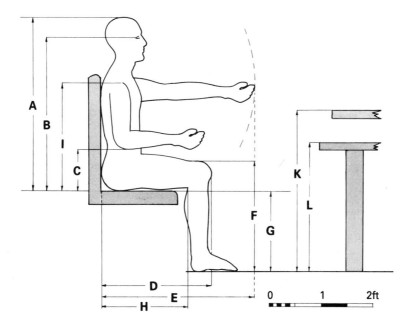

**Fig 10** Ergonomic design dimensions

**B** Eye height sitting. A measurement of around 34in (863mm) is about right for the vertical distance between the seat surface and the inner corner of the eye. This is useful if you want to be able to look out of cabin windows and, more important, to get a good view forward over the bows from a seated steering position.

**C** Elbow height sitting is the vertical distance from the sitting surface to the bottom of the elbow. This is important for armrests and is about 8in (203mm).

**D** Buttock–knee length is the horizontal distance from the most posterior point of the buttocks to the most anterior point of the knee. This dimension is approximately 26in (660mm) and is a guide to the distance from the lowest part of the backrest of a seat to the dashboard engine instrumentation or front bottom edge of the steering wheel. Note that extra space should be calculated into this dimension to allow for the helmsman to stand at the wheel.

**E** Anterior arm reach of about 37in (940mm) should be allowed when designing into the control position the distance between the top of the helmsman's seat backrest and the controls around the engine instrument panel.

**F** Knee height sitting is the vertical distance from the floor to the uppermost point of the knee — about 23in (584mm). This distance is important for working out a reasonable clearance under fixed tables, such as the lower surface of a navigation desk.

**G** Popliteal height sitting is the vertical distance from the floor to the underside of the thigh immediately behind the knee. A reasonable dimension to work on is 18in (457mm). There has to be some compromise in cabin seating arrangements, but these dimensions can be a starting point.

The problem is complicated by the need to make seating do three things: provide seating and give a comfortable position for eating, allow for lounging when the body is relaxed and for sleeping when the seating becomes a berth.

It is uncomfortable to have the seating too high so that your feet dangle in space; seating too low gives you a cramped abdomen and is unpleasant when eating. If the forward part of the thigh is left unsupported it causes the muscles to tense rather than relax.

In designing any seating, make allowance for the thickness of cushioning. I used 4in (101mm) Dunlopillo for seating in the forward cabin and 6in (152mm) for berths in the main sleeping cabin aft. (Polyurethane foams can be a lethal fire hazard. If you use them on your boat get the best fire-retarded types with covering materials that minimise the risk.) Take into account the fact that cushioning compresses when someone sits on it.

**H**   Buttock–popliteal length is important in determining the squab length of seating. Narrow seating with a back near vertical is uncomfortable. Again, the full length of the seated thigh should be supported. This dimension is about 21in (533mm).

**I**   Shoulder height sitting. A length of about 25in (635mm) is a guide to working out the length of a seat backrest.

Note that all these dimensions are a guide and take no account of extra small or large people and certainly not the encumbering thickness of foul-weather gear.

Standing room is the only dimension that can be solved by having a larger boat. If you had been finishing off a wooden boat in Henry VIII's time you would have been able to have head-room in a smaller craft than today. Average height was very much lower than today, when, with better nutrition and health care, each succeeding generation gets taller. In fact, the average US citizen is taller than his UK counterpart.

My hull could accommodate 6ft 4in (1,930mm) standing head-room in the wheel-house and 6ft 2in (1,880mm) in the forward cabin. When deciding on standing-room height in the main cabin it is sometimes possible to gain height by leaving a minimum amount of space under the cabin beams on which the sole rests. However, in a displacement boat (Fig 11) and sailing yacht the standing area becomes more restricted by the curvature of the hull.

Raising the cabin sole a few inches increases the floor area and allows level standing right up to the sides of the cabin superstructure side. On the same figure you can see how, by raising the dinette seating above the cabin sole (N), a view out of the windows is gained. Also, by setting the storage locker just back from the lower edge of the superstructure at the turn from the side deck, it is possible to give some shoulder room (O), giving more space and comfort to two people sitting side by side.

Finally, on Fig 11 I will mention the unmentionable, the ergonomics of the WC. Whether yachtsmen are squeamish or

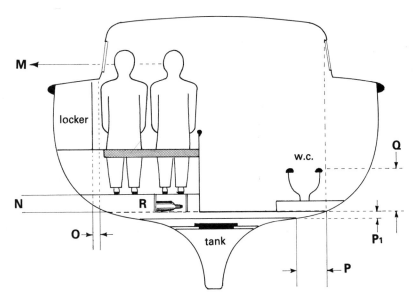

**Fig 11** Effect of cabin sole and platform height on ergonomic design

simply like to keep their constipation to themselves, I have never seen the design of the WC discussed in detail. There are some diabolical WC installations about, including a few which make normal bodily functions an achievement akin to an Olympic decathlon. Surely it is as important to have the correct repose in this compartment as it is to have comfort in the cabin? Marine toilet manufacturers design their wares to be squat so that the uncaring boatbuilder can cram the unit into as small a space as possible. By raising the WC unit (Q), so creating a throne, a more comfortable height is achieved. The household toilet seat is about 18in (457mm) from floor to seat top. The Blake Lavac toilet I got for *Sea Hound* was only 8¾in (222mm) high, so it had to go on a good-sized platform to get it to working height. Full and easy access to the inlet and discharge valves was provided by flaps in the right places. I will go into greater detail about the WC later, but please don't imagine that the toilet compartment isn't worth bothering about.

In any cabin without full standing-room you must aim for a design where it is possible, at least, to sit in comfort without banging your head or bending your back to uncomfortable limits.

Walkways through forward cabin space should be at least 20in (508mm+) wide. Bulky wet-weather gear will still catch on the furniture but this is a reasonable space to walk through on a small boat. See that entrance hatches are of similar dimension although, with sailing boats, to gain extra strength it is common to taper the hatch towards the deck. This is because legs, even in heavy gear, do not require the same space as the body.

The escape hatch is mandatory in some countries. One must be provided when the main hatch leads you through or over the engine space. Many sailing boats need a hatch to give passage to the sails from foredeck to sail locker. While you can get sails through a small hatch, stick to the 508mm clearance for crew members. Beware of hatches with 508mm as the outside dimension; the actual hole will be much smaller.

## Ergonomics for Engines
Have you ever stood on your head to get at a sump oil plug? Or dived headlong into a quarter berth to try and top up a battery in darkness caused by your mass blocking off all light? If so, you will hardly wonder that a lot of engine failures are caused by the disgraceful way mechanical installations 'happen' in most boats, whether sail or power. They seem to have been made by fiends who will never have to service them and if something goes wrong, repairs become very expensive — not because of the cost of the replacement part, but because to get at it the boat has to be dismantled and rebuilt! Later I will deal with this subject so that you can make annual maintenance and repairs as easy and pleasant as possible.

## Galley Design
Few people enjoy cooking in the confines of a boat. The term 'galley slave' is all too true in many small boats, where cramped conditions, poor ergonomic design and lack of ventilation, turn even the eager cook into a harassed skivvy.

Several design factors are critical:

*Height* to work upright. Even in a small boat this can be arranged by having the galley area near the main hatch where the coach-roof can be given extra height without spoiling the lines. On sailing craft the galley is often arranged to port or starboard of the main companionway. This gives the cook head-room as well as daylight. It also allows ventilation, but this can be a mixed blessing in bad weather with rain and wind coming through the open hatch. Try to keep the cook dry and arrange ventilation by means of an extraction fan.

*Cookers* may have to be gimballed, which will take up extra space. They must be installed carefully and safely to prevent fire hazard or accident to anyone nearby. If the cooker is not gimballed it must be bolted securely in place. Choice of fuel is up to you and you must be aware of the hazards. Gas will explode if it escapes and builds up in cabin spaces. Paraffin under pressure can

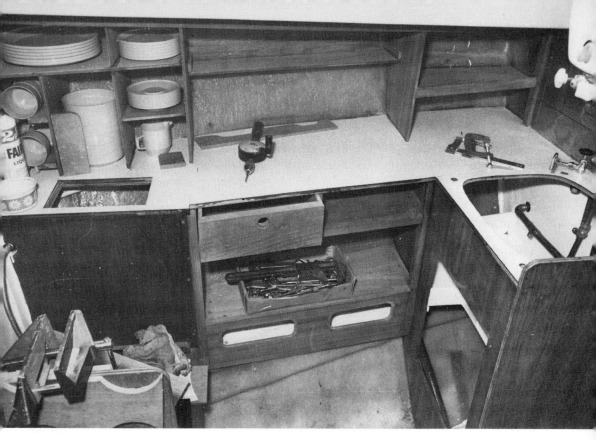

Fig 12 The way to a man's heart is through his stomach; galley design and sound construction are vital for a happy ship

spray out or be spilled to cause fire. Alcohol stoves have flames invisible in sunlight and spillage is again a hazard. Tragedies have occurred when people have tried to refuel alcohol stoves thinking that the stove was out when the flames were merely invisible. Cookers must be installed using the best materials as specified by the maker. They should comply with safety regulations or local bye-laws. The manufacturer should be able to advise you on these.

*Working space* must be sufficient so that you can stand square to the cooker or the sink without catching elbows. Have a work-top that can be reached from both sink and cooker areas. Many designs are dreadful in this respect and make dishing out a meal or clearing crockery a major operation. Normal working surface height is best at 34–35in (865–890mm).

*The sink* My pet abomination is the toy

sink — the ones into which a dinner-plate jams when you are washing up. Dinner-plates do not shrink in size because they are used on a boat. So many fittings put into yachts seem doomed to make life difficult. True, space is limited but if a builder can cram six berths into a small boat, the least he should do for the cook is ensure that six people can be catered for comfortably. Builders' merchants carry stocks of excellent stainless-steel sinks, often at a price much lower than the Wendy House models that appear in chandlers' catalogues.

*Garbage* If you are to avoid filthing up the sea and the rivers, not to mention the boat, you will consider the provision of garbage disposal. A garbage-collection point in the galley will ease disposal ashore. Plastic bins and liners are most convenient, provided you make room in the galley for them.

*Crockery and pans* Heavy things are best stored low down. I designed space for pans under the cooker. Crockery space should be designed to hold the specific size of dish, cup or plate, so that they do not crash about or get thrown out on to the floor. Buy the crockery first to get dimensions for storage.

*Food storage*  Maximum use should be made of the best areas to store food. Items such as vegetables that need to be kept cool can be stored low down near the bilges or below the water-line. Higher up, cabin space is warmer and, perhaps, drier. The old joke about the cruising boat whose crew did not know what was coming next for their meal because the labels washed off the cans stored in the bilges, should not apply in a well-designed modern boat. Put heavy tinned foods in lockers that keep them dry and immobile. I made a deep locker to the left (Fig 12) with access from the work-top. It is insulated from the heat put out by the stove, is perfectly dry and tins cannot jump out of it.

### Sketching and Drawing up Plans
If you intend modifying the drawings supplied as part of a kit or, like me, you plan to create a new interior, a good deal of time must be spent roughing out ideas and then examining them in detail to check that they will work. You will need correctly dimensioned plans so that when you get down to the actual construction you will know exactly what is wanted. It is easy and inexpensive to rub out a few pencil lines or rip up a sheet of paper. It is very expensive to dismantle and replace wooden or GRP mistakes. To give you plenty of ideas for interior design, there are many excellent books available. *Classic Yacht Interiors* by Bill Bobrow and Dana Jinkins is packed with pictures of exotic yacht interiors. Perhaps your boat will be less exotic, but there are many design features you might be able to modify to suit a more modest craft.

During planning and construction I kept A3-sized layout pads to hand. Detail paper is thicker than tracing paper and slightly less translucent. Even when you have drawn up scale plans you will find the sketch pad necessary for taking actual dimensions off the hull as they will certainly

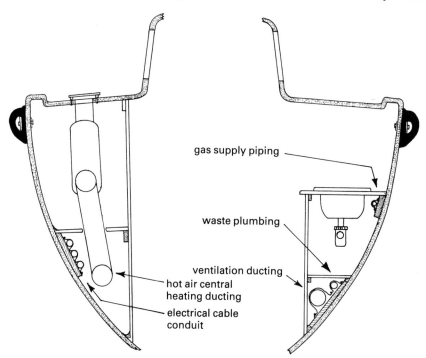

**Fig 13** Utilisation of triangular-shaped spaces for services

vary from the moulder's drawings.

I wish I could say that I hit on the perfect design at the first attempt. Before the hull arrived I had done some detailed planning, but when the hull arrived I found I needed to install orange boxes and other makeshift rigs to see if my ideas worked. Some of them didn't! Many rough sketches, mock-ups and rough-dimensioned drawings later, the final working drawings were prepared by a friend, Alan Prior.

If you are not familiar with boat design you must call in a professional designer. Without his help and advice you could be building a maritime disaster.

With a full kit boat you may only want to make minor modifications and in this case the kit supplier should be prepared to advise if the modifications are acceptable.

In planning my boat I saved cost by such simple measures as putting the galley sink back-to-back with the WC compartment, both sharing the semi-bulkhead. This reduced the runs for water and gas piping and made the waste plumbing that much easier. In Fig 13 you will notice the triangular shapes left by side-locker bases and the curvature of the hull plus the locker face. I utilised this space as service trunking. Hot air for fore and aft cabins was led through flexible ducting; plastic electrical conduit carried wiring as well as the copper tubing for water and gas supplies.

In the average boat volumes of expensive space are wasted. If designers were made to pay back cash for lost space, boats would cost a great deal less. As it was, I pictured a kind of chess game to be played with myself and dry rot, which I was convinced would spring up in every bit of unreachable timber. This private phobia created a lot of work in designing access to every part of the boat and I used thousands of extra screws making every floorboard or entrapped space accessible. However, if at any future date it is necessary to remove skin fittings or parts of any mechanical installation, there will be no problems in getting to them. This sort of operation would be impossible in many boats without tearing them to pieces.

## Ordering the Moulding

Crunch time comes when dreams have turned themselves into sketches, the brochures have been digested and every last penny calculated in the budget. Now, the order for the boat has to be placed and before you part with the cash, you have to be certain that you are getting value for your money.

There are considerable differences in what goes into a GRP hull construction. You can price bare hulls of similar form and length with different builders and find as much as a 300 per cent variation. Some cost more because they are moulded to the specifications of a classification society, such as Lloyd's. These moulders have a reputation to maintain. You may get a clue to quality when you see large orders for GRP hulls being placed with a moulder by pilot agencies, port authorities and naval forces. At the other extreme are moulders who have purchased a set of moulds from second-hand or bankrupt stock and use them in a broken-down shed. With no reputation to risk they turn out first-class rubbish.

The moulder's workshop is the first major contribution to the production of a first-class hull. Before you order, visit the moulder's workshop and give it careful scrutiny. See if the business seems well organised, don't be put off by slick sales talk, but ask questions about the technical side of the moulding procedure. Try to take a look at boats previously moulded by the firm and, if possible, talk to their owners who will complain about any faults such as fading colours or osmotic attack.

## The Constitution of a Good Hull

There was a time when glass-reinforced plastic was hailed as the most perfect and fault-free medium the boatbuilder ever had at his disposal. It is only comparatively recently that it was realised this perfect material could develop serious faults in the structure of the laminate. In the early days of GRP, there were plenty of minor moulding faults, such as wrinkling, pinholing and fish eyes that were immediately visible when the boat was removed from the mould. In time, as materials and moulding techniques improved, these faults were eliminated or remedied by the development of new resins and release agents. What was not understood was that, by the nature of the minute voids unavoidably created when resins did not completely surround every glass strand, conditions would be created which could lead to serious cosmetic problems, surface blistering and later to severe delamination and structural damage to the laminate. This new bogey was osmosis.

### Osmosis

Osmosis is a kind of blistering with several forms. It takes place when certain qualities of GRP have been immersed in water for some time. Molecular particles of water pass through the gel coat which is acting as a membrane. It finds its way into the voids around the glass strands of the mat containing fluids of different density. The density of these fluids rapidly increases and blisters are forced up on to the laminate surface. Pressure within these blisters can be as high as 90lb per sq in. Large voids producing these kinds of pressures will do worse than blister, they will cause structural delamination and loss of strength. Osmotic attack is worse in fresh water than salt. It is costly to remedy so you must be sure that the hull you buy conforms to moulding practices that, at the present time, minimise the possibility of the problem.

When looking for the best hull and checking over the moulder's workshop, consider the following points:

**1** Does he leave completely clear resin/mat below the water-line? This is highly desirable. It gives the least water-permeable lay-up. You can bolster this watertightness by applying water-barrier paints which I shall recommend in the chapter on painting. In the meantime, a clear bottom allows the moulder to see if any serious voids in the laminate have been accidentally created. Be assured that clear laminates are the best way to produce a sound bottom to a boat. The gel coat — the smooth outside layer of laminate that is painted on to the mould of the hull — should be $20/_{1,000}$–$22/_{1,000}$in (0.5–0.55mm) thick when wet and a good moulder will be able to measure this with a special wet film thickness gauge. Poor moulders guess the thickness and leave the gel coat as thin as $5/_{1,000}$in (0.12mm) — a perfect thickness for inducing osmotic attack. To get even coverage and thickness over the mould, two applications of the gel coat are best, allowing the first to cure partially before application of the second. Timing is important to get a chemical as well as a mechanical adhesion between these coats.

**2** Check that there is a resin-rich layer behind the gel coat, reinforced with surfacing glass tissue. This should not be rolled so that it is forced into the gel coat dangerously near the outer surface. If it is, it may act like a wick to introduce water into the voids and induce osmosis.

**3** When laminating commences, are layers of glass and resin built up gradually and thoroughly rolled to ensure that minimal amounts of air are trapped? What methods of control are used to ensure that the right numbers of layers of glass cloth are moulded into place? Tylers used dye of different colours spotted on to the glass before it was moulded into place. It was easy to check the different colours and count them to see that the correct weight of lay-up had been achieved. Some poor moulders wet out great wads of glass cloth and lump them into the mould where it is impossible to eliminate pockets of air, even by the most frantic rolling.

**4** How does the moulder control workshop environment? Temperature and humidity should be controlled within fine limits to produce the correct cure of the hull moulding. A resin that is not fully cured is more permeable and this is the best way to encourage osmosis. In some bad workshops the moulder is so eager to get production runs to the maximum that the hulls are pushed out into the open yard before a full cure has taken place. With many of the resins, this sudden change literally kills the reaction and cure. Some resins can be stopped and will later start to cure when put in a higher temperature. However, putting a hull out into the rain and cold is not a practice to be recommended.

5 The resin makers go to enormous lengths to test and check their resin mixes. The resin, accelerator and the catalyst are mixed precisely to gain the necessary characteristics for specific applications. In the past (and perhaps in the present), moulders have altered these mixes for their own convenience. For example, he might extend the gelling time by altering the amount of catalyst so that the workmen can have their lunch before the resin goes off — fine for the workmen but rotten for the resin. Loading structural resins is another way for the less scrupulous moulder to save money. When resin prices rocketed in recent years, they were extended by incorporating much less expensive materials to make them go further. These soon weathered and produced serious problems for the unfortunate boat owner. It is, I may say, perfectly all right to load resins to the resin-maker's specifications for such jobs as filling voids around propeller shafting, for smooth fillets to streamline 'p' brackets and the like. Fillers such as colloidal silica, microballoons (tiny hollow phenolic spheres) and microspheres (hollow glass spheres) when used in the correct mix with complete resin/hardener mix, are perfectly legitimate materials. The problem is that you cannot see what the cheapjack moulder puts into his mixes or where he misuses them. You will need to know the correct mixes for glassing in and to keep to the mix as recommended by the supplier.

There are many variables in the production of a GRP hull. Only a moulder of the highest integrity is likely to achieve the standards necessary for a quality hull. To meet such demands costs money.

The better car manufacturers are now guaranteeing their products for several years against corrosion. Perhaps one day the GRP hull will be similarly guaranteed against osmosis. In the meantime, a Lloyd's moulding certificate has much to recommend it and for those who might wish extra protection, the services of a professional surveyor might well prove to be a worthwhile investment.

## Built-in Reinforcements

The boat designer will have specified on the lay-up plan all areas of the hull that must be specially reinforced with top-hat sections and the like. Reinforcing materials include these special GRP sections formed by laminating over a core material which may be end-grain balsa wood, marine plywood or light alloy. Alternatively, they can be areas where extra thickness of glass mat is provided for strength. Although these are the responsibility of the designer and moulder you may need to specify extra reinforcing to certain areas to provide strength for special units that you intend installing. Items such as the area around a leg (which is bolted into place to keep a boat upright as she dries out on a falling tide), for powerboat transom trim tabs, for areas where stabilisers are to be built on to the hull and for foredeck areas where a powerful anchor winch is to be installed, all these might call for reinforcing.

When it comes to your own work on the hull, you will need to know what reinforcing has been used and the way to deal with it so that you don't weaken it with your own handiwork. You must have methods of dealing with problems created when fasteners and items of equipment pass through reinforced areas. I will deal with these problems later, but ensure that you discuss all severe stress areas with the moulder or designer before the hull is moulded. I have come across two boats where the designer had so underestimated stress areas that, in one of them, the bulkheads broke away from the hull as it twisted in a bad sea; in the other, large free areas of hull had no reinforcing and consequently fractured.

Interior moulded GRP furnishing modules create a great deal of extra strength. Tankage for water, fuel and waste all contribute to strength. Tanks should be separated by a coffer dam to prevent liquids permeating and contaminating one another. Make sure that the moulder knows the best possible tank gel coats for the specific liquid contents.

## Glass Mat

Glass fibres are made into several different forms to produce the material that is reinforced with resins to produce GRP. Chopped strand mat must be type 'E' glass, best quality, conforming to Lloyd's and British Standards (or equivalent) specification. It is tailored in the moulder's workshop almost like a bespoke suit so that when it is wetted out into the mould it drapes and fits the shape perfectly with no unnecessary overlapping. Perhaps many customers are not interested in seeing the moulder's lay-up plan which gives the quantity and type of glass mat being used, but it does reveal a great deal about quality and strength. True, when you cut holes in the hull you will find out how thick it is, but knowing this before you buy can be reassuring.

Chopped strand mat is bought in various widths and lengths on a roll. It is designated by weight per square foot, the most useful weights being 1, 1½ and 2oz per sq ft. Different weights of mat need different quantities of resin. A safe ratio, resin to glass is between 2:1 and 2:5.1. So for 1sq yd of 1oz mat with a weight of 9oz, you would need $2.5 \times 9 = 22.5$oz of resin (1.4lb).

The glass has a binder to hold the strands together until it is wetted out with resin. Basically, there are two types of binder — emulsion and powder. The emulsion type has, in the past, been most commonly used in boat moulding, but with greater knowledge of osmosis, it is now recognised that this breaks down more readily in the presence of water. The powder types will probably now take over to reduce the possibility of osmotic attack. They should be used in the initial layers, at least, of reinforcement behind the gel coat. For your own use inside the boat, the glass mats with emulsion binder will be perfectly adequate if the more modern types are not available.

Woven glass cloths or woven rovings come in weights between 4oz and 24oz per sq yd. These glass materials have a variety of weaves which give them particular characteristics. Basically, these provide areas where high tensile strength is needed with a degree of flexibility. They also have the blessing of providing a quick build-up of thickness while having the disadvantage that to impregnate them and avoid the dreaded air voids or resin-starved areas is quite difficult. For finishing, you will generally have no need of them.

Glass tapes are made with an open weave of glass in various widths from ½in (13mm) to 6in (152mm). They are most useful for temporary fixing of bulkheads into the exact glassing position, for glassing in supports, for wiring and other light jobs that require fixing to the GRP hull. They are easily impregnated with resin and the open weave makes them conform to curved shapes very well. I used tapes of 2in (51mm), 3in (76mm) and 5in (127mm) wide, which covered most jobs around my boat.

## Resins

Quality resins which conform to Lloyd's and British Standard marine specifications are best. It has been found that isophthalic acid resins give better results in precluding osmosis than the orthophthalic acid resins. For safety reasons, most resins are sold pre-accelerated. Cobalt is the most commonly used accelerator and as it is already in the resin you do not need to worry about spoiling the mix by not getting quantities right. All you do is add the catalyst. The catalyst most commonly used is called MEKP and it is critical that the resin manufacturer's instructions are followed as regards its proportion to the resin. It is generally about 2 per cent.

Resins are inflammable and could be a fire hazard as they burn fiercely. In Chapter 8, I refer to their use in construction. Here I am concerned with their storage in liquid form during the building. They have a shelf life of between three and nine months and as catalysts are organic peroxides they present a special fire hazard. They should be stored in a separate area, outside, which is dry and well ventilated. Combustible materials such as rags or paper that have become contaminated with a catalyst can ignite spontaneously and should not be left lying about.

These chemicals are irritating to the skin and highly dangerous if they get into the eyes. First aid consists of washing vigorously with clean water but a doctor or casualty department of a hospital should then be consulted. Several other materials used in fitting out a GRP hull are also dangerous if not used properly and I will refer to these as I go along.

## Gel Coat Colours

I repeat, pigments added to the gel coat below the water-line are not to be recommended. They make the gel coat more permeable. The degree of permeability depends on the colour itself, some being worse than others. The more permeable they are, the earlier the owner can expect osmosis to start. Dark blue, red and dark green are most vulnerable as, compared to other colours, they incorporate greater quantities of plasticiser. The best moulders never use coloured gel coats below the water-line, although I have seen the unknowledgeable aghast at seeing clear day-light through the hull bottom!

The second consideration should be the colour's resistance to fading or change and the way it shows up scratches. Red is a notoriously unstable colour and John Tyler did everything in his power to dissuade me from having it for the hull above the water-line. However, he agreed to do this specially for me, provided I would have the most stable of the reds, cadmium red, as the colorant. Cadmium is much more expensive than other reds which do not last well in the marine environment.

As you know with cars, some colours seem to show every speck of mud while others look clean for a long time. Light colours show scratches and dirt much less than dark ones. Dark colours also absorb a lot of heat — not generally a problem in our climate, but a consideration for boats kept in more sunny places.

Despite giving a boat every attention, she will need painting one day. Delay the evil hour by using a moulder who knows about the colours he is offering you.

# 3 TOOLS AND MATERIALS

Wooden sailing ships and men-of-war were built with little more than an axe to chop the trees down and an adze to finish and shape the planks. *Mary Rose* raised off the sea bed after over four hundred years is perhaps ample testimony to the strength of such constructions, which were held together with wooden pegs called treenails or trennels. However, we are expecting something more sophisticated and certainly more comfortable than the old shipwrights were able to offer, and we have at our disposal a wide range of tools to cope.

Most of you will have a selection of tools that you feel will take you a long way towards finishing the hull. However, a few notes on some of the tools I used might help the less experienced. These are shown in Fig 15 (see p50).

## Marking-out Tools and Measures

A chalk line and plumb bob are needed from the beginning to set up the hull vertically with the water-line running level. The centre-line of the inside of the hull has to be drawn so that bulkheads, semi-bulkheads and floors to take cabin soles can be marked out true. Although a long level is excellent for accuracy, I found the Stanley aluminium 24in (600mm) ideal for confined interior space. A small 10in (254mm) level helps in really tight corners. 6in (152mm) and 12in (305mm) set squares were used for small cabinet work and for checking larger jobs when I had to measure and mark to square off the bulkheads. I found some specially selected straight sections of Dexion aluminium angle most helpful for marking out long lines, but I had to be careful not to knock them out from their true straight edge. A carpenter's marking gauge completed the marking-out kit, plus a number of pencils and a Stanley knife to sharpen them.

## Cramps, Vices and Other Holding Tools

What holds a lot holds a little as regards 'G' cramps but they are quite expensive in the larger sizes. Paramo of Sheffield make excellent and powerful cramps and I had a couple of their 6in (152mm) and 3in (76mm) models for controlling lumps of teak that wanted to escape from the curve into which I was trying to force them. Less expensive but ideal for light work are the American Stanley 3in (76mm) and 6in (152mm) 'G' cramps. I had eight of the various sizes and this was just about the minimum needed. Sometimes I had every one in use and could have done with spares.

I had a pair of sash cramps as I do a lot of home cabinet work and these are most useful if you make a lot of doors or drawers that need cramping after assembly and gluing. Paramo make a good set of cramp heads and these can be fixed to any length of wooden batten of suitable cross-section and strength to provide a sash cramp of size to suit the job. In this form they are much easier to store. The batten merely has to be drilled to take the two heads at the correct distance apart so that the work fits between.

The Stanley aluminium vice shown in Fig 14 was very useful when working inside the hull away from my main bench vice. It is portable and strong.

## Hand Tools

These will consist of your own selection of planes, screwdrivers, chisels, files, hand drills and bits, saws and hammers. If you buy wood finished from the timber merchant it will need further cabinet finishing with a smoothing plane. If grain is difficult, as with some teak, a scraper will also be needed. I always scrape wood to a

**Fig 14** 'G' cramps, vice and sash cramp heads supply the extra 'hands' needed during the construction

fine finish with a newly cut piece of window glass. A strip of sticking plaster on the top edge prevents you from cutting your fingers. As the glass becomes blunt discard it and cut a new piece.

All sharp-edged tools should be kept sharpened on a good honing stone. This makes for accuracy and safety. Burma teak and many of the fine hardwoods are tough and soon take the edge off saws. Expect to spend quite a lot of time sharpening tools. You can get special plane-blade and chisel holders from James Neill of Sheffield. These keep the tools at the correct sharpening and honing angles.

Tools I found of special value were a set of Screw Mate drill and countersink bits. They save a great deal of time by complet-

ing two operations at once. Footprint do a similar set of drill/countersinks and they have the added advantage that they will, by means of an adjustable collar, drill, countersink and sink screws ready for taking screws or wooden plugs. A set of plug cutters to match these bits proved useful. By inserting the grain of the plug in the same direction as the main wood grain a neat finish is achieved.

You may have sets of conventional screwdrivers, but I found a Stanley No 131A Heavy Pattern spiral ratchet screwdriver indispensable, especially when I had to drive numbers of largish screws, like the 400 I used in the teak planking floorboards. The smaller Yankee Handiman handled lighter jobs with equal speed. A screwdriver bit that could be used in a brace drill was ideal when real strength was needed to drive 4in (102mm) No 12 screws.

**Fig 15** Selection of hand tools used in boat construction

1 Stanley smoothing 2⅜in plane   2 Marking gauge   3 Ball pein hammer 1lb   4 Pin hammer Warrington pattern   5 Claw hammer 20oz   6 Steelmaster axe   7 Set chisels: firmer bevel edge ¼, ½, ¾ and 1in   8 Stanley 131A heavy duty Yankee driver   9 Bradawl   10 Cramp heads   11 Double-pinion enclosed-gear hand drill   12 Electrician's ratchet brace drill (compact for boat spaces)   13 Try square 12in   14 Try square 6in   15 Three square file (saw sharpening)   16 Electrician's screwdriver ³⁄₁₆in tip   17 Yankee Handyman driver   18

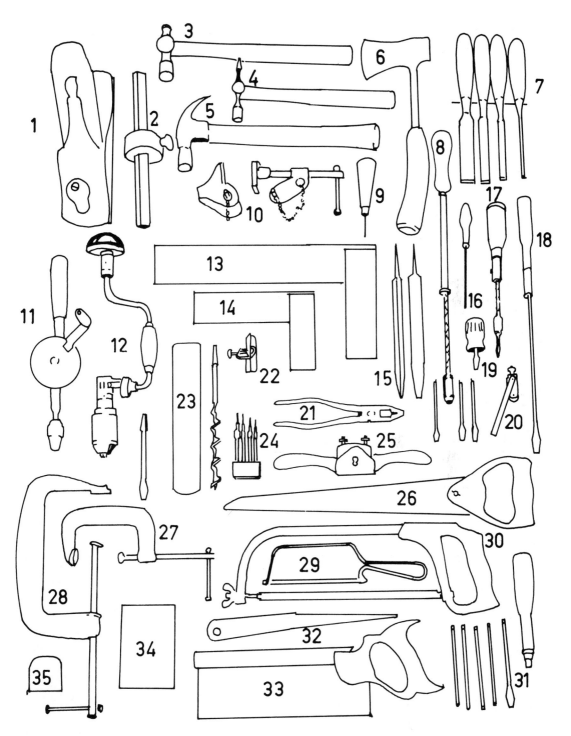

Screwdriver 10in with ⅜in tip **19** Screwdriver for small spaces **20** Stanley honing gauge **21** Pliers **22** Auger bit depth gauge **23** Auger bits ¼, ½, ¾ and 1in **24** Screw sinks (countersinking and counter-boring bits) **25** Spokeshave **26** General purpose saw (James Neill) — saws anything **27** 3in 'G' cramp **28** 6in 'G' cramp **29** Junior hacksaw **30** Hacksaw **31** Footprint ratchet screwdriver **32** Keyhole saw **33** Tenon saw **34** High speed drills **35** Stanley Powerlock rule (Not shown Stanley 24in level)

While most of the heavier woodwork is screwed and glued together, brass pins are used for edging and some fine work. A pin hammer with a ball pein head, 4oz (57g) or 6oz (170g), is best suited for these jobs. Brass pins bend easily and should always be inserted in pre-drilled 1/16in (2mm) diameter holes.

## Hole-saws

These are an excellent investment (Fig 16). I used them for precision cutting of cabin window corners, which were then finished off with four straight cuts between them, using a jig-saw. All locker faces were finished off with rounded corners, as described in Chapter 4. There are, in fact, a great number of larger diameter holes required in a boat — to take skin

fittings, deck fillers, piping, etc, through bulkheads — so a variety of diameter and matched arbors are necessary. Larger sizes need a powerful industrial drill to swing them but a good-quality drill will turn up to 2in (51mm) diameter hole-saw without being overstressed. The sizes I selected from the Milford catalogue were 3/4in (19mm), 15/16in (24mm), 11/16in (27mm), 11/4in (32mm), 15/16in (33mm), 19/16in (40mm), 2in (51mm), 21/16in (52mm), 21/4in (57mm), 23/8in (60mm), 29/16in (65mm), 3in (76mm), and 4in (102mm). Note that I was expecting to use 1in (25mm), 11/4in (32mm), 11/2in (38mm) and 2in (51mm) pipes and fittings. I allowed a clearance of 1/16in (2mm).

## Electric Power Tools

Good lighting aids accuracy and power tools reduce effort and construction time.

I would suggest that, in any large project, a minimum of 3 per cent of the budget is spent on a quality industrial drill, a jig-

**Fig 16** Large hole-saws need a powerful drill to swing them and various arbors to match. Quality counts as GRP is vicious on saw-edged tools

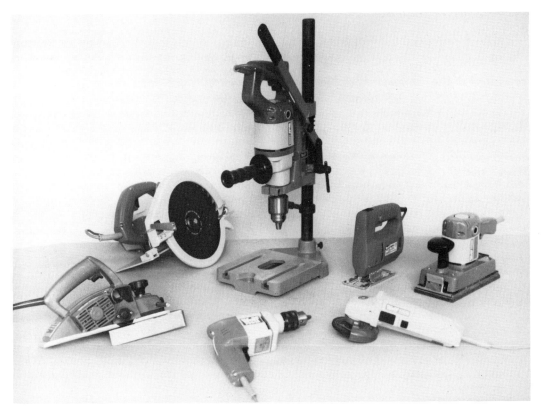

saw, circular saw and Grinderette. Fig 17 shows a selection of the tools I used. These represented 4.8 per cent of building costs. In case you wonder why I bought individual tools, rather than the kind with a range of accessories, I would emphasise that the DIY man sometimes does not realise how much he is expecting of an inexpensive drill which is really designed for making small holes, rather than driving a multiplicity of attachments. One set of bearings in the drill has to bear a heavy burden and the windings on the motor hardly have time to cool before it is on again. The fact is that drills are rated for short bursts of speeds. Circular-saw motors are designed to run for much longer periods. Changing tools gives them all time to cool. Also, as time is something I am always short of, I did not want to waste it taking one attachment off and putting another in its place.

By buying the electric planer and circular saw I saved a considerable sum by having all the teak and iroko delivered straight from the ship in its rough-sawn state. The saw coped with teak planks up

to 2⅓in (60mm) thick. The calciferous deposits that are a hallmark of Burma teak made the sparks fly and the first ordinary blades I used did little more than 80ft (24m) of cutting before they had to be resharpened. Later, I used tungsten carbide-tipped circular saws and they made a tremendous difference. In fact, they lasted through the whole project and showed no signs of distress after hundreds of feet of ripping. Eventually, they do have to go back to the maker for sharpening as it cannot be done by the amateur.

The Grinderette proved an excellent tool for grinding back GRP round window openings and roughing up cured GRP previous to bonding new work in place. Sanding discs of 24 and 26 grit gave very fast stock removal while 50 and 89 grit discs were suited to preparing some of the special steel-fabricated items, like auto-pilot bracket and beam supports, before they were painted.

If your budget only runs to one drill, I recommend the compact variable speed model. The variable speed is a great bonus when dealing with a variety of materials, from stainless steel (low speed or it will burn the drill tip out in seconds), plastics, woods, rubber to aluminium, steel and compound materials, as when drilling through a deck covering into GRP with balsa reinforcing.

For drilling the heavy-section rubber fendering around *Sea Hound* we used the heavy-duty Wolf four-speed back-handle drill on a mortice drill stand. Taking out ¾in (19mm) plugs from 1in (25mm) thick rubber was hard work, even when a trickle of water was kept on the rubber as lubrication. Great care was taken to keep the water away from the drill and in the end we succeeded in making the eighty holes needed to let in the bolts. The large industrial drill is necessary for larger diameter holes.

This tool kit should enable you to complete work on the hull.

I must confess I had the advantage of owning a Coronet Major woodworking machine which I have had for many years and which has helped me in major fitting work around my house. However, Wolf make a very compact saw table which will handle timber up to 1½in (38mm) and if you do have a workshop, this extra power facility would be a boon for cabinet work cutting. The Coronet has a tilting saw table, 10in (254mm) disc sander and 2½ft (762mm) centre lathe on which I turned various items including the flag-pole.

## GRP Moulding Tools

*Brushes* sufficiently stiff to press the resin through the glass mat. 1in (25mm) and 2in (51mm) will be sufficient. They should be used with a stippling action to impregnate the glass mat without disturbing the fibre distribution.

*Acetone* is a highly inflammable liquid which must be stored safely, and used with good ventilation. It is volatile and is used for brush and roller cleaning. It will damage GRP gel coats and must only be used,

in an emergency, to wipe a surface that has accidentally become contaminated with resin. It is good practice to mask off any areas of work with newspaper and 1in (25mm) masking tape. Surfaces below the working area should be protected with polythene sheets.

*Rollers* come in various forms, with metal or plastic washers on an axle. They are used to consolidate the laminate and drive out air. A single-wheel roller will be useful for consolidating laminate between bulkheads or furniture. The wider roller of 2–3in (51–76mm) will do for most other work.

*Plastic buckets or bowls* in which to mix resins. A child's plastic bucket is ideal for mixing small quantities. It is better to work with small quantities as, if you are working slowly, the resins will start to set before the job is completed. Old washing-up bowls are good for thick mixtures and paper cups for very small amounts. When resins set in plastic ware they can be removed cleanly by cracking them out.

*Rubber gloves* may feel cumbersome and hot but, particularly if you have a sensitive skin, they are a must when dealing with resins, etc.

*Barrier creams* such as Kerodex Kero 71 are highly advisable especially if you work with epoxide resin systems. These creams give excellent protection and aid later cleaning of the skin.

*Skin cleaning* is best done with Kerocleans or a similar preparation. On no account should acetone be used for, although it is a solvent, it will merely thin polymers and epoxides so that they penetrate your pores.

*Dust mask and goggles* should be worn at all times to protect eyes and lungs from dust when cutting cured GRP. If inhaled in quantity it could be dangerous. Inhaled sawdust can also damage your health, so wear a mask when reducing or sanding timber.

*Measures for liquid hardener* are available as syringes or automatic plastic dispenser bottles. Exact measuring is essential if the polymer resins are to work properly. A drop extra for luck will not do. Spring balance scales are needed for weighing some resins, if specified.

Some hull suppliers will supply you direct with small quantities of all the above materials but a good alternative is to go to one of the big companies now specialising in this market. Some are listed in Appendix C.

## Materials

You will need to know about traditional materials — wood, plywood, glues, etc — as well as the modern materials that have so much to offer, although they may not have originated with the boatbuilding industry. Be careful, though, with these introduced materials, in case of environmental problems.

I found several practical products from outside the boatbuilding industry. Ferodo products, for example, have excellent non-slip characteristics for deck and step areas. TBA Industrial Products offer materials which reduce fire risk. If fire-resistant materials can be substituted for inflammable ones this can only be to the good. The aircraft industry has many products with high specifications that are only a little dearer than the inferior ones on the market. It is a question of finding out about them and checking whether they will stand up to the marine environment. (See Appendix C for addresses.)

## Wood

Wood such as teak is expensive, but its long-lasting beauty, strength and resistance to rot and fungi attack keep it top of the list as a timber for use in a boat.

Iroko is an excellent substitute for teak, with similar properties but not quite such a good colour. Both woods darken after being sawn up and often the only way of

**Fig 18** Storing timber and plywood
1 To keep damp from bottom plank place polythene sheet over lower sticks
2 Bottom sticks might be of varying thickness to get the first bottom plank level; the rest must be of equal thickness
3 Fully seasoned wood can be stored plank face to plank face — full sticking is only needed for unseasoned timber; the end grain of planks can be candle-waxed to stop fast drying and end splitting
4 Place sets of sticks vertically over each other and at about 2ft intervals throughout the length of the plank
5 Do not let damp contact exist on stored marine plywood sheets
6 Weight of sheets stored improperly will bow them
7 Plywood should be supported off the ground and on rear face with 4 × 4in sticks to keep if off ground and wall
8 Plywood remains flat and damp-free with air space at back and face sides

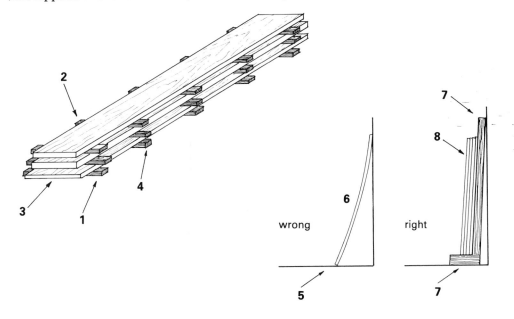

to vary a great deal and it would be best to cut off the same long plank.

To keep timber in prime condition it must be stored correctly after delivery. Fig 18 shows the usual method. The atmosphere should be neither too hot nor too damp. My unheated garage was ideal, far better than the workshop which held the central heating boiler and was therefore too dry.

### Timber Preparation

With huge power planers, circular saws and band-saws at his disposal, the timber merchant can supply you with timber ready for use in cabinet work. This extra machining costs money. It also wastes timber. If, for example, you order a plank 1in (25mm) thick, planed, it will end up ⁷⁄₈in (22mm) thick. If you specify a width, the edge sawing again wastes timber that could well have been used after the sap wood along the edge had been removed. However, it is no good ordering 2⅓in (60mm) thick planks if your circular saw will only cope with a depth of 1½in (40mm). But if your saw can deal with this kind of depth you should be able to reduce all plank stock to the sizes you need. The method is illustrated in Fig 19.

It is necessary to support the plank over its whole length so that your attention can be given to the straight cut of the saw. After securing the plank to the cutting bench and starting the cut at the overhang, small battens are secured with 'G' clamps to take the weight of the strip being removed. Even at the end of the cut, both plank and strip will be supported. Accidents happen when saws jam or falling timber knocks them on to the user. If rough planks are to be reduced, first plane the face side and one face edge so that they are at right angles to each other. Then the saw will run smoothly and each succeeding piece will have right-angled corners.

**Fig 19** Large planks being ripped up with a circular-saw must be properly supported throughout their length to avoid accidents; 'G' cramps and battens are used to hold the main plank in place and stop the sawn section falling off

differentiating between the two is by the spicy smell of teak which iroko does not have.

Teak is imported into Great Britain in sawn planks of random lengths and thickness. One supplier openly offers 'thousands' of different sizes. This offer is certainly worth consideration. You can save money if you are able to use 'shorts' — short length planks as opposed to the more expensive long planks planed and cut to size. It is convenient to handle and cut small cabinet-work items from shorts. If, however, you are keen on exact matching of colour and grain, then shorts are likely

### Marine Plywood

Buy the best quality you can afford and certainly nothing less than BS 1088 WBP from a reputable supplier. The 'reputable' is important. Foreign plywood which does not comply with BS 1088 but still carries the specification mark has been coming into the country for years, as more than one yachtsman has found, to his disadvantage, when the wood begins to delaminate in the glue-line. The 'WBP' stands for Weather and Boil Proof and, as it suggests, boards of this grade glued together with phenolic adhesives to BS 1203 will stand seventy-two hours of immersion in boiling water without deterioration of the glue-line. British sailing waters never get quite that hot, but the specification ensures delamination is avoided for many years. All the same, good ply construction should ensure that no edges are left exposed to constant weathering. Poor-quality plywoods have many voids in the core. Water can permeate from the end grain and frost will cause delamination.

Although sapele, utile and khaya woods are sometimes used in marine-ply construction, by far the best is makore (otherwise known as cherry mahogany). This is the only wood classified in BS 1088 as 'very durable'. Cheap imitations of marine plywood often incorporate gaboon — a wood not recommended in BS 1088. Check exactly what you are ordering — makore throughout, makore-faced with durable core, or something less satisfactory.

Teak-faced marine-grade plywood is available and although usually supplied with a single $^1/_2$oin (1.5mm) face, can be obtained with both sides faced, at a price. The single-faced boards are usually sufficient.

All my marine-grade plywood came from one source, Thames Plywood Manufacturers of Barking, regretfully now out of business. Thames Plydek had the appearance of a traditional planked deck but was basically Thames Marine on one face, made from alternating strips of makore or teak 2½in (63mm) wide and a contrasting insert of light or dark timber about $^1/_{16}$in (3mm) wide running in the long direction of the sheet.

All plywood should be stood on the long edge, vertically, so that bowing does not occur. If you have the space, it would be better laid flat. Edges must not get wet and care must be taken to protect faced plywood from damage. This is particu-

larly important when working them on the cutting bench.

Matching faced plywoods for colour and grain can make a lot of difference to the look of the finished item (Fig 20). When cutting faced plywoods with a jig-saw that cuts in the upward stroke, mark out and cut from the back of the panel to avoid chipping on the faced surface. When sawing on a downward cut, mark and cut from the face side.

Fig 20 Matching plywood grain on steering console helps make cabinet work up to professional standards

Standard size for plywood boards is 8 × 4ft (2,440 × 1,220mm). The merchant may have undersized boards which will be cheaper than standard stock. Incidentally, Thames also had a service which enabled them to manufacture boards up to 35ft (10.6m) long with meticulously machine-made scarf-joints. Other manufacturers may still be able to do this.

## Head-lining and Soft Furnishing

Fire-resistant materials from the aircraft industry offer obvious attractions. ICI

headlinings are lethal when set alight because of toxic fumes. Upholstery foams
used in furnishings can now be encased in
fire-retardant coverings. The UK furniture industry has standards for fire-
retarded and protected upholstery foams.
Anything of a lower standard must not be
taken on board a boat.

Head-linings for cabin roofs are made of
3/20in (4mm) plywood panels cut about
3/32in (3mm) short all round. This is
sufficient for the lining material to lap
round the edges and bring the panels up to
size. Small light panels can be Velcro
tacked behind to provide a concealed
fixing. Heavier panels need greater support. A joint-covering strip screwed along
the long edge is excellent, although the
screw heads will show. However, if raised
countersunk head screws are used they not
only look attractive but will enable you to
remove panels for inspection of wiring, or
for future modification.

When the plywood head-lining panels
have been cut, try them in place before covering to make sure the right allowance has
been made for the covering material overlap. Placing them on the wrong side of the
lining material (Fig 21), mark the material about 3in (76mm) out from the panel
and cut it out. Using a large sheet of fairly
rigid plywood, stretch the lining down flat
and pin with thumb tacks. Cover the right

'Vynide' and 'Ambla' are fire resistant and
are usually used in panel and seat finishing on aircraft. They are available in about
forty different finishes and colours, with
weights from about 12 oz (340g) to 22oz
(624g) per sq yd (0.8m²). John Cox and Son
Ltd of London distribute them for ICI and
local suppliers can be found. The materials
are fixed to panels with special adhesive.
The supplier will give you details.

Although foam sticky-backed lining
materials are available. I am not in favour
of their use in boats because of fire risk.
Plastic foam in mattresses, seats and

**Fig 21** Headlining and window detail
A GRP cabin top
B Aluminium window frame set in general pur-
pose mastic or better still silicon rubber sealant
C Glass if window is not set on curve, acrylic if
on a curve
D Interscrew
E Swish curtain rail
F Pelmet
G Celuform quadrant
H Head lining panel
I Flat board to work on for head lining covering
J Lining material has corners cut away to
avoid overlap; do not cut right up to panel
corner
K Tensioning tacks to get covering material
under slight tension
L 4mm marine plywood

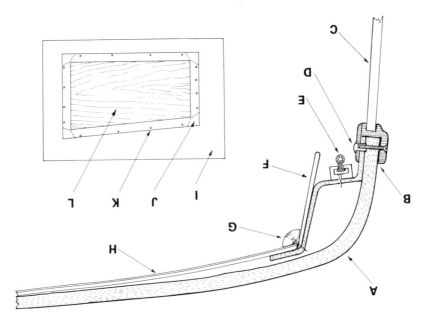

side of the panel with the recommended adhesive and place carefully on the lining. Cut the corners as shown so that no overlap occurs, as this would result in an extra-thick area and poor fit. Put adhesive on the overlap area of the panel and stick the lin-ing down all round. Battens and bricks can be used to hold the material in place while the adhesive sets. If you are careful not to pierce right through the panel you can use thumb tacks to hold the material in place.

Celuform is a thermoplastic material with a low-density cellular core and a tough homogenous outer shell. Made by Celuform Ltd of Aylesford, Maidstone, Kent, it is a first-class material for cover-ing strips to head-linings, edge-finishing and other edgings found in boat construc-tion. It is self-extinguishing and flame-spread resistant. The sections I found most useful were quadrant flat, half round, rect-angle, square and 'D' sections. The latter was perfect for the head-lining covering strips. The square section was used around the top edges of the battery covers to make a safe place to put down tools when work-ing on the engines. It is available in a number of finishes, but the white Celuform is easily painted.

Working it requires no special tools but it cuts best with a fine-tooth saw. Epoxide resin adhesives are excellent for fabrica-tion jobs. Pin with brass panel-pins, but do not overdrive the heads into the softer core. By immersing them in boiling water, the flat sections can be bent to any re-quired curvature.

## Asbestos-based Products

Accepting that there are great health hazards from the wrongful use of certain types of asbestos, this material has excep-tional advantages when it comes to provid-ing fireproof barriers and heat shielding. If you take simple precautions when work-ing the following materials, there should be little risk. Always wear a face mask when sawing and remove the dust straight away with a vacuum cleaner. The asbestos particles are embedded in resin and once worked, there is no chance of asbestos fibres becoming free so the materials are safe to use inside or outside the boat.

*Duraform* is a thermoplastic PVC sheet material reinforced with chrysotile (white) asbestos. It gives a high fire-resis-tant performance with low flame spread, no flaming and is self-extinguishing. It is available in thicknesses from $1/20$in (1.5mm) to $1/4$in (6mm), in 8 × 4ft (2,440 × 1,220mm) boards with fourteen decorative plain colours and gloss, satin, matt or em-bossed surfaces. The material has low water absorption and high chemical and weathering resistance. It has been used successfully on cladding panels on inland waterways boats. I used it as an interior finishing cladding for the forward cabin sides, louvres on engine-room air intakes and covers for battery tops. It can be worked with normal hand tools, which is preferable, as they make less dust than powered tools. I found epoxide adhesives excellent with Duraform, but leaflets are available from TBA Industrial Products which give full technical information.

*Heatshield* is another Turner & Newall Ltd material originally developed for the automotive industry for heat shielding around exhaust systems, bulkheads and around units prone to heat radiation — alternators, petrol pumps, fuel tanks, and so on. Heatshield is a phenolic resin-bonded asbestos material sealed with an aluminium reflective surface, or with one aluminium surface and the other finished with aluminium foil.

It is supplied in $1/10$in (3mm) thick sheets, though for production runs it can be moulded into components. It is an excel-lent material for engine-room bulkhead cladding, fuel-tank protection and as a heat shield above and behind cookers and water heaters. It will operate continuously at 482°F (250°C) and withstand heat soak temperatures up to 572°F (300°C). It re-duces sound emission, has low resonance, low weight and is resistant to vibration fatigue. Flat sheets are easily worked with hand tools, with the usual health precau-tions taken during working. When using the material as cladding, I fixed it to the bulkhead with large-headed brass panel-pins before permanently fixing it with round-head screws with a small washer underneath to spread the clamping load.

Heatshield is not affected by water (fresh or salt), by petrol, oil, diesel, anti-freeze or rust inhibitors, so it is ideal for engine spaces. It does, of course, add to the cost, but the protection it offers must be balanced against this.

## Stainless-steel Tiles

Although Heatshield has excellent in-sulation properties, it does not have a decorative finish. I found a practical and decorative answer, for use in the galley or toilet compartment, in Styles stainless-steel tiles, made by the Zealand Engineer-ing Co Ltd of Ashford, Middlesex. Alloy tiles are made in various parts of the world but they are not as durable in a marine environment.

The tiles can be fixed to marine plywood, glass-reinforced plastic or any material provided it is free from dirt, grease or flak-ing paint. I put them straight on to the Heatshield I used as a lining behind and over the heater and oven, with epoxide

**Fig 22** Epoxide resin adhesive was used to fix Styles stainless-steel tiles to galley walls covered with fire resistant Heatshield

resin, type ET-17 and EHL-17. As this was slow-setting I used pads and battens (Fig 22) to hold the tiles in place for about an hour. Rubber-based contact adhesives could be used, but they are not waterproof and could cause the tiles to loosen later. I cut the tiles with ordinary heavy house-hold scissors, dabbed epoxide resin adhe-sive at each corner and pressed them into place. Working from the bottom upwards, they proved sufficiently self-supporting for a couple of rows to be fixed before a pres-sure pad was put in place.

## Swish Furni-Glyde

This was developed from the plastic curtain-rail system made by Swish. Some fourteen co-ordinated nylon fittings ena-ble what was a curtain-track system to be used for a number of interesting applica-tions. Since *Queen Elizabeth II* was fitted out with over a mile of it, I thought this sufficient precedent to use it on my boat. Some of the components available are shown in Fig 23 together with the uses they can be put to as drawer runners, stops and on sliding doors. Fig 24 shows the track being used overhead, on a drawer, to give support and act as a stop so that it can-not fall out, even when off the drawer catch; the latter should always be fitted al-though it is not shown in the figure.

Lightweight sliding doors save the swing-ing space of the hinged door. Fig 25 shows Swish items in this context. No doubt many other uses will be found for this ver-satile product. I found that, heated care-fully in boiling water and bent to shape, the track formed an excellent oblong shower curtain-rail. Don't be tempted to make corners too tight, or the track will distort. Have a try-out with a small piece before starting on a long length.

## Fendering

Fendering should be a tough and func-tional part of your boat. Inevitably, boats have to take knocks, so give them adequate protection from the start, rather than prissy bits of wood, alloy and plastic that might look decorative and enhance the sheer-line, but do little else. They soon have to be replaced at great expense. How-

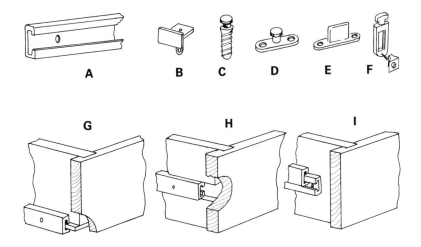

**Fig 23** Swish Furni-Glyde components
**A** UPVC Swish curtain track
**B** Stop-end for track ends on drawers and curtains
**C** Barbed slider for use on sliding doors
**D** Plate slider (alternative to C)
**E** Pilot
**F** Adjustable end slider for doors with sufficient thickness
**G** Method of using Swish track to take the drawer base
**H** Method of using Swish track in conventional way instead of using wooden runner
**I** Method using two sections of Swish track within each other

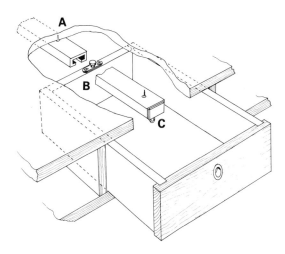

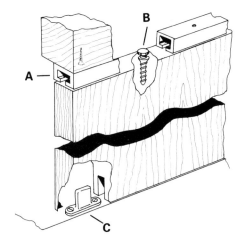

**Fig 24** Furni-Glyde used for overhead drawer runner
**A** Swish track
**B** Plate slider
**C** End stop to prevent drawer falling out

**Fig 25** Furni-Glyde used for sliding door arrangement
**A** Swish track
**B** Barbed slider
**C** Pilot

ever, they are easy to install with light bolting through the hull and many have a plastic strip to cover the screw heads. A special tool will probably be needed to force the plastic into the alloy. This can be difficult in cold weather when the strip is less pliable.

A wooden fender near the sheer-line is easy to fit; it does take some hard knocks but is easier to replace than the toy fendering previously described. Wood should never be screwed through the hull but properly bolted with bolts sunk and plugged over with wooden plugs cut from the same material as the fender strip.

Fig 26 illustrates the points that should receive attention when fendering a hull.

**A** Large backing washers or plates spread stress loads over a large area on a GRP hull. I cut and drilled my own from strip steel which were later galvanised. Before tightening them on the inside of the hull, they were covered with silicone rubber to act as a final water seal.

**B** Many fender sections need a flat metal strip through the centre section to reinforce bolt location and spread loadings. I used 2 × ¼in (51 × 6mm) strip which was first cut to the necessary lengths before sending, along with the plate washers to

HM Dockyard, Plymouth, for galvanising. Galvanising is done at many shipyards and the charge is usually estimated by weight. After galvanising, I finished the strip and plates with a full epoxide resin paint system. Metal strips should not terminate at the end of one fender section but must extend far enough into the next fender so as to be anchored by at least one bolt.

**C** On large-section fenders, centres for bolt holes should be 15–18in (381–457mm) apart. Drilling the outer part of the 'D' is best done with a water-lubricated holesaw. Electricity plus water can kill, so take great care to use only a trickle of water with the drill kept at a low speed of 200–250rpm.

**D** Rubber plugs to fill the bolt holes are available from the merchants. They are fitted in place with silicone rubber compound and driven home with a wooden mallet, taking care not to overdrive them.

**E** My hull had a complex lip to take a fender moulding that had to be specially extruded. This is a fairly expensive item if the hull manufacturer has not got a standing contract with a rubber supplier for this special shape. Mine had not but, through *Yellow Pages,* I found a small manufacturer prepared to make the extrusion

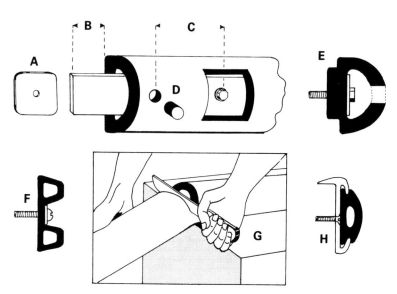

**Fig 26** Fendering a hull

moulds and manufacture the section I wanted. The moulds were moderately expensive but the final bill was less than a bulk-produced product from one of the larger manufacturers.

**F**  This is a 'B'-section fender, now available also in PVC and rubber. Larger sections have hollows in the top and bottom sections. They are easily fitted and the flat retaining strip is decorative, especially in stainless steel. PVC tends to scuff and become dirty but is reasonably durable.

**G**  Cutting small-section rubber strip can be done with a sharp knife. A fine-tooth saw will be needed for larger sections. Both methods are easier with water lubrication. Bend the strip being cut downwards, holding the cut open to prevent the rubber from pinching the blade.

**H**  Many fender sections are available with a covering lip for the hull-to-deck joint. The one shown here is made of aluminium and has a rubber insert. If the insert is small section and more decorative than fender-like, avoid it. With a decent 'D'-section insert, the fender can be effective but expect hard work when inserting the rubber or PVC extrusion strip. A special compressing tool might be needed; enquire when ordering. Plastic strip can be softened by heating it gently in hot water. Both rubber and plastic can be eased into place with washing-up detergent.

### Fendering: Bow and Stern Quarters

In certain section fenderings, the manufacturers offer special sections extruded to a bow section angle, and 90° angles for the stern quarters. On my boat the large sections were mitred for the stern quarters and a teak finishing piece was placed either side of the bow (Fig 27). I engaged two shipwrights to help me with the fendering since each 11ft (3.3m) section

**Fig 27** Fendering at the bow is finished off with teak run into the extruded rubber section that forms the main fendering; the stem-head roller clears the teak and a chafe plate allows a clear lead for mooring lines

weighed nearly 110lb (50kg) and had to be roped into place and supported while it was drilled and bolted: one person working and one supporting outside and the third putting on plate washers and bolting up inside. The teak bow pieces were fitted down inside the 'D'-section rubber at their aft end, to give firm location, and the bolts were plugged over with matching teak. All joins in the rubber part of the fendering were sealed with black silicone rubber.

## Fasteners

Nuts, bolts, washers and screws of various kinds play a large and vital part in yacht construction, both for woodwork and engineering installations. They are needed in quantity, so buying a few here and there in a plastic packet is out. Find your nearest industrial fastenings supplier and see if his catalogue and prices suit your requirements. I found that GKN Stainless Steel Fasteners of Bordesley Green, Birmingham, had the full range I required. Why stainless steel?

In 1979 official sources estimated that corrosion cost £10 million a day in the UK. When cadmium-plated brass and copper fasteners were used so much in boatbuilding, yachtsmen had to spend a great deal of money replacing corroded fasteners. Copper dezincifies in salt water, steel and iron rust and in no time boats become costly if not downright dangerous. A fastener failing at a critical time can cost life.

Fasteners are available in two types of austenitic stainless steel: A2 or 18/8 (18 per cent chrome and 8 per cent nickel) and A4 or 18/10/3 (18 per cent chrome, 10 per cent nickel and 3 per cent molybdenum). Both grades are corrosion resistant but 18/10/3 has greater freedom from surface staining in a marine environment.

A rather more expensive material is Monel which is happy in the severest underwater and chemical environments. Stainless-steel fasteners must not be used under water. They perform perfectly well in all applications above the water-line, both inside and outside the hull. A4 fasteners are slightly more expensive than A2, but for quantities used in a single construction the price differential is not great.

It pays to minimise the number of different types of fasteners so that full boxes of a small number, rather than small numbers of many types, can be bought. With bolts, there is some difficulty in knowing exactly how long they should be as the GRP thickness of the hull will vary. Where work is out of sight, such as the engine-room, it is best to buy studding (threaded rod) in lengths of 39in (1m) which can be cut to the required lengths and finished with a nut at each end. One nut can be fastened by punching the edge of the thread on opposite sides. This prevents the nut from coming off.

Washers are important, especially on the engineering, where they not only spread load but prevent fasteners from coming undone with the vibration. Single coil and crinkle washers are available in A2 and A4 stainless steel.

## Metrication and Thread Forms

The progression to world metrication is a slow business and although the implementation of the isometric system reduces the number of bolt diameters to ten (M5 to M36) from the original fifty-six imperial diameters, the boat industry still lags behind. Imperial thread forms are still used, namely BS, Whitworth, BS, Fine, Unified Coarse, Unified Fine and BA. I did most of the bolting work on *Sea Hound* with M6 (approximately 1/4in (6mm) diameter) and M3 (approximately 6BA/0.110in (3mm) diameter). A number of items from chandlery catalogues have threaded holes but are not supplied with bolts. This is understandable as the manufacturer does not know the length of bolt required, but I found it wasted a great deal of time sorting out what thread had been used in order to get the suitable bolt. The less thread sizes you have aboard, the fewer spanners you have to carry, but the position today, when we are still a long way from full metrication or any kind of standardisation in the industry, means that you have to carry the whole range.

## Woodscrews

Slotted-head woodscrews are best bought in stainless steel and with a modern head,

| | | | |
|---|---|---|---|
| countersunk head woodscrew slotted | | machine screw pan head slotted | |
| | | machine screw raised cheese head slotted | |
| raised countersunk woodscrew slotted | | machine screw raised countersunk head slotted | |
| | | machine screw cheese head slotted | 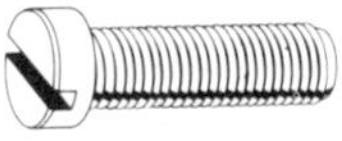 |
| round head woodscrew slotted | | machine screw countersunk head slotted | 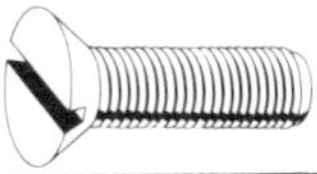 |
| countersunk head woodscrew superdriv/recess | | cotter pin | |
| raised countersunk head woodscrew supadriv/recess | | flat washer | |
| round head woodscrew supadriv/recess | | spring washer | |
| hexagon set screw | | self-tapping screw countersunk head supadriv/recess top-type a bottom-type b | 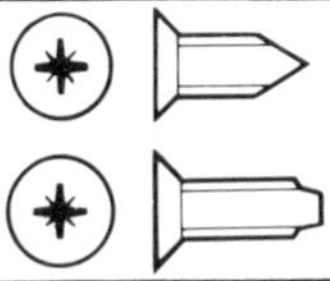 |
| hexagon bolt | | self tapping screw raised countersunk head supadriv/recess top-type ab bottom-type b | 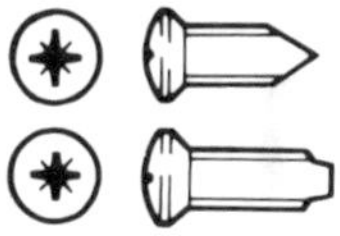 |
| plain nut full (lock nut-half) | | self tapping screw pan head supadriv/recess top-type ab bottom-type b | 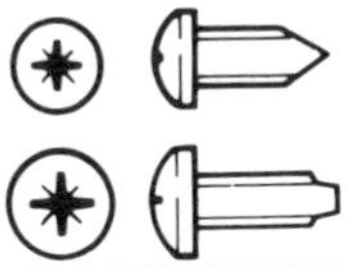 |
| castellated nut | | self tapping screw mushroom head supadriv/recess top-type ab bottom-type b | 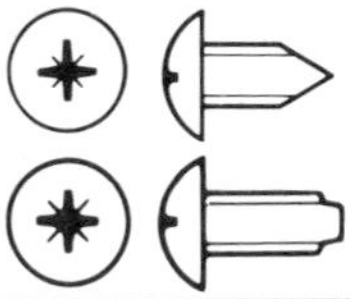 |

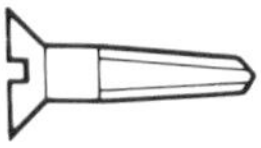

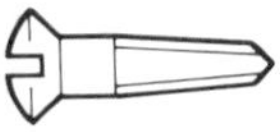

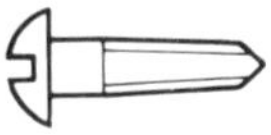

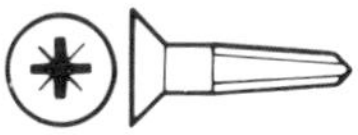

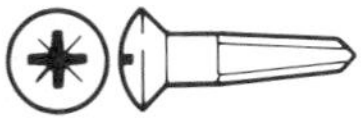

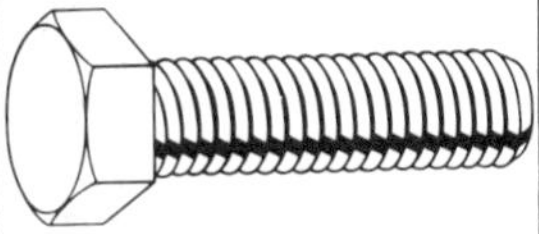

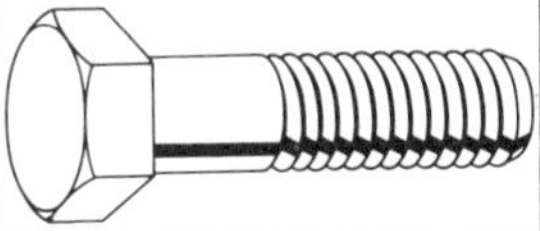

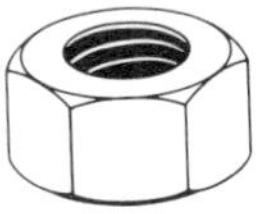

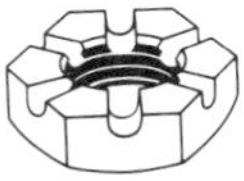

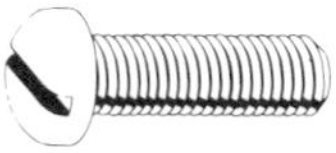

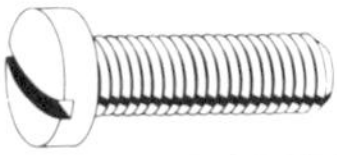

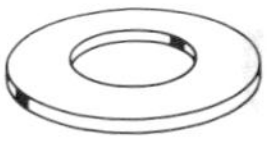

**Fig 28** Fasteners identification chart

such as the GKN 'Supadriv' range. The problem with driving any screw is cam out, that is, the screwdriver jumps out of the slot as turning pressure is applied with the result that the slot — and possibly the screwdriver — is damaged. This happens a lot in boatbuilding when it is awkward to get a vertical drive and maximum pressure on to screws in a difficult location. Phillips-head screws were the first cross-head screws to try to solve the problem and later GKN produced their Pozidriv cross-head. The latest, Supadriv, is a great improvement and should prevent painful fingers from metal splinters. The cross-head drivers for Pozidriv and Supadriv are compatible and will also drive Phillips-head screw heads.

Be careful when fastening such items as cabin doors. Woodscrews are fine for the door hinge but should not be used to fasten the hinge into the GRP stile. Use self-tapping screws, perhaps type AB with the pointed tip, for this. Even with these a word of warning is necessary. On no account should this type of screw be used for any application where severe loading could rip it out. It is bad practice to use self-tapping screws for deck fittings, grab handles and the like, but it is not unusual to find that even professionals use this dangerous method.

All screws, but especially self-tapping ones, should be counterbored with the correct size drill bit. On my boat, light-duty self-tapping screws were inserted, with tips dipped in epoxy resin as an extra safeguard. For woodscrews, there are bits which will drill a complete hole and countersink in one operation. They give the fastener maximum holding power with no possibility of splitting the material into which it is inserted. With self-tapping screws into GRP there is a great danger of splitting out the glass or jamming the screw so tightly that the screw head breaks off.

When you find a suitable manufacturer, get a copy of his full catalogue so that, initially at least, you can put in one big order. From Fig 28 you will understand why I plead for sensible rationalisation of all these items.

### Fasteners Under Water
Usually, the manufacturer of any item that requires through-bolting under water supplies suitable nuts and bolts that are compatible with the fitting. Silicon bronze or, for larger bolt sizes, aluminium bronze fasteners perform well under water. They should not be used in conjunction with dissimilar metals which would set up galvanic corrosion and, as with all underwater metal parts, should be protected with some form of cathodic protection. Firms offering this service will recommend the size and disposition of anodes to be fitted on shafting or through-bolted on the hull.

While stainless steels are unhappy in an environment where oxygen is unable to keep their outer surfaces protected with an oxidised layer, I find that silicon and aluminium bronzes cope well if given paint and sealant coatings that isolate them. I used an epoxide undercoat and finishing coat on underwater bolts on the housing of both echo-sounder transducer and log. They were also coated with silicone rubber sealant as they were fed into place.

### Deck Covering
The traditional teak-laid plank deck undoubtedly looks superb when properly laid and maintained. It is, however, costly to build and difficult to keep clean, due to the inevitable fuel spills or oil from beaches carried aboard on the crew's feet.

If teak planking is to be used, the water-tight integrity of the GRP deck can be maintained by:

**A**  Through-bolting using wooden plugs on the bolt heads on the outside, epoxide adhesive under the planks and Arbokol 2175 for deck seams.
**B**  As above, but using woodscrews from below. The only difficulty with this method is to get the correct screw length through varying thickness of GRP laminate for sufficient grip on the planking to keep it in place while the adhesive sets.

Although I am all for tradition, I believe there are available more practical deck-covering materials which provide excellent non-slip properties. GRP is very slippery and dangerous and the simplest and cheapest way to overcome this is to give it a coat of non-slip deck paint after masking off surrounding areas.

Then there are the plastic and rubber coverings which are glued into place. Among these are Dunlop Trakmark, Walker's Treadmaster, 3M Safety Walk and Ferodo Decktread. When considering any deck material look at the specifications, think how comfortable it will be to walk on, how it retains its friction properties when wet and if it deadens noise.

I chose Ferodo Decktread as it was being manufactured to Admiralty specifications for use on warships — a good recommendation. When used on public transport, this material has a life expectancy of eight years or so with a traffic flow of a million people a year. Even in a marina I didn't expect so many people aboard! After eight seasons (Fig 106) it is in excellent condition despite the occasional fuel spillage, dropped anchor, etc. Oil resistance is excellent and the surface is easily cleaned with liquid soap or detergent and then rinsed well.

You will have to make paper patterns of the area to be covered and send them to Ferodo. The reason for this is that Decktread has to be cut with a diamond-cutter. I neglected to specify the cut-outs for the two after gas tank hatches, with the result that I wore out a jig-saw blade every 8in (20cm) — an expensive mistake, but such friction ensures that when Decktread is wet it gives excellent grip. A bonus is that Decktread is fire resistant to BS 476 Class 1, relating to the surface spread of flame, and if it should burn it does not produce toxic fumes.

It is available in a number of thicknesses from $^1/_{16}$in (2mm) to $^1/_4$in (6mm) in plain and slatted, and five colours. I chose a slatted red Decktread which was carefully cut at the works to give the appearance of a laid deck with parallel planks. The Decktread was easily fixed to the GRP decks with epoxide adhesives ET-17 and EHL-17. The decks were first scratched up to offer a degree of mechanical bond and

then both deck and Decktread panels were given a thin coat of the adhesive. The panels were laid in place and the air squeezed out, but the edges had to be weighted down to hold them in close contact with the curve of the deck. I used plenty of clean bricks for this and inside twelve hours the deck was ready to walk on.

**Adhesives**
One directory lists over two thousand adhesives, each one designed to do a specific job. The adhesives used in boatbuilding have to be extremely efficient and strong to perform well in a hostile environment. From the point of view of convenience and cost, it is best to limit the number of types. Higher cost is only justified if it achieves superior results.

I used an epoxide resin system. This, though expensive, has advantages over polymers for amateur use. Generally, a glue-line derives its strength in two ways — chemical and mechanical bonding. In chemical bonding the molecules of the adhesive combine with those of the material in the surfaces being bonded. This happens to perfection when new layers of GRP are bonded on to ones that have not fully cured. Because chemical reactions are influenced by temperature, full reactions will not occur below 50°F (10°C). When a GRP hull is delivered the laminate is fully cured and although it is then impossible to get a chemical bond you can make reliable mechanical bonds.

Mechanical bonds depend on the surfaces of the material being sufficiently rough and perfectly free of grease, dust or other dirt so that glue molecules can be forced into the microscopic mountainous landscape and grip it as the set takes place. All GRP surfaces must be scratched with a sharpened file to roughen them and expose some of the ends of the glass fibres. All this dust must be removed. I used a domestic vacuum cleaner. Any dirt or oil must be thoroughly cleaned off before the scratching as you do not want these, or a cleansing agent, to contaminate the fibres as they are exposed. The epoxide resin family of adhesives provides a superb mechanical bond and has the advantage that it can be used for joining many types of composite materials — light alloys, plastics, acrylics, glass, wood, perspex, and so on. With one family of resins there is chemical compatibility which is carried over to the paint system if you use epoxide resin paints.

Table 2 shows the adhesives I used. There are equivalents from other manufacturers that can be substituted, but the ones listed are acknowledged by the Admiralty, Lloyd's register and equivalent bodies throughout the world.

All adhesives have to be used in a controlled way. Always study the manufacturer's literature and make sure you understand it before you start work. Many adhesives have a definite shelf life. These should be bought fresh and only stored in small quantities if you can use them within a reasonable time. Some are hygroscopic. They absorb moisture from the air and will deteriorate if kept in damp conditions. It is important to store all of them out of direct sunlight and heat.

Industrial hygiene should always be observed in your working area, even though you are only building one boat.

Acetone, cellulose thinners or similar solvents can be used to clean equipment before epoxide resins have hardened on it. Epoxide resins do not stick to polythene, so use the recommended plastic containers for mixing. Hardened resin is removed from a polythene bucket by flexing the sides when the mixture has set. The Cascophen and Cascomite glues can also be removed from the mixing container by flexing.

It is important to clean your hands properly. All synthetic resins have a skin-irritation potential, and can cause dermatitis. There will be no problems if the following procedures are observed:

1   Always use a suitable barrier cream on any skin that might come into contact with a synthetic resin.

2   Always clean off wet resin before it sets. Use a skin cleansing cream, *never* a solvent which will encourage the resin to

*Table 2:*   ADHESIVES
*Source: Wessex Resins and Adhesives Ltd – Epophen and Gougeon Systems*

| Product | Description | Uses and Comments |
| --- | --- | --- |
| Epophen ELE-17 Hardener EHL-22 | Two-part product mixing to thick grey compound. Mixed 1:1 by weight. Working time for mix 1 hr at 68°F (20°C). | Enormous strength for direct contact bonding of large items like cabin beams, decks and superstructure to hull. Excellent for fairing-in on structures inside and outside hull. Lower cost because grey content is resin filler. Excellent for gluing plastic laminates (eg Duraform, Formica) to GRP as fixed cabin linings. Rough up GRP before gluing. |
| Borden Epophen EL-5 EHL-15 } West System (WRA) Gougeon (USA) | Two-part product. Mix 100:50. Working time 35–45min for 1lb (454g) batch at 68°F (20°C). Thin gold tinted syrup when mixed. | All matting in of components — bulkheads, cabin beam ends, encapsulated plywood reinforcement areas. The syrupy liquid mix soon wets out all types of glass mat. |

| Product | Description | Uses and Comments |
| --- | --- | --- |
| Epophen ET-17 Hardener EHL-17 | Two-part product. Thick white and thick golden brown. Mix equal parts by weight. Working time 1½hr at 68°F (20°C) for 2lb (908g) mix. | Approved by Lloyd's for bonding teak to GRP for decks. Excellent for workshop fabrication of items using different materials — steel, alloy, wood, cast iron, GRP, plywood. Used for all wood-to-wood joints where a water-proof joint without staining is essential. Used for fixing stainless-steel tiles in galley. Rough up GRP; degrease and roughen steel; etch light alloy before gluing. |
| Epophen Epoxide Resin Putty Pack (Wessex) | Two-part product. Thick like putty when needed. Grey in colour. Cut off and mix equal lengths from sticks. Working time ¾hr at 68°F (20°C). | Hull and deck fairing on wood, metal or GRP. Fairing-in skin fittings to hull lines and 101 jobs in and around the boat. |
| Cascophen RS216M (resorcinol-formaldehyde) Resin with catalyst RX58 | Two-part mix. Red liquid plus white powder hardener. Mix 5:1 by weight. BS/1204/WBP. | Excellent weatherproof quality — a must for all timber joints with glue-line exposed to elements and below water-line and bilge areas. Red staining may preclude use for fine cabinet work but is no problem for woodwork that is to be painted. Excellent for bonding decorative laminates to wood but must be immediately cleaned off decorative surface. Clean off with water-damp cloth. |
| Cascomite 'One Shot' (urea-formaldehyde) | White powder — simply mix with water. BS/1204/MR. | Moisture-resistant and gap filling. Very easy to mix and use. Ideal for fine cabinet work. Clean off with water-damp cloth. Use for interior woodwork and cabinet work. |
| Contact adhesives (various brands, Superstick and others) | Spread over both surfaces, allow to dry out for a few minutes, then bring surfaces together. | Used for decorative laminates in dry areas — not WC compartments. Not waterproof. Highly inflammable vapour given off drying surfaces. |
| Specialised adhesives recommended by manufacturer for bonding his product | | Bonding soft trim materials to plywood backing. Bonding acoustic lining material to engine compartment surfaces, etc. Care needed to ensure compatibility with trim, etc. |

penetrate the pores. Rozalex, Kerodex and Wessex have products for barrier and removal applications.

3 For blending epoxide putties, throwaway polythene gloves are available from Wessex. If you are not a clean worker they should be used at all times, although they do make your hands hot.

### Usable Life

All synthetic resin adhesives have a definite period between mixing and beginning to set — the working time as laid out in Table 2. The actual time depends on the temperatures of the adhesive, the surfaces it is applied to and the ambient temperature. Only mix quantities that can be used in the time given, making allowance for the fact that setting will take place much quicker in higher temperatures. The epoxide and polymer resins are exothermic — they produce heat in themselves as they begin to set. I gave myself a shock when, on a hot summer's day, with the temperature inside the hull at over 90°F (32°C), I tried to glass in some shelving. I mixed the epoxy resin in a small bucket, put it down and started glassing in. I looked around a few moments later and thought I had a smoking time-bomb behind me. The exotherm was so great that in the few moments of putting my brush back in the liquid resin it had set and was giving off smoke that made me think it was about to burst into flame. It went over the side at lightning speed!

The exotherm is excessive if you try to build up a large volume or thick layers of GRP too quickly.

### Gluing Timber

Although timber that has been impregnated under pressure with wood preservatives has obvious advantages in boatbuilding, it has certain problems when it comes to getting a reliable glue-line. It is recommended that preservative treatment be given after all the wood is fixed together. Copper salts, often a constituent of wood preservatives, can adversely affect the setting of epoxide resins. Take technical advice when pre-treated timber is to be used. Preservatives alter the colour of

wood and tend to darken it. I only used preservatives on out-of-sight woodwork and have kept the beautiful warm brown of the teak cabinet work natural in colour.

Teak has a bad reputation for gluing, but I had no problems. Ensure that the wood is dry and that it has been rough sawn for some time before planing and making it up into cabinet work. If you come across a particularly oily piece of teak you can wipe off the surface with acetone and allow it to dry thoroughly before using epoxide or resorcinol glues. If you do not let the solvent evaporate completely, you will get a glue-line that will probably fail.

Moisture content is important in achieving a good glue-line in timber. Ask your supplier about this when ordering kiln-dried timber for your project. Urea resins prefer a 12–15 per cent moisture content while the resorcinol glues will work better with a higher moisture content of 15–18 per cent. Even if kiln dried to these levels, the timber must be given dry storage, but not on a damp concrete floor where moisture will be extracted into the timber and certainly not in the open.

### Sealants

Sealants perform a number of functions, not only sealing out water and damp but acting as jointing which will absorb both compressive and extensive movement. You will need a range of sealants with differing characteristics. I found that Adshead Ratcliffe & Co of Belper, Derbyshire, had the products and the technical literature to enable me to get perfect results. No doubt there are other manufacturers in different parts of the world with a similar range of products. Table 3 lists some of their products which are of value to the home boatbuilder. Basic precautions should be taken with these, as with any chemicals, as some contain toxic compounds which may give rise to dermatitis. A number are two-pot compositions which must be mixed and used within a given time. Setting time varies, so giving you a choice for slow jobs or speedier ones.

Most sealants have a definite shelf life, some as little as twelve months, and many

*Table 3:* CAULKING AND SEALANTS
*(Based on products from Adshead Ratcliffe & Co Ltd, Belper, Derbyshire)*

| Sealant and Appropriate Cleaner | Work Life/ Cure Time | Sealant Type and Normal Joint Preparation | Typical Applications on Boats |
|---|---|---|---|
| Arbosil 1081. Colours: white, black, grey, bronze, translucent. Arbo Cleaner No 13. | Skin 5min. Tack free 1hr. Cure 2–7 days. | One-part elastic silicone rubber sealant, gun applied. Arbo Primer 2650 for porous surfaces, 2172 or no primer for plastics. No primer for most other surfaces. Surfaces must be dry when sealant applied. | Suitable for joints in GRP, aluminium, glazing, ceramics, deck fittings, sanitary ware, etc. |
| Arbokol 2175. Colour: black. Arbo Cleaner No 13. | Work life 1hr. Solid cure 24hr. Full cure 7 days. | Two-component poly-sulphide rubber sealant. Arbo Primer 327 for good adhesion to timbers. Gun applied. | Deck caulking and bonding timber deck to GRP or aluminium decks. Chemical (oil, petrol, diesel) resistance. Good chemical resistance and ageing properties, even under severe conditions. |
| Arbokol 2150. Colours: grey, black. Arbo Cleaner No 13. | Work life 1hr. Set 24hr. Full cure 7 days. | Two-component poly-sulphide sealant curing to tough rubber. Arbo Primer 327 required on timber. No primer required on most other surfaces. | Heavy-duty underwater sealant. Adheres to GRP, ferrous and non-ferrous metals. Suitable for sealing joints in keels, through hole fittings, etc. Also used for caulking in hull timbers. Good petrol, oil and chemical resistance. |
| Arbomast GP sealing compound. Colours: natural, grey, black, white, teak. Arbo Cleaner No 13 or white spirit. | Skin 24hr. | Oil-based sealing compound intended for general-purpose caulking above the water-line. Particularly suited to use in timber constructions where joints are to be painted. | Painting joints between timber components and bedding cover strips, etc. Should be painted. Low cost. |
| Arbomast BR sealing compound. Colours: grey, black, white and translucent. Arbo Cleaner No 13 or white spirit. | Skin approx 48hr. | One-part butyl rubber-based sealing compound. | Suited to joints not exposed to ultra-violet light and particularly suited to bedding cover strips, beads, etc. |
| Arbokol 1000. Colours: grey, black, white, teak, bronze. | Skin approx 1hr. Through cure 14–30 days. | One-part polysulphide sealant. Cures from the surface inwards. Surfaces must be dry and clean. Porous surfaces primed with Arbo Primer 925 or Arbo Primer 327. | Sealing deck and skin fittings where a slow cure is acceptable. Also suited for general-purpose pointing and sealing on super-structure. Chemical resis-tance and durability good. |

will deteriorate if stored in heat or direct sunlight. Buy only as much as you need. Most sealants, including Arbokol 1000, 1081, 2150 and 2175, are sold in cartridge form and are applied with a skeleton gun available from most sealant makers. There are various sized nozzles to fit the cartridges, but probably the handiest type is the blank polythene one which you can cut to get the right size 'squirt'. When using one-part sealants it is advisable to seal the nozzle with a piece of polythene sheeting and an elastic band, otherwise the sealant will solidify in the nozzle.

Be prepared to clean off tools, joints and yourself, especially with the quick-setting varieties. The single-component items should be wiped off, then clean finished with a little Arbo No 13 cleaner on a cotton rag. This cleaner does not affect GRP but it is foul smelling, as are some of the polysulphide rubber sealants.

When bolting up skin fittings you will inevitably get some sealant on the spanner. Again, it must be cleaned off right away or it will be difficult to remove. When working alone, try to select one of the slower curing sealants, as it takes time to put a fitting on the outside of the boat, bolt it in place, then nip inside to put nuts on bolts and tighten them up.

When a joint is in full view, give it a smooth, fine finish. Use masking tape to protect surfaces outside the jointed area and tool and wipe the joint. Pressing a knife dipped in solvent over the sealant will often improve adhesion. The wipe will give a smooth surface. With Arbokol 1000 and 1081, tooling with a knife dipped in water containing a small amount of detergent will give a good finish. Masking tape is best removed soon after tooling so that the edges of sealant settle down and are not torn up as they would be if the masking is removed later in the cure.

Teak-laid decks give any yacht a touch of luxury and, with modern methods of laying the planks using epoxy adhesives and Arbokol 2175, one can produce long-lasting, practical deck surfaces, fully up to professional standards. This caulking sealant is greatly superior to the old methods using oakum and tar, as the adhesion of this two-part polysulphide ensures adjacent planks are not only watertight, but they can flex without fear of any movement disturbing the integrity of the joint.

Whatever make of sealant you decide on, get the relevant technical literature and understand it fully before you order and use the material. This will enable you to estimate quantities and to use the sealant properly. Do not be like the yachtsman trying to repair a deck, who was awash in a treacly mass because he forgot to add the second component of a two-component system.

**Paints and Painting**
The time has long gone when the PR men hailed GRP as a material that 'never needed painting'. Not true!

Paint is needed for protective and cosmetic reasons. The protection side is the most important. Bits of boat cost a lot of money and when you have struggled to afford them, it is not pleasant to see corrosion and weathering eating them away.

Over the years I have been associated with a number of marine-paint manufacturers and my boats have occasionally been used as floating test beds for marine paints. Except on wood, I favour the epoxy and polymer paint systems. In the early sixties, when these paints first became available for the amateur, I realised that they had properties which would be invaluable in a marine environment. Both cure by chemical reaction and, with a correctly prepared surface, have superior adhesive qualities as well as hardness and long life. They are waterproof compared to conventional paints which is a favourable point in relation to GRP boats and fittings. Generally speaking, I am not in favour of using such waterproof coverings on wood because wood is not a stable material. Its moisture content varies with the weather and immersion; as a result it needs to 'breathe'. The vapour barrier created by these modern paints is not suitable for wood. It could be argued that if a dry wooden structure was completely sealed with a moisture-barrier paint it would remain perfect. The trouble comes when part of the paint film is damaged and water seeps into the substrata. It then begins to lift off the paint with vapour pressure.

I always use a conventional paint on any wood that is likely to get damaged. If there are parts of the internal wood construction that are completely hidden and are unlikely to get damaged, then I use an epoxide resin or polymer paint. The two-can polymers keep their gloss better than the two-can epoxide resin paints. However, the latter do seem to have greater covering power and certainly stick well to a properly prepared surface, rather better in fact than the polyurethanes. I do find that the sheer adhesive quality of an epoxide seems to ensure a better glue effect when compared to the polymer, which really must have perfect surface preparation to do its job equally well.

But to get down to the practical side: what needs painting on a brand new construction?

### Pre-painting Metal Fittings

Skin and exhaust fittings, steering gear, torque tubes, valve bodies, bolts and bolt-on panels all benefit from a protective coat of paint before they are built into the boat. When they are fresh from the factory they will probably be oily or greasy. First, then, clean them with a degreasing solvent. Underwater fittings or those that are to be housed in damp conditions should be given an etching primer followed by epoxy primer and two coats of epoxy resin paint. It is easier and better to do painting before assembly then when the items are fitted in. If fittings do get accidentally chipped during assembly they can be easily patched in and given a final pristine coat. Boatbuilders would scorn the idea of wasting so much time and money — a cost that would have to be passed on to the client — but DIY has a great advantage here! You are doing this extra work for your own benefit.

Blakes of Gosport have a range of paints in both two-can and conventional paint systems, which I now use. All yachtsmen will have their own trustworthy favourites and it is a good plan to keep to one manufacturer. I would not recommend the home builder to go in for experimentation

as I sometimes do. The fewer types of paint you can manage with, the better. Read and understand the manufacturer's technical literature so that you do not run into problems.

### Interior Painting

As you build the interior of the boat you will have parts behind panels and under floors that will be very awkward to get at in the future. These must be painted as you go along. I did find it annoying to have to stop work and start clearing dust from the cabin in order to do a spot of painting, but actually this did no harm. After painting I could see what had been achieved and went on to the next part of the work with a clean start.

I repeat, do not put wood preservative on timber before glassing in. With the bonding completed and thoroughly cured, preservative can be applied. Let it dry out very thoroughly before applying the paint system.

I took the car from the garage to give me room to pre-paint the forward-cabin plywood ceiling lining-panels. The floor of a paint shop should be wetted before starting to paint, to keep down dust. Three gloss coats over two primers, rubbing down between each coat, have lasted eight years without yellowing or going dull. In this situation they get plenty of steam from the galley but little ultra-violet light which speedily destroys paint. Most paints and varnishes incorporate a UV filtering medium.

The beautiful grain of fine-grain timbers should be preserved. Varnish is excellent outside where it will take the weathering, but inside, many owners prefer a matt finish. You can get varnishes that will give you this matt finish but I have found that they tend to darken with age. For me, the modern boat must be light and airy, not a black cavern, so I decided to try a melamine finish, used by the furniture industry, which does not darken. I obtained this from Jenkins of London and it looks very good either as a satin-sheen finish, as applied, or, when rubbed down with steel wool, as a matt finish. It is not suitable for use where it will be in contact with water or the colour will leach out of the timber. In a dry cabin (yes, we do get them on motor boats) the finish looks good and lasts well. It is easily renewed and has one advantage for the amateur — runs do not happen often and when they do can be easily rubbed off and coated over. Coats dry in fifteen minutes and overcoating can proceed quickly. With quick drying time dust is not such a problem as it is with varnish.

Perhaps one of the easiest finishes for wood is an oil called Deks Olje, made in Norway. It consists of two special oils, one which saturates wood deep into the surface, and the other which complements it as a surface finish. The product should be used as per the maker's instructions, but basically all that is needed is to flow coats of the first material on to wood surfaces until a heavy saturation is achieved. This is allowed to dry out and then the finishing coats are given. Although it does take time to saturate new wood, the treatment is long lasting. There is little darkening although you do get some blackening of badly treated areas of timber after prolonged weathering. Restoration is easy if this weathering is caught in time and cleaned off before re-treatment. I would only recommend this material for new wood.

**Bottom Painting**
If you do this work properly first time it will last many years. If you skimp on time or materials, or deviate from the instructions given in the technical literature, you will pay dearly for your mistake by having to do future rectification work.

It is now considered essential to provide a water-barrier coat between an antifouling and the gel coat on the hull moulding. Either of the two-can epoxy or polyurethane systems can be used, but I prefer the epoxy systems because they have greater build up towards the required thickness. Polyurethanes are thinner and more coatings are needed for a similar thickness. The exact painting specification and sequence is available from the paint manufacturer.

All paint manufacturers will tell you that the biggest problem on a new hull is to rid it of mould release agent. Paint will not adhere to contaminated areas. Incidentally, never use silicone polishes on a boat. These make any future painting almost impossible without a an expensive removal programme.

Once degreased, the hull bottom should have the shine taken from it. Rub it down thoroughly with 3M Wet or dry (220 grit) used wet. That will take the shine off the gel coat. The fine scratches produced ensure that good mechanical adhesion will follow. The better the coatings stick, the less you will have to do to them in the future. The priming coat is designed to be the strong link between the surface to be painted and the coating itself. High-performance paints must be applied in the right weather conditions, as specified by the manufacturer. They depend on a chemical reaction when the two cans are mixed and this is affected by ambient temperature and humidity, just as the original resins used in the construction were. Too cold and the reaction is slow, too hot and the reaction is over too quickly. Pick the right day to begin and see that the weather pattern will allow you to give overcoatings at the recommended interval. The overcoating time is always a bit of a problem with two-can systems. If the first coat is overcured, the adhesion of successive coats will not be as good as it should be. In any case, you will have to rub down between successive coats to flatten the surface, so there should be no real panic if there has to be a delay. When this does happen, give a dry rub down with a 180 grit 3M Wet or dry to give a little extra roughness to the overcured surface. It means more work, but you are always at the mercy of the weather when working in the open.

Present research suggests that a two-can paint system should develop, in total, a thickness of $8/_{1,000}$–$10/_{1,000}$in (200–50 microns). Check the paint-maker's specification sheet to see the dry-film thickness the paint should give. Blakes' epoxy dry-film thickness is approximately $2/_{1,000}$in (50 microns), therefore four coats would get you the lower of the recommended limits. Blakes recommend only their epoxy system for waterproofing, but other manufacturers offer a two-can polyurethane system. These have a thinner dry-film thickness of about 35 microns and, to get a minimum build up, will require more coats.

When *Sea Hound* was built it was not generally accepted that waterproof coats were needed under a GRP boat and only a GRP primer was specified, with anti-foulings put straight on top. The first rumblings of osmosis problems were about when an accidental oil spill in local waters all but stripped off the anti-fouling. I decided at that point that the boat should have proper protection. The oil company compensated the owners for the damage to the yachts, so all the old system was scraped off, taking care not to gouge the surface, and finally cleaned off with 120 grit 3M Wet or dry used wet. This seems rather a coarse paper but it did achieve the overall dull matt finish I wanted as well as removing the last traces of old paint. I then gave four coats of black epoxy resin tar. This is a high-build material producing a 75 micron dry-film thickness on each coating. It is no good using it if you want a coloured anti-fouling, but I thought the Blakes Tiger black anti-fouling with white boot top and red topsides looked well. This system has proved excellent: no flaking or cracking, and no osmosis. Mind, the boat does come out of the water each winter. I believe a lot of the trouble with osmosis has been caused by people keeping their boats in marina berths all the year round, only bringing them ashore for anti-fouling at the beginning of the new season. Long immersion meant that saturation was pretty constant, with no chance for surface moisture in the gel coat to dry out — perfect conditions for the development of osmosis.

Every new GRP hull should now have full osmosis protection before launching. The paint should be carried to the top of the boot top as the slightly raised temperature in this area encourages the first osmosis blisters to develop.

When brushing either type of paint system, there is always difficulty in getting even coatings at wet edges. For this reason, it is best to use alternative colours which will enable you to see if patches have been overbrushed or not coated at all. Various colours of epoxide resins are made and they are quite safe to overcoat with an anti-fouling.

After applying the water-barrier system, mask it off at the boot top and give it the required colour anti-fouling. Masking tapes have the habit of becoming part of the boat if they are left on too long and are exposed to strong sunlight. They are the devil to remove when this happens. It is less wearing on the nerves if you are held up on a job to strip off the masking and reapply it at a later date. Don't leave it on for more than three days in strong sunlight.

## Anti-foulings

Anti-foulings sometimes appear the next best thing to witchcraft! There is no single 'best' anti-fouling made. Miracle claims are made by manufacturers but the whole subject is complex, with so many variables, that most of the claims are 99.9 per cent advertising puff. The best approach is to ask local yachtsmen what they use — probably the product of two or three manufacturers — then send for literature and price lists. As I mentioned earlier, it is always best to get the whole of the paint system from one manufacturer. He will have tested the compatibility of his range and you will have no problems in that department.

Although highly efficient, the use of tri-butyl tin based anti-foulings was banned some years ago for the use on yachts although it is still used on commercial vessels. Manufacturers have had to revert to the old less efficient copper based anti-foulings. Thankfully the emulsions holding the copper salts are now improved enough to make the new anti-foulings both acceptable to environmentalists and the yachtsman.

The important function of the emulsion is to ensure that its leaching will provide a constantly renewed sterile surface which will last the length of time that the boat is in the water. Another approach has been to provide a slippery surface based on Teflon which will not allow fouling species to adhere to it. Copper-based anti-fouling must never be used on light alloy underwater units, like outdrives, as it will produce bi-metallic corrosion. Cathodic protection must not be painted over. Anti-foulings are always rubbed down with 'Wet or dry' so that you do not breath in their poisons.

## Estimating Quantities of Paint and Anti-foulings

The manufacturer's technical literature will give the covering rate for paints in either square yards or square metres. You should work out the areas and convert these to quantities from his figures.

To estimate the area of the bottom of the hull, the following method gives a rough approximation:

**1**   Motor boats, heavy displacement boats with a long straight keel and beamy shallow-draught yachts:
water-line length × (beam plus draught).

**2**   Medium-draught sailing boats with well-rounded bows:
0.75 × water-line length × (beam plus draught).

**3**   Narrow-gutted keel boats with short keels:

0.5 × length × (beam plus draught).

Measure in metres and you will get an answer in square metres, in yards and you will get the measure in square yards.

## Keeping Paints and Brushes

One big advantage with the two-pot systems is that they seem to keep in perfect condition for a considerable time without skinning or deteriorating. This is most useful when you come to paint small items. I used a tablespoon to mix the right quantities of hardener and base paint. Thorough mixing is needed and give a few minutes for air bubbles accidentally stirred in to settle. This will produce a better finish. The cleaners used for epoxy adhesives seem to work well for brushes. Having the correct cleaning material for each type of paint saves the cost of ruined brushes. Some thinners and brush cleaners do not get on well with other paint systems. If you are changing paint systems, use a new clean brush or thoroughly wash the old one in detergent and hot water. Allow it to dry before use.

When you go through the manufacturer's literature you will find that paints can be a fire and health hazard. Follow the advice given for safe use and storage.

# 4  GETTING DOWN TO CONSTRUCTION

With the boat safely delivered and sitting plumb on its building site, you will climb aboard and wonder, as I did, at the gaping GRP cavern that is to be the forward cabin and, in my case, the equally large pit that was to be the after cabin. You will realise then the enormity of the task you have taken on. But, first things first. Make the working area as clean, safe and comfortable as possible.

## Access, Safety and Weatherproofing

If, like me, you are building outside in a garden, you need clean access. Old railway sleepers make a good pathway (Fig 29). I put sleepers all around the hull which, as well as giving a firm working area, provided a hard surface to support the step-ladder safely. Contact the engineering superintendent of your nearest railway station to find out about the availability of sleepers.

Safety is important as you will be lifting a lot of weight aboard. The height of the hull will determine whether you can use steps or ladders. You will probably be working in bad weather, even frost and snow, so they must be secure. I secured the step-ladder in position on the sleepers with locating battens so they could not slip. After the first gale had blown them down, leaving me inside the hull, I ensured that they were secured by a lanyard at the top.

As well as being marooned aboard, another hazard is falling into holes. You will be eager to start on the real building, but take time to cover over the engine compartment with a 4 × 2in (102 × 51mm) frame and 3/4in (19mm) chipboard floor and make some safe steps down into the holes. Loose boards and boxes are dangerous.

Choosing the time of the year for delivery is a help in ensuring that, before winter comes, you have the boat weather-proofed. I was so pleased to get the hull after years of dreaming and planning, that it arrived in February. I really had to get going to make sure it did not become a reservoir. A stout tarpaulin was secured over the wheel-house, once the wheel-house was bolted into place. If your boat has a separate wheel-house moulding you will find through-bolting in to the hull, with a rubber sealant in the joint, a straightforward job. My boat was supplied with the bolts and, while the crane was on site, I had the wheel-house lifted into place. I raised it on some timbers so that I could get plenty of silicone rubber sealant into the joint, then lowered it into the final position and bolted it into place. The joints on either side were covered later with the teak name boards, the one across the front with a Celuform strip, shaped at the ends by immersion in hot water, to make a snug fit.

## Windows and Port Holes

Acrylic plastic sheet, either clear or tinted, is the least expensive material for glazing windows on boats. It can be set into the GRP moulding with an extruded rubber seal around its edges or, even more cheaply, screwing directly over the opening which has been previously lined with a trim. I am prejudiced against these methods, although they are common practice on professionally built boats. I believe that any weakness created by a hole in the hull should be replaced by something which brings strength up to, or very near to, that of the original moulding (Fig 21). Putting bolt holes or, worse, screw holes in acrylic plastic creates stress which, as the hull works, can lead quite easily to breakage. They might be acceptable on inland waterways or estuary cruising boats, but for sea-going craft they are no competition for the aluminium-framed window.

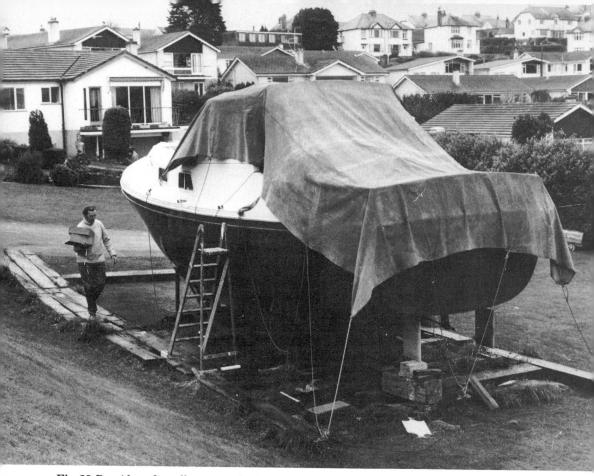

**Fig 29** Provide safe walkways to the hull and make it weatherproof; secure those ladders to avoid accidents

Templates of brown paper were cut to the inside (hole size) of the windows taken from the General Arrangement drawing. One copy of each template, marked port or starboard, was sent to the Essex Aluminium Company factory where they were used to make up the windows, while I kept the second copy Sellotaped on to the superstructure to mark out the position for cutting the aperture. Check that they look well lined up from the outside and that they are in the right position not to interfere with interior arrangements. When the window units arrived they were checked against the markings and, in fine weather, the holes were cut with a hole-saw for rounded corners and then a jig-saw. They were fine finished with a Grinderette to give a slight clearance to the window. Gaps between the GRP hull moulding and the cabin GRP lining were filled with epoxide resin ELE-17 to make the hole

watertight and prevent crushing of the two laminates. All internal linings had to be in place; the best windows come complete with aluminium inside trim which gives a neat finish and adds extra strength. Windows were first fitted 'dry', then fixed with a general-purpose sealant. On looking back I think I should have used a polysulphide sealant which would have made a superior job.

### The Forward or Main Cabin
For a start you will need pencil, rules, levels and a chalk line. When the boat has been in position a few days, check that it has not sunk or shifted. Next, determine the centre-line of the hull, which is not quite as easy as it sounds. It is important as all fitting measurements will be taken from it and no two hulls from the same mould are exactly alike inside.

Determine the centre of the main bulkhead and put a nail in it to secure one end of the chalk line. Now, stretch the other end of the line to the stem, securing it temporarily with sticky tape. Bring the level up to the line and, making sure that you are holding it vertically against it, mark with a carpenter's pencil several points through the cabin's length. Once you are sure you have the true centre, scribe it along parts of the GRP as a permanent reference. The eye is a good judge of a true line, so get down and take a squint along it. If you are lucky to have tanks which are perfectly centralised or keel bolts, so much the better. Make it a habit to check measurements frequently when working.

## Moulder's Bulkheads

The main bulkheads are usually placed in position by the moulder (Fig 30) who is conforming to the Ship & Boat Builders National Federation scheme mentioned earlier. Check that bulkheads are vertical and not warped. It is not unusual for the vertical to be fractionally out and when you are building in furniture you will need to shape some timber so that items like doors hang perfectly. I found one bulkhead bowed some 3⁄8in (10mm) in its 6ft (1.8m) height. By shaping the vertical door-post and panel on either side to conform to the bow, it provided a perfect side to work to.

Bulkheads are often supplied oversize and need vertical cutting back. After marking out to plan size, cut away most of the length with a jig-saw and finish top and bottom ends with a pad-saw.

## Cabin Sole and Cabin Beams

Cabin beams are the equivalent of a house's floor joists, with the cabin sole in place of floorboards. But do not refer to the cabin sole as the floor. The floor is a special term for the part of a wooden boat's construction that binds the two sides of a frame together at the lowest point near the keel. Draw the position of the cabin beams at right angles to the centre-line.

As a rule, you can space the centres of beams as you would in a house, that is, at 16in (406mm) centres. You will not have this decision to make if you are building to a kit plan. The depth of the beams determines the standing head-room after allowance for the thickness of the sole. However, a guide to thickness should be taken as 3⁄8in (10mm) for each length of 39in (1m),

Fig 30 The gaping hole inside a GRP hull when it is first received is frightening. At least I have fitted the cabin beams, hatchways and my first semi-bulkhead (left centre) is about to be fitted

as a minimum for beams up 9.8ft (3m) long. The beams on *Sea Hound* were 6in (152mm) deep × 1¼in (32mm) iroko. Rather substantial, but as I had to carry ballast forward anyway, I decided it was better to carry most of it in the form of heavy construction.

Each beam in *Sea Hound* was to rest on a tank top, with ends shaped to be 3⁄4in (20mm) short of the curve of the hull line. It is good practice not to have a hard end butting on to the GRP hull, so I fitted a foam insert under the ends and, by glassing in over a large area either side of the beam, allowed the load to be properly spread. Limber holes were cut with a hole-saw to give a rounded top, and then sawn out to give good drainage should water accidentally get into the bilges.

With the beams fully shaped, they were given a 'dry run' in the marked positions to check that they were level athwartships and fore and aft. The level, plus a 10ft (3m)

**Fig 31** Interior of forward cabin showing beams and tank access hatchways, all made in Iroko. Full painting after Cuprinol treatment was completed as certain bilge areas were completed.

piece of straight Dexion Angle, were used.

For the hard land on the tank tops I used epoxy resin Epophen ELE-17 plus EHL-22. The GRP was roughed up with a file to give a good mechanical bond, then vacuumed as dust is no help to good adhesion. Next, polyurethane foam was cut and placed under the ends of the beams after the first resin had set. This was to be the first bonding using glass mat plus Epophen EL-5 and its hardener EHL-15. The glass mat was cut to a rough pattern and shaped to give the spread of load I wanted.

## Bilge Access Hatches

Hatches in the cabin flat to give access to bilge tanks will influence the spacing of the cabin beams. Provision of decent access to tank-top fasteners, pipes and their clips will be appreciated later on. Fig 31 shows the beams in position and the hatch openings outlined with 1¼in (32mm) timber using simple housing joints into the beams. I used resorcinol glue and stainless-steel screws for joining the hatch-opening timbers.

Where weight and cost are important, Douglas fir or red pine make lighter and cheaper timbers than can be successfully used for beams and hatch bases. Since timber preservatives can destroy the bonding properties of both polymers and epoxide resins, no treatment was given to the timber for a couple of months after the bonding was completed. This did not hold up work, as it is best to put down the planking last thing so that it does not get dirty and dented during the building. For comfort and safety, lengths of chipboard will give a good walkway, but screw them down temporarily so that they do not get up and hit you.

When making hatches, ensure that the joints of planks or plank-effect plywoods match up. They should have ¹⁄₁₆in (2mm) clearance to allow for easy removal as they always swell slightly. In traditional constructions hatches were often made as a wooden grid to increase ventilation of the bilge area. This is still a useful idea, so long as you put a plastic tray below the grating to catch the dirt.

## Cabin Sole

In traditional construction this is often made of tongue and groove boards; in modern boats, sheets of plywood. I am not keen on either for, once down, they can seldom be removed easily. Builders don't worry about the wrecking and contortions the owners will have to do later to carry out repairs or maintenance. I used teak strip planking, machined as in Fig 32. When the time came for fixing, they were screwed down to the beams with 1½in (38mm) Pozidriv stainless-steel screws — four hundred of them. I can remove any small section of planking in order to carry out maintenance or inspection, with minimal disturbance.

If a plywood sole is specified, ensure that no cabin furniture is built on it. At some future date, it may have to be taken up which would be almost impossible if it is built over. For the after cabin I used Thames Marine deck plywood. This had a plank-simulated veneer, looks good and is a good substitute for the real thing. If you decide to put down the sole early, protect it with a hardboard covering.

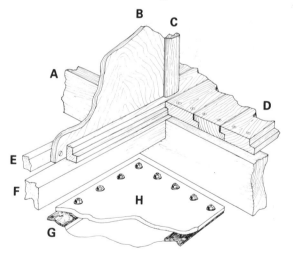

**Fig 32** Cabin sole planking detail
**A** Cabin beam
**B** End panel
**C** Finishing strip
**D** Machined teak strip sole
**E** End panel locating strip
**F** Hatch frame
**G** Sealing Strip to fresh water tank top
**H** Tank top cover

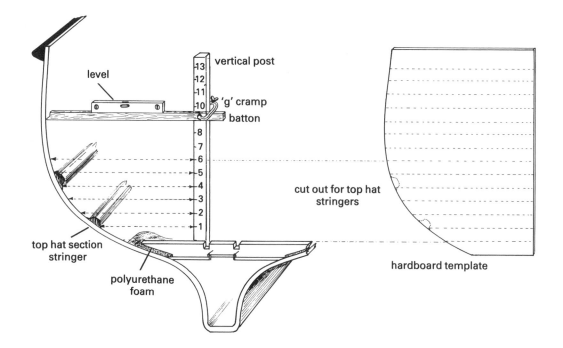

Fig 33 Measurements for semi-bulkheads

## Semi-bulkheads

With plenty of space available, the professional builder can loft the shape of bulkheads from the plans. Being limited for space, I found the easiest way to get their shape was to use the method illustrated in Fig 33. The shape was then drawn out on hardboard, which makes for less expensive mistakes than 5/7in (18mm) marine ply. The method of taking the measurements is self-explanatory. The graduated vertical timber was usually held in place by a stout 'G' cramp and I braced this again with a short length of batten and a couple more cramps at either end. Make sure you place the vertical so that you always take the measurements from the inside where the graduations are marked on it. In the final drawing of the hull curve, subtract an amount equal to the thickness of the polyurethane foam you will use to isolate the bare wood from the GRP hull. When the time comes for glassing in the semi-bulkheads, make sure they are held well in place vertically with clamps, battens and even battens pinned across the tops from existing units, so there is no possibility of movement. A few tack patches will give

added strength once the real glassing begins.

Sometimes it is possible to join the bottom of the semi-bulkhead to a cabin beam. It can be screwed and glued or through-bolted. If it is run down to the bottom of the beam where it could be in bilge water, the edge can be painted with resorcinol glue or, after joining, with an ordinary paint system.

## The Dinette Area

The seat ends were made first. Working from the plan, I drew each end out full size directly on the plywood. If you use a jig-saw, work on the opposite side to any face veneer to prevent the blade from chipping it. A batten was screwed across the tops of the beams just the thickness of the plywood and back from the ultimate position for the outside face of the seat end. At the wheel-house end I found I had to join the seat end to the GRP at the top, and the wood of the main bulkhead at the bottom. Batten and glue was sufficient at the bottom, plus a bit of glassing in using 3in (76mm) glass-fibre tape where the land was on GRP.

Many dinette areas have to be raised above the normal cabin-sole level. On *Sea Hound* I did this with 3/4in (19mm) ply mini-bulkheads which were bolted to the cabin beams and glued.

So as not to waste the space under the raised dinette, I made a hatch with access to a bottle store, dry above the bilges yet cool enough to keep wine and beer in excellent condition, even in hot weather.

## Seat Construction

My method (Fig 34) was to fit a strong beam $3\frac{1}{2} \times 1\frac{1}{5}$in (90 × 30mm) running from the main bulkhead to the semi-bulkhead that was to form the forward end of the berth. This was supported on two $3/5$in (15mm) U-section plywood pieces, glued and screwed in place on the bulkheads at the outboard side of the seating. This would support the front of the lockers and cupboards. It was made strong enough to allow all athwartship seat pieces to be let into it with simple housing joints.

The forward edges of the dinette seats had to be shaped to take the table-top dropped into position when the double berth was made up. They also had to be raised sufficiently to keep cushions in place. I used the housing joints at the outboard end of these and dovetailed them to the inboard pieces that were, in turn, screwed and glued to the plywood ends. By careful design, the space now enclosed under the seats could be sub-divided into smaller compartments to take crusing gear. I think it is important to sub-divide so that you are not grovelling around in a mass of equipment to find one item. The largest space was for storage of life-jackets. They are easily reached, but don't get chafed on other gear. Small cases will fit into the other underseat spaces, although guests are encouraged to use soft bags or holdalls.

Many yacht-construction books advocate covering seat-tops with plywood panels and then cutting small access

**Fig 34** Dinette seating depends on the long outside beam and the faced plywood ends for main support; front edges of seating are rebated to take table top which forms the double berth when it is lowered

hatches in them. While this can save weight in construction, which could be an important factor, it does limit access. All the seat-tops I built have complete access through removable plywood panels. The panels are divided where necessary so that they are not too cumbersome to move.

Sloping seat-backs often waste space in that the length of a berth is reduced. Upright seat-backs, even with good cushions, are uncomfortable. Some compromise is necessary, but do ensure that you provide some comfortable seating on a cruising boat. Again, seat-backs are usually glued in place, but I preferred to have a light batten framework and screwed the backs in place. This gives full access, if needed. I made small removable hatches in the seat-back to give access to such items as autopilot, distribution board and the like. No potentially usable space was wasted.

**Fig 35** Dinette table detail
**A** Cabin side location of table top
**B** Right angle screwed locating plates
**C** Reinforcing plywood
**D** Hinge
**E** Bolt

## Tables

Drop-leaf or bracket-support tables, or modern designs using aluminium tube with a table sliding up to the cabin deckhead are all ways invented to overcome the problem of the table being in the way. With dinette designs where the table is lowered to form the middle section of the sleeping berth, the only problem is the design of the supporting leg which has to fold when the table is in the lowered position. One method is shown in Fig 35.

More sophisticated and expensive systems are available — even the kind which has a gas-pressure system to adjust the height of the table. Where alloy tubing is to act as the main support of the table-top, you may be able to arrange it so that the space under the raised dinette area houses the tube in its lowered position. Hunting the hardware is great fun but, in the end, simplicity is the key-word.

A fiddle around the table edge prevents a wash or wave from spreading crockery and food around the cabin. Corners of the fiddle should be cut away so that crumbs can be removed. Some designers prefer removable fiddles located with brass dowels

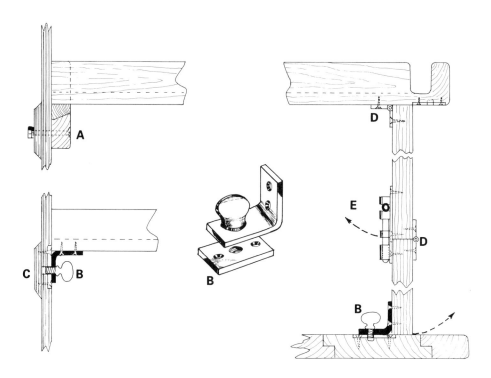

into holes on the table-top. This is a boon when charts have to be perfectly flat for reading and working on, but these fiddles tend to loosen with age and can be accidentally knocked off.

## The Galley Area

Fig 36 shows the basic construction of the galley. The two nearest end panels for the gas stove and sink were made first and, by means of ¾in (19mm) battens, placed correctly fore and aft, secured to the cabin beams. Once in place, I worked towards the hull side, first with the cooker front and then the sink front. These had to be shaped to the hull sides. The cooker front panel had to accommodate a reinforcing top-hat section that ran into it at this point.

The working-top and storage spaces that were to link stove and sink areas were tricky to make as they had to follow the shape of the hull at the back, with the front angled correctly to form the U-shaped galley. Here was where the sliding bevel came into its own for marking the angles for the carcass and the drawer construction. At

**Fig 36** View of the basic construction of the galley

this stage, the holes had been made for the gas supply to the cooker and on the drawing you can see the flexible pipe end hanging down ready to be connected. All the time you are working you should be thinking of other jobs running parallel to the one you are doing, so that you can save time by moving smoothly from one area to another.

All cross-shelving was attached to the ¾in (19mm) battens, screwed and glued into place, and not one woodwork joint was used in the carcassing. True, I had some difficult joints to make in the corners of drawers, but even these were not too hard with the bevel still set to the angle required.

Fig 37 shows the construction a little more advanced, with provision being made for crockery storage. Nothing is more unnerving in a heavy sea than the crash of crockery flinging itself about the cabin. Limit the movement of the crockery and

Fig 37 Crockery storage has to be made to measure for your own particular ware; the locker just in front is for storage of tins

Fig 38 Copper pipe and fittings were used for plumbing in the hot-and-cold-water system but more modern plastic fittings would make for an easier job.

prevent it from slipping out of the space provided. Immediately in front of the crockery storage space, I cut out a hatch in the working surface to give top access to space for the storage of tinned foods.

The large access hole for the full-sized sink (Fig 38) made it easy to finish the hot-and-cold-water plumbing. To the right of the water-heater is storage for washing-up liquid bottles, scourers, soap, etc. The heater side of this storage unit was lined with stainless-steel tiles to protect it.

Finally, Fig 39 shows the galley finished. Note the small BCF hand fire-extinguisher near the stove. It would be no use in a major outbreak, but excellent for a small flare up. The decorative laminate galley-top working surface was fixed with resorcinol adhesive since contact adhesives are not waterproof. When using this glue, weight the surface down while the adhesive sets.

### The Toilet Compartment

Construction began with the small semi-bulkhead (Fig 40) that was to form the front of the base to take the WC. This was glassed into position and the two valves for inlet and outlet were fitted. I provided ac-cess through a trap door in the front of the semi-bulkhead and through the top of the panel that was to take the WC. Framing for the structure of the basin unit and stor-age cupboards was made from $1\frac{1}{4} \times 1$in ($32 \times 25$mm) iroko or, for light parts, $\frac{3}{4} \times \frac{3}{4}$in ($19 \times 19$mm) iroko. Platforms for the pumps were made by glassing in short cross-pieces to the hull side and screwing the other end to the batten that was to provide the land for the covering panels.

The water- and sewage-pump platforms were made from $\frac{3}{8}$in (9mm) marine plywood. The ceramic sink was really de-signed for wall mounting and had to be adapted for use on the boat to fit into the counter top. However, with the hole cut to sink it to the depth I wanted (and this necessitated quite a bit of work with a rasp file) I got the correct placement. After the decorative surface laminate was put in place, the basin was fixed from beneath with epoxy putty. The gap on top between laminate and basin was sealed with polysulphide rubber sealant. All out-of-

**Fig 39** The completed galley

**Fig 40** Basic construction of toilet compartment, framing is 1¼ × ¾in Iroko, the Blake Lavac electric toilet pump is seen at the right-hand side

**Fig 41** Forward end of toilet compartment showing carcasing to wash basin unit and the Stuart Turner freshwater pump

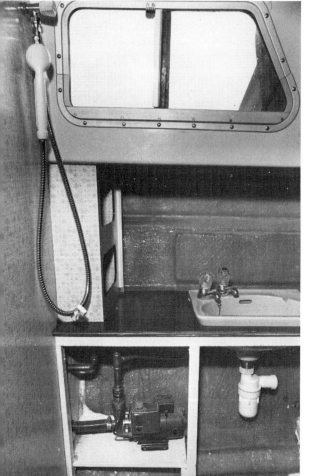

sight wood was treated with Cuprinol wood preserver and painted white at the end of construction.

Fig 41 shows the forward end of the compartment and all surfaces being covered in waterproof decorative laminate. Incidentally, immediately behind the sink you can see the huge reinforced area that Tylers put in to take the strain of legs. In Fig 42 the final panelling and WC are shown put into place. The shower tray, shown in position, had to be specially moulded. First I had to make the mould to the inside shape of the tray. To save cost I made it from softwood and ordinary grade plywood. I took measurements for the end pieces to determine the flat and curved sections. I used the sliding bevel to take the angle between front and ends and then cut ends to shape, joining them with a softwood framework at the correct bevel angle. All I had to remember was to keep the right dimensions to allow for the 1/4in (6mm) thickness of the GRP. The tray now looked like a bit of a World War I wooden aeroplane with two solid ends joined by stringers. The last job was to take a piece of 1/6in (4mm) plywood and bend it round, fastening it with plenty of glue and pins to the flat and curved section of the bottom. Pins were later punched well down when the glue had set. The corners were rounded off to a fine finish with Surform tools, files and glass-paper. To get a perfect surface on which to mould, three coats of undercoat and filler were given and rubbed down between each coat. The slightest blemish must be eliminated, so on top of that I put three coats of epoxide resin two-can paint, rubbing down between each coat to get a glass-like finish. I took this mould to an industrial moulder, though having done the most difficult part of making the mould, I dare say I could have done the job myself.

In the photograph you can see the pieces of teak waiting to be made into a traditional grating. The angle for the tray was kept on the sliding bevel and the pieces of teak marked to get the correct angle. A grating consists of halving joints — and a lot of patience to saw and chisel them out. Use a waterproof glue to fasten the grating together.

Fig 42 Toilet compartment nearly completed; at rear of toilet, holes give access to diverter valves from holding tank

## Forward Desk Area and Wardrobe

Fig 43 looks like a complex heap of Dexion, firewood, 'G' clamps, etc, but it demonstrates the way to start filling the area between the forward bulkhead and the semi-bulkhead I fitted on the port-hand side. This rig is to establish what will be the forward edge of the desk and then, from the vertical piece of timber just right of centre in the photograph, to take the measurements for the midsection semi-bulkhead, the mini-bulkhead that forms the knee-hole to the desk.

Fig 44 shows the results of these measurements. The carcass construction is done and then reinforcing GRP put in with 3in (76mm) tape and resin at the parts that are out of sight, to bond the structure on to the hull. It was difficult to take the shape off the front panel that was to go across the top-hat reinforcing section in the lower part of the picture. A pencil line was drawn on the GRP of the hull itself to mark the back edge of where the

**Fig 43** Batten, level and 'G' cramps all help when it comes to taking fine measurements off from what will be the forward edge of the desk

**Fig 44** The desk semi-bulkhead and top were first made from the measurements in Fig 43, then the rest of the carcass built up using ¾in square batten for the lands of the other small panels in the desk.

**Fig 45** Sliding the panel into place under the covering strip above the forward desk unit

panel would come. Vertical measurements were taken down to that line from the top edge. The drawer was designed to accommodate a portable typewriter and had a lifting lid. Both lid and the front edge of the top were given a raised teak edging so that when linoleum was fitted to the top it would be flush. Linoleum has proved an excellent surface and is not too slippery in use. All panelling above the desk top (Fig 45) was finished with teak-faced 1/6in (4mm) marine plywood and the knee-hole with Ambla fire-retarded lining material. To keep the forward end of the boat warm, an outlet from the cabin heater was provided in the knee-hole.

From the plans of the starboard side of the forward part you will see the wardrobe and chart drawer. The construction of these was straightforward once the bulge in the bulkheads had been taken into account and I had the verticals from which to hang the doors. The top of the wardrobe was finished with the same linoleum as the desk top.

All doors in the boat have louvred ventilation. On a sailing boat you would have to have some means of closing main hatchway louvres to keep out water. This was not a problem on *Sea Hound*. I put louvres on the wardrobe doors as nothing is worse than the smell of musty clothes kept in an unventilated space. The method of making the doors and louvres is shown in Fig 46.

**Door Construction**
The door shown can be adapted to either a twin-panelled version or one with louvres in the top section. A haunched tenon (D) fitting into the mortice of the stile allows you to cut the groove for the panel right through the stile without leaving an ugly gap at the top when the tenon is put in place. The door can be changed to a louvred

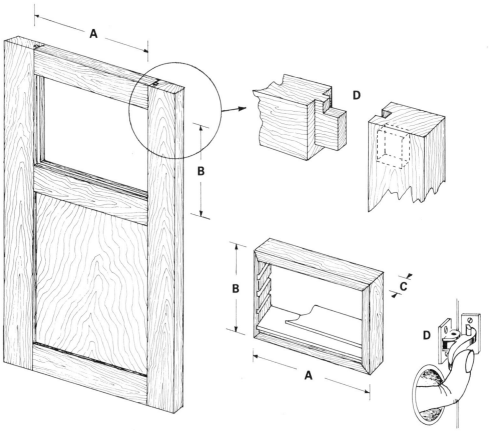

**Fig 46** Method of making doors and louvres

version by stopping the groove at the middle rail and then making up the louvre by mitring four pieces of wood to fit A to A and, in height, B to B. Depth C of these pieces should be the thickness of the door stile plus ¼in (6mm) for small doors and ½in (12mm) for cabin doors. The side pieces are marked with a sliding bevel to the 45°, into which the louvres will fit, and then cut with a fine-tooth saw and chiselled out. The pieces are glued and pinned into place in the top section of the door. I used teak for the louvres for interior furniture; the engine air-intake louvres, made of Duraform, were made on the same principle. The louvres were cut ⅕in (5mm) thick and made over-wide so that after gluing into place and setting, they could be planed down to the face and back of the surround. Very small doors, such as those to the drinks cabinet and below the sink unit, were made from marine plywood faced with teak, with a solid teak edge pinned and glued on to this.

With care, you should be able to remove a door-sized panel from the main panel by using a series of small drilled holes at the corners of the marked-out door to let in the jig-saw without wasting timber. It is not purely a matter of economy. Nothing looks more professional than matching colour and grain when the door and panel are finally fitted and polished. Whenever possible, take advantage of the beautiful grain in wood.

Wardrobes look best if a pair of doors is fitted and they are more practical as you need less swinging room for them. The left-hand door of a pair I made was fastened top and bottom with bolts; the right-hand door then fastened to the other with a bird-type door catch (Fig 46D). The access hole was finished with a teak trim. Flush and out-of-sight door furniture on a boat means that it does not catch in clothing when you are moving about in a confined space. Hinges should be of a marine specification and are available in brass, chromed brass, stainless steel and nylon. Pins should be of brass or stainless steel to avoid seizing. If you have undertaken the building of a boat, you will be pretty experienced in fitting hinges and hanging doors, so the choice between letting butt hinges into the door alone for a sufficient depth to give the stile clearance from binding, or letting it into the jamb and stile in equal proportions is up to you. From the practical point of view it is easier to sink the hinge into the door stile while it is in the workshop and fix the other side to the door jamb flush, without any cutting. I always put a piece of old cardboard, the thickness of the clearance I want, under the bottom of the door before marking out the hinge fastening points.

The pins of hinges must be in proper alignment, otherwise the door will not swing smoothly and you will shorten the life of the hinge. Brass butt-hinges are available in narrow and broad suites. For cabinet work, where you have sufficient thickness in the door stile, the narrow suite hinges are ideal. For cabin doors and large wardrobe doors with some weight, the broad suites will be better. Butt hinge sizes usually give length first, then the width when they are opened out. Halve this latter figure to find if the hinge will fit the thickness of the door stile. Doors made out of a single thickness of, say, ⅜in (9mm) ply can have small butts, but strap hinges which lie on the surface look attractive and are much stronger.

### Security on Doors

Judging from most chandlers' catalogues, one would think, from the absence of quality locks, that boats never get broken into. The sad fact is that theft from boats of all types has increased enormously in recent years. Some would argue that a determined thief will break down anything and, it is suggested, that if you strengthen a door and put on a decent lock, this will only result in more damage.

But a thief who sees easy pickings will take them. He will not struggle and make a lot of noise breaking into a boat if he can help it. With security devices you buy time. The longer a thief takes to break in, the better the chance he has of rousing someone's attention.

The main problem with locks is that while they are easily obtained made with brass cases, their works — especially springs — are made of steel which quickly corrodes.

Rim locks are surface mounted and mortice locks are let into the door stiles which accommodate their mechanism. The thickness of the doors will dictate which type, although the mortice lock always looks neater. Rim locks are made either left or right handed and you determine which you need by looking at them from the inside face of the lock. If when you lock it the bolt shoots to the right, you are looking at a right-handed lock; if the reverse is the case you have a left-handed lock. Mortice locks are normally not handed, although it is worth checking that the bolt is reversible to provide for doors opening inwards or outwards.

When a break-in occurs, it is usually the surrounding woodwork that breaks or the screws that hold the lock that tear away. With a bit of ingenuity it is possible for even a small lock to become much more effective. Strengthen the doors in the area of the keeper and lock with stainless-steel plate drilled to match the lock and keeper holes, and with additional screw holds securing it to the wood. Instead of using woodscrews, through-bolting gives much better strength. No matter whether screws or bolts are used, they must be hidden from view or of a type that cannot be removed with an ordinary screwdriver. Screws can often be countersunk and plugged over to conceal them.

With the scarcity of decent door-locks specially designed for boats, it is hardly any wonder that the hasp and padlock is still a popular way of securing doors and hatchway entrances. They look rather untidy but provided they are fitted correctly with concealed bolts, they give good security. Cheap padlocks made with a couple of levers so that they can be picked with a hairpin are not suitable. High-security models, made of all brass with five-lever mechanisms and bronze shackle, are available. Stainless-steel ones are also on the market, but check that the inside of any lock has a mechanism that is the same material as the outside. Bronze pins, bronze springs inside a bronze housing, are best.

Hasps should be fitted in the woodwork so that they provide a minimum of space for a thief to get a jemmy under. Sometimes this can be done by countersinking the head of the hasp and the eye so that when the lock is in place there is little or no room underneath any part of the hasp.

Although electronic burglar alarms for boats have found a ready market, and they do good in a limited way, if you can afford the outlay, I still think that it is best to spend more on primary deterrents before opting for secondary protection.

**The Wheel-house**
The priorities here were good visibility all round when manoeuvring at close quarters, being comfortable on a long run with the auto-pilot on but still keeping a lookout and protection from the weather. Sailing men like to feel the wind on their faces and often complain in motor sailers with inside steering that they are uncomfortable, especially when they cannot see the set of the sails. I no longer enjoy the trickle of rain-water down my face, but that is a personal preference. You must each decide on your own requirements. Comfort has its basis in ergonomic design of the seating and the positioning of the instruments and steering-wheel.

**The Steering and Instrument Console**
Fig 20 shows me fitting a panel to the steering and instrument console of *Sea Hound*. Long before this, I had done a lot of designing on paper to check the depth of the main steering bevel box of the Mathway gear. In fact, every item that was to be installed — engine-maker's instrument panels, steering torque tubes, engine control and cables, auto-pilot, secondary instruments, depth and log-repeater heads — all had to be measured and worked into the plans. Important instruments have to be sited where you can see them clearly without dazzling reflections. Other instruments, such as engine-hour meters and battery-condition meters that you do not have to refer to constantly, can be sited to one side or, as I did, below at the right-hand side of the console. On a sea-going boat the compass must be the second most

important item after the steering. It creates design problems since so many other instruments, for engine monitoring and for navigation, do nasty things to compasses. I shall say more in Chapter 7 about engine instrumentation, but be prepared to question manufacturers if their literature does not specifically state how far instruments should be mounted from the compass. The height of the compass head is important so that you can read it comfortably when you are either standing or sitting. The Sestrel-Moore I use is available with a bearing sight so it was important that the height of the top of the sight should be clear of any obstruction on the forward part of the boat. This is why the centre section of the forward instrument console was made lower than the two sides. Each make of compass will have particular characteristics that you must take into consideration when designing the mounting.

Fig 47 shows the console a stage further on, with the steering torque tube connected, the Kill-Fire extinguisher hung on its bracket, with a deal of cable to connect to the electrical test unit and the Wynn windscreen-wiper water-supply bottle held in place with a stainless-steel bracket made from strip. I found many uses for stainless strip. It was bent to form all sorts of retaining clips during the construction.

To the lower right-hand side of the photograph is the reservoir for the engine Thermostart starting aid. A needle valve to close the supply is situated just beneath it. For economy of space I decided to have the one reservoir supply both engines from a tee joint. The two Egatube conduit sections to the right of the reservoir are to house the engine instrument-wiring loom and for protection of the throttle control cables. I had to set the Morse twin-throttle control unit on a specially shaped plinth (Fig 48) to obtain a good lead down to the engines. This compromise was forced by the need to have the instrument panel itself at an angle which would allow the instruments to be read easily. This produced the wrong angle for the Morse head and cables. Your boat will create its own problems and when it does, take time to think

**Fig 47** The steering console has all front panels removable to get at the units it houses

the design through; there are always plenty of other jobs to be getting on with while you come to a satisfactory solution.

### Wheel-house Roof Lining

With an open wheel-house the lining material has to be durable and I used ¹⁄₆in (4mm) marine plywood, varnished. The roof was divided up so that at the forward end, where several lots of electrical cables from the electric horn, windscreen-wipers, searchlight and the VHF aerial had to be housed, I could get speedy access by undoing either left- or right-hand panels. At the aft end of the panelling they were made to fit right from side to side.

Panels were screwed into place close to their edges and the screws covered with a finishing strip of teak, again screwed at intervals. Sometimes there will not be sufficient web sections to screw the panels

**Fig 48** The finished console; the Morse twin engine control unit was set on a plinth to give cables a proper lead

in place. In that case, glue and bond small scantling timber in place to form a fastening grid. A bonus is that this will reinforce the moulding.

Certain areas of the wheel-house roof might need strengthening pads glued and bonded in place. Rigging eyes, where considerable strain will be imposed, need well padding up to spread stress over a large area and, preferably, as far as other main structural items. Mounting pads for searchlights, aerial sockets and the like can be fixed with screws through the GRP from below. They are better not glued in place in case they need renewing in the future. If they are sealed with silicone rubber sealant (Fig 49), the bond will keep out water and make for easy removal later.

**Fig 49** Fittings were not bolted directly on to GRP; here the deck pad is secured from underneath with screws and sealed with silicone rubber sealant

## Engine Hatches

The design of hatches over the engine compartment raises some major design problems. In sailing boats where hatches occupy the cockpit floor area they are usually supplied as a GRP moulding. All you then need to do is find a suitably sectioned rubber moulding for the edge of the hatch to provide a seal. Hatch fasteners will keep it in place, but check that it is watertight when you have finished, as just a couple of fasteners will sometimes bow a moulding, letting water in at the ends furthest from the fasteners. A teak lifting grating is the most practical way of covering this type of hatch to provide a non-slip area. A quicker method is to glue a deck covering on it. Try to see that the cockpit drains are at a position and level to drain the area round the hatch as well as the whole cockpit.

With power boats, the business of providing engine hatches is more difficult. They must be reasonably waterproof, give access to a big area and yet not allow too

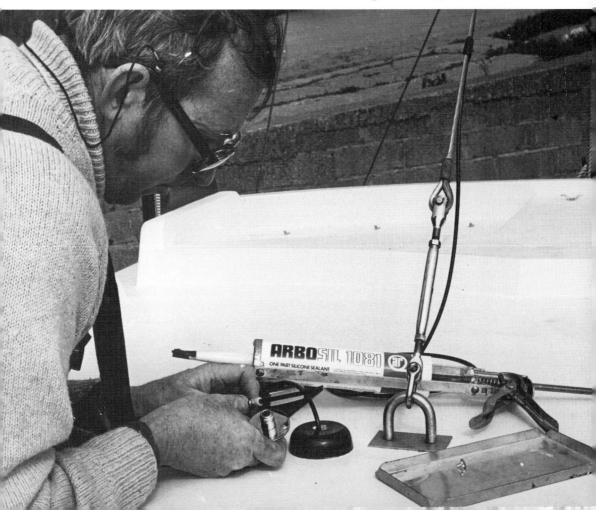

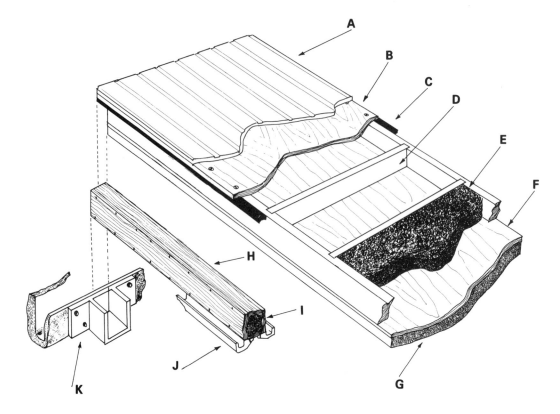

much sound to escape from the engines. Many firms offer great heavy GRP hatches, which need a good deal of muscle power to lift them. These may give good access, but they could be dangerous, especially if you are lifting them about in rough weather. Other moulders put a criss-cross of beams for the hatches to rest on. The result is something like the Grand National when you want to service the engines. By Sod's Law, they will always be where they cause maximum obstruction at the place you need to reach most often.

I wanted maximum access with minimum weight. I had noticed that in the design of wooden gliders, the wooden box section spars for the glider's wings gave an enormous strength over a long span. The beams to take the hatches were made like these spars and held on fabricated steel brackets at either end. Each individual boat will require specifically designed brackets, but to give you some ideas, I have drawn the type I had fabricated by a local engineer in Fig 50 which shows all details of the hatch construction.

Engine compartment hatches should be

**Fig 50** Engine hatch construction
**A** Ferodo Decktread non-slip deck material
**B** 6mm marine plywood
**C** Neoprene rubber edge sealing strip to prevent noise escape
**D** Reinforcing members; special thought must be given to arranging reinforcing where heavy bolting of seating might be placed
**E** All voids between the skins filled with polyurethane foam with self-extinguishing characteristic
**F** 4mm marine plywood lower skin
**G** Soundproofing material
**H** Box section (marine plywood) beam to support hatch covers made of 12mm ply
**I** Box beam filled with polyurethane foam
**J** Celuform architrave drainage channel to stop water dripping on to engines; the channel was drained to the bilge at the aft end and stopped at the forward end
**K** Fabricated steel bracket bedded true on epoxide resin putty before being bolted to main GRP structure

sound-proofed. This is dealt with in detail in Chapter 5, but from the drawing you will see that foam was used as infilling for beams and the hollow hatch sections. Apart from adding strength, the foam also acted as a sound-absorbing material. I also added a layer of sound-deadening material below the lower panel surface where it could absorb engine noise before it could be reflected off the solid panel surfaces.

The finished hatches were not light but, as they are of a reasonable size, they can be lifted out and handled by one person, are of great strength and keep noise levels down.

Another possibility these days is the use of lightweight honeycomb-core materials. The aircraft industry uses light alloy honeycomb cores, bonded with epoxide resins, to make strong cargo hatch floors. Since these adhesives are most suitable for composite construction, I believe very light hatch covers could be made which would, by combining acoustic materials in the design, be more sound-proof than the ones I made. The company making composite sandwich panels is Technical Resin Bonders Ltd of Huntingdon.

## The After Cabin

The sleeping space on a sailing boat is different from a sleeping berth on a motor boat. Sailing men expect to sleep when the boat is well heeled and bouncing about. They require narrow berths that will keep them snug and secure. The motion of a motor boat in a rough sea just about precludes all thoughts of sleep, so it is rare, though not unknown, for motor boats to have berths designed to hold the occupant in place. Sailing men have all kinds of ploys to keep them in their bunk, including large pieces of canvas with a rod through them, that act like the sides of a baby's cot.

Deciding that I would never sleep in rough weather anyway, I decided to have civilised quarters for my wife and myself. I designed berths 6ft 3in (1.9m) long (actu-

Fig 51 The after cabin where the main problem was to design the furniture round the Mathway steering system. The ducting for hot air central heating rests on the 'P' brackets and their reinforcing web; above my head are the two tanks that hold the gas bottles

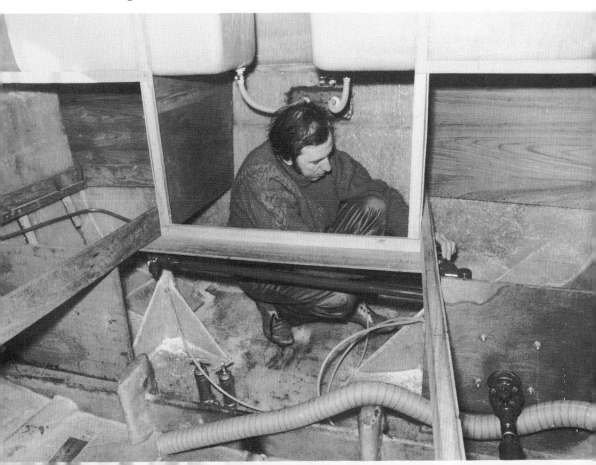

ally 6ft 5in (1.95m) across the diagonal because of the curved shape of the transom) and a full 2ft 6in (0.7m) wide, with sides parallel. The critical factor was not the berths but the correct installation of the steering gear (Fig 51). When that was worked out (see p159) the frame for each berth was constructed, side and ends being made of 5 × 1in (127 × 25mm) teak. The corners were dovetail jointed for strength and the sliding bevel was used for finding the correct angle for the end of the bunk near the stern. The frames were made up but not glued to see if they could be manoeuvred into the aft cabin in one piece. They could, so they were removed and glued up, checking with the bevel that

they were setting at the correct angle. The construction method for the framework to take cross- and side-pieces which support the plywood tops and front panel is shown in Fig 52.

**A** The bunk frame was sufficiently deep to keep the mattress in place, but not to keep the occupant in. The height of the mattress actually comes above the side so that the edge does not dig into someone sitting on the side of the berth.

**B** Cross-pieces were housed with a halving joint into the side rails at either end. They were not glued in place so that they could be removed, along with top panels, to give access to the storage compartment

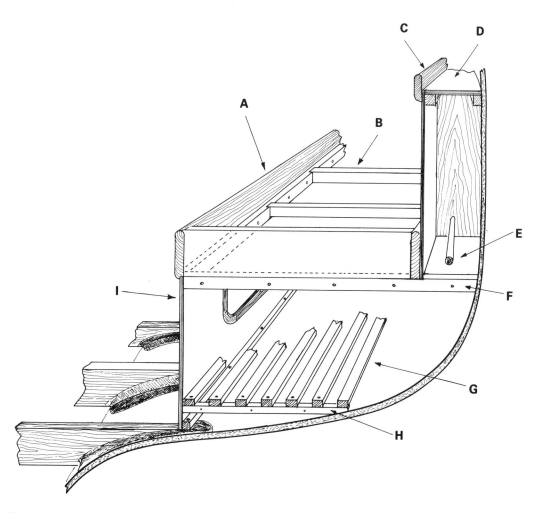

**Fig 52** After cabin bunk construction

below. This method is quite strong enough when cross-pieces are spaced at 15in (381mm) centres.

**C**   Fiddle rails keep items like watches in place.

**D**   Although only narrow, this top panel is removable for easy access. Apart from my phobia about mushrooms growing in shut-off areas, I also worry about meeting an over-zealous customs officer who might want to look behind the panelling! Mind, when you leave the boat, as you do when cruising, it is not a bad idea to have a compartment built in somewhere to conceal valuables. Wherever the gap between hull and panel is sufficiently large, lockers should be provided. Use every inch of dry storage space. Professional boatbuilders do not do this because of the expense involved. The amateur builder has no excuse.

**E**   Services can be run in behind panelling where they are well protected and dry. Conduit is easily installed so that should you need to remove wiring there is no need to disturb the panelling.

**F**   When you start to build in the furniture, fitting that first batten to the bulkhead is the most important piece of construction. Get horizontals level and verticals vertical from the start. In the illustration, the batten, along with the semi-bulkhead that took the steering reduction box, was the main support for the bunk frame and cross-pieces. You may have to shape the support piece at the hull side where the bulkhead lands (Fig 53) to allow for the thickness where glassing in has been necessary. Never grind away the GRP which will weaken the structure and possibly create a stress-concentrated zone.

**G**   Bilges accumulate water, even on a sound GRP hull. It sometimes comes from condensation but, no matter, the space in bilges must be kept ventilated and this simple batten system is most effective in keeping these spaces free from mould and water.

**H**   A batten, again on the bulkhead, is all that is necessary to screw the locker bottom battens in place.

**I**   Locker fronts can have doors or open access. For ventilation and quick access I have open locker fronts low in the boat while, higher up, it was a question of what needed to be kept out of sight to keep the boat looking tidy.

Fig 54 shows the completed after cabin with the seat and wardrobe filling the aft space between the berths and a foot well at the end of each berth created by the panels that hide the gas lockers. On the outboard end of these it was found possible to build overhead open-fronted lockers which are useful for stowing bulky woollies and the like. The construction was simple. The vertical and horizontal battens that were to take front panel and seat-top were screwed and glued to the berth front

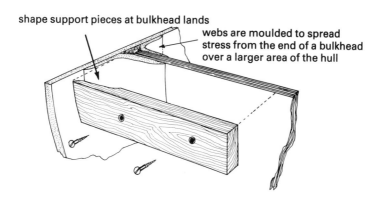

shape support pieces at bulkhead lands

webs are moulded to spread stress from the end of a bulkhead over a larger area of the hull

**Fig 53** Fitting a batten on to a bulkhead

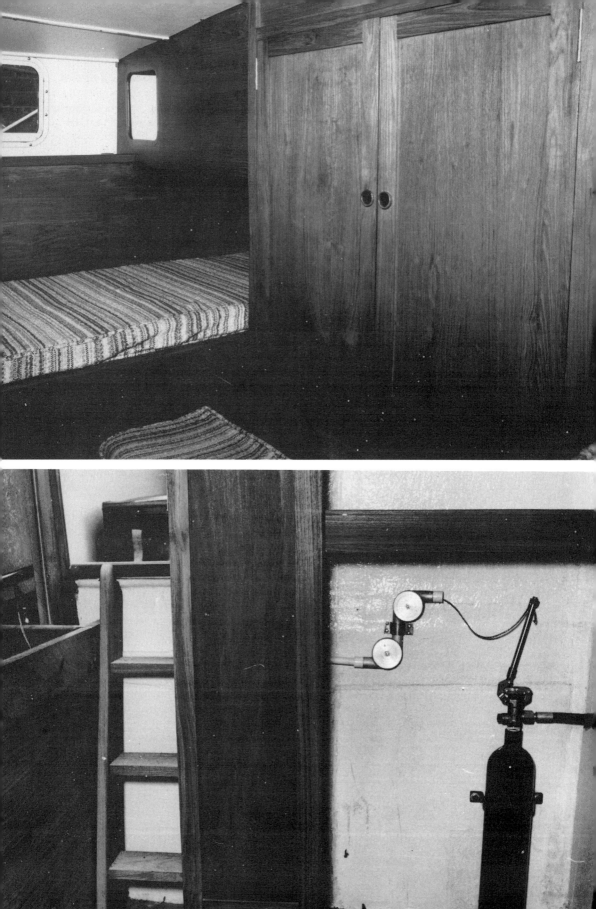

**Fig 54** The completed after cabin

**Fig 55** The after cabin showing the wardrobe that houses the 6lb Pyrene BCF fire-fighting system cylinder and its handpull over my bunk

panels and filled in. The seat-top was hinged to give access to the space beneath. The small shelf below the wardrobe door was necessary to give clearance to the steering tie rod and drag link. The shape of the furniture is often dictated by the things underneath and you will encounter this design problem on your boat. A fiddle rail was put across this shelf.

The starboard berth locker houses a hefty pair of legs for when the boat is on a drying-out berth. Bilge-keel sailing boats avoid this problem, but if your boat carries legs make sure you provide accommodation for them. *Sea Hound*'s 7 × 5in (178 × 127mm) legs are 5ft 6in (1.6m) long and even though made of pine still need lanyards and grips so that they can be lifted into place. They have leathered faces to prevent them from scuffing the GRP when they are bolted into place with 1in (25mm) diameter stainless-steel bolts with 3in (76mm) diameter washers specially made to spread the load from the bolt. There is still space in the same berth locker to take the emergency storm warp

and drogue, the mizzen sail and a suitcase. Engine oils are carried in a special tray under the seat and bathing ladders in the bottom of the wardrobe. There is a shelved cupboard immediately to the left of the cabin entrance (Fig 55) which takes small items. In the bottom of this cupboard the battery master switches are housed in an Ega box installed after the photograph was taken.

The cabin sole was made from Thames Marine Plydeck which was simulated planking on plywood; this has proved excellent for this cabin where wear is minimal. With good flooring like this there is no need for carpet. Personally, I am not keen on carpeting for small boats anyway as it tends to get damp and smelly.

**Open-fronted Lockers**

Too many open lockers can make a boat look untidy; however, they are handy for items that are in constant use and for emergency items that may have to be reached quickly. Every compartment on

**Fig 56a** End and edge finishes to plywood
**A** Hand grip seat end capping finish
**B** Part of teak quadrant (56B2) used for capping
**C** As above for 90° bend
**D** Cover strip
**E** Door opening with teak edging
**F** Door opening ply to ply

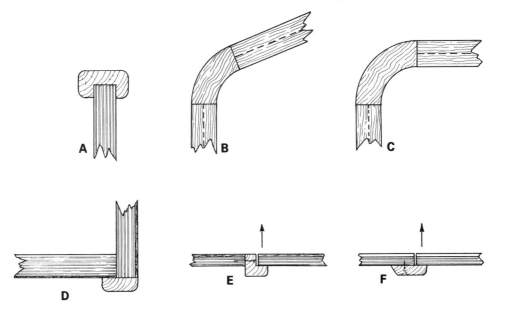

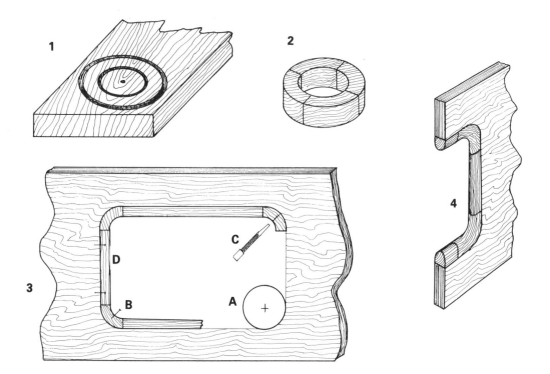

**Fig 56b** Method of finishing open lockers and edges of cabin furniture

my boat has some open-fronted lockers, which is a help with ventilation. They can be left lined or unlined as you think fit.

The simplest method of making the locker opening is to jig-saw it out and put in an edging that is mitred at the corners. As I wanted only rounded edges on cabinet work to minimise accidents, I made them as shown in Fig 56b.

**1** Using a hole-saw in an electric drill, two concentric holes were cut from solid teak slightly thicker than the plywood surround. I did not cut right through the wood on either of the two concentric circles first time, but reversed the wood and, cutting from the reverse side first, cut the outer circle so that the piece dropped out of the plank. Then, gently holding the piece in a wood vice, I finished cutting the inner circle, leaving a ring of teak as in 2.

**2** The ring was quartered with a fine-tooth saw.

**A** To cut the correct hole shape in the panel, I set out the oblong shape of the out-

side in pencil and, from this, the four centres for the radius that would form the curved corners. Using the hole-saw, I cut out the four holes from the face side to get a clean cut without chipping the face veneer.

**B** With a $1/16$in (2mm) drill, I drilled the quarters for gluing and pinning as shown. They stood slightly proud in thickness so that they could be planed down to the faces after the glue had set.

**C** All pins were punched well down and the holes filled with teak dust and glue. There are teak wood-fillers available but these usually do not match too well.

**D** The straight midsections of solid teak were cut so that they butt jointed tightly on to the corners. These were pinned in place and the pins punched below the surface as for the corners.

**4** When the glue had thoroughly set, the sections were planed down to the faces, then a Surform file or rasp was used to get the rough form shown. It was finished off first with a coarse glass-paper to get rid of file marks and then with a fine paper to cabinet work standard.

Fig 56a shows methods of finishing edges of cabinet work.

## Through-fixing on Cabin Roofs

A number of items, such as ventilation fans, deck fittings, grab-rails and outside handholds need extra care in their fitting. Problems arise when you have to through-fix through a compound structure in GRP. Many hulls have a plastic foam, plywood reinforcing, end-grain balsa wood, or other form of filler between two skins of GRP. Composite structure of this kind increases the strength of cabin roofs and decks but can suffer, if made of soft materials, when you through-bolt or screw and put them under compression. This will crush the in-filling material and damage the GRP in the compressed area.

## Grab-rails

Fig 57 shows a typical situation I had to deal with in the forward cabin roof when fixing grab-rails. Tylers had made the forward cabin roof very strong by using two reinforcing methods at right angles to each other. Athwartships they used strips of plywood and created corrugations by spacing them to form a single and double skin alternately. On top of this were four longitudinal top-hat sections running the full length of the outside of the cabin top and these were foam filled. From the figure, you will see that when I came to fit the grab-rails to the outer top-hat sections, I had to use some cunning. The rails were made first. Two teak strips of the correct cross-section and length were cut from a plank. What was to be the underside of each rail was put face-to-face with the other and a strip of newspaper and a few spots of glue were used throughout their length to fasten them together. The newspaper was to ensure they did not stick too hard as they obviously needed separating when the shaping was completed. After marking out in pencil, the holes at either end of each handhold were drilled out with the electric drill and hole-saw. I put some extra 'G' clamps in place as each part was sawn so that there would be no danger of the area being worked splitting open. A jig-saw then removed the section that is heavily dotted on the diagram. The next stage was to plane them, still in one piece, to get the taper on their sides. Finally, a round Surform tool rounded them off so they had a comfortable grip. After sanding, the two were separated and were then ready for fixing.

**Fig 57** Making and fixing grab-rails
**A** Foam-balsa core material must be removed
**B** Epoxide resin/glue replacement for core material
**C** Hardwood plug
**D** Grab-rail epoxide-resined to GRP stringer
**E** 2 grab-rails spot-glued back to back
**F** Hand-holes, hole-saw and jig-sawed out
**G** Hole-saw

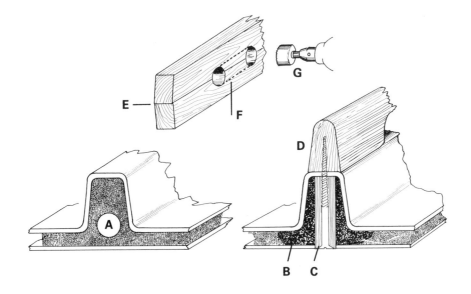

The points at which the fastener was to pass through the top-hat section were marked on the outside top and a pilot hole drilled downwards, passing first through the foam, then through the inner GRP skin or through ply, and then the inner skin. Next, a hole-saw, used from the inside, removed a ¾in (19mm) hole through the lower skin. The foam was cleaned back from the hole with a small file, and a ¾in (19mm) wood dowel was inserted, marked for length and cut off. Finally, the void had to be filled around where the dowel would be replaced, to spread stress over a larger area. I used epoxide resin, injected with a gun, then fixed the epoxy-glued dowel. When it had set, it was easy to drill through the dowel from the outside, then counterdrill and countersink from the inside in order to fix it with 4in (102mm) No 14 stainless-steel screws. Some builders would prefer to use through-bolting on a handrail, but I was quite satisfied that with the underside of the teak rail being epoxy-bonded to the top of the top hat, and with such large screws inserted, I would have no trouble. I needed the largest screwdriver I had to drive these screws and the help of an assistant on the outside in order to bend the grab-rail to the curve of the reinforcing section.

**Design and Building up Forward**
Both sailing and motor boats may have a couple of berths in the fore peak as shown in Fig 58 on the General Arrangement drawing of a Sadler 26. The division, with either a single or, as in the drawing, a double bulkhead, is to reinforce the area to take the huge downward thrust of a mast mounted on the cabin roof. Where a double bulkhead is used, the intervening space can be used for a WC compartment plus, on larger yachts, a shower and hand-basin. Doors on both bulkheads keep the compartment private from the main and forward cabins. In some smaller boats, only one door is provided, it being assumed there will be no occupants in the forward cabin when the WC is being used. Such arrangements are not very satisfactory as this compartment should be private.

The design of the forward berths needs some thinking out as the space also has to function for anchor-chain stowage and for storing the sails. It might be an idea to sacrifice one berth and have the opposite side of the boat devoted solely to sail bins, but once the design has been decided the first job is to glass in the semi-bulkheads (A) that are to support the middle sections of the berth. Next, the side-pieces (B) are cut from ⅜in (9mm) marine plywood to the outside curve of the hull, the inside edges reinforced with batten to give a land for the loose plywood tops. These are glassed in and screwed down to supports at the main bulkhead and across the top of the semi-bulkheads. The bunk tops and panel fronts are assembled next and these can have openings as shown, or doors. In sail bins there is always the danger of damp and dark setting up mildew on the sails. The more air you can get into the compartment and the better it circulates the less chance you have of mildew. Keep sails off the side and floor by means of slatted wood shelves.

The floor area (C) is minimal in some designs. Try to have a reasonable amount of standing space as this will help in getting sails through the hatch to the foredeck.

A problem for the occupants of a small forward cabin is solved by a shelf (D). When the crew take off their clothes there is often no place to put them except on the floor. Dry clothes and wet outdoor garments should be kept separate, and provision should be made for this.

Anchor-chain stowage (E) is the third function to be catered for in this small space. Anchor chain is heavy, even for a small yacht and, unfortunately, this weight comes just where it is not wanted — where it affects the pitching movement of the boat. Functionally, however, it is best up forward where it can be led through a hawse pipe up to the deck outlet. These days, consideration should be given to limiting the amount of chain carried on coastal cruising boats. There should be enough chain to weigh down the anchor and with an inboard length to prevent chafe, with rope for the middle section. Modern ropes are pleasant to handle and strong enough to provide safe anchoring,

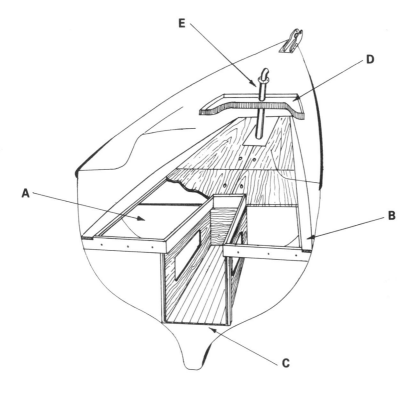

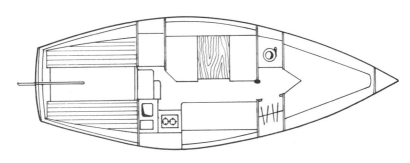

always ensuring the right catenary curve is achieved so that the anchor digs in properly.

The chain locker must be drained to the aft bilges, so that water and mud brought aboard can escape and not build up to a stinking mess in the locker. The compartment is best lined with wood slats to prevent the chain chafing the GRP of the hull.

On my own boat, as you will see from the General Arrangement drawing, I have two bulkheads forward. The first, from the

**Fig 58** Construction of small forward cabin and plan view of general arrangement of Sadler 26

stem, is a collision bulkhead down to the water-line where I stow 15 fathoms of chain to aid the trim and provide good anchoring. The next space to the second bulkhead is a bo'sun's store for paint, adhesives and sealants on the port-hand side and electrical and engine spares on the starboard-hand side.

# 5 POWERING

When the naval architect designs a boat for a production moulder, both know the kind of powering it will need. This is critical. Whether the boat is to be used on inland waterways or at sea, underpowering could be dangerous. It is not unknown for boats to be swept over weirs, or for currents to drive a boat backwards when it is supposed to be making headway. On the other hand, overpowering wastes money — in the initial outlay and then in fuel and running costs. Certain types of hull when overpowered can be just as dangerous as underpowered ones. If certain engines are recommended for your kit boat, do not alter the power unit before consulting the design department. It is possible to substitute one make of engine for another, similar, one but there is more to it than choosing one of the same horsepower rating. The weight is important for one thing. This affects the sailing performance of a yacht or the ability of a power boat to get up on the plane. The power-to-weight ratio of different engines should be examined.

Physical dimensions are also critical. Length determines if there is sufficient room between gear-box and inboard propeller-shaft gland to make the correct shaft connection. A shorter unit might make for better installation prospects. The height of the engines could determine final choice. One type might fit comfortably beneath the wheel-house sole, while another needs accommodating in special raised boxes, easy enough to make, but destroying ease of movement about the deck.

If you have scale plans of your boat, it would be worth while contacting the various engine manufacturers who may be able to supply scale tracings. These are printed on transparent paper in 1:24, 1:20, 1:12 and 1:10 scale, and are valuable if you are planning a complete engine installation in a new boat, as I was, or if you wish to substitute an alternative engine to the one offered as standard in the hull. Calculations for correct diameter and pitch of any propeller is provided by the engine or propeller manufacturer.

**Costing the Engine Installation**
As this is the biggest outlay after the hull, it should be considered carefully. It is more complex than merely comparing the price of the unit. First, work out the full costs of the engine plus stern gear. Some planing hulls will take conventional shaft-driven propellers, outdrive units or outboard engines. Some sailing boats will take an inboard engine and outboard or saildrive unit. The advantages and disadvantages of each type are as follows.

**The Inboard Engine**
This type of engine is sheltered from the environment and out of sight. It gives the designer some leeway in getting weight distribution right, though when placed forward the engine will begin to intrude into valuable living space. By using a remote or built-on 'V' drive the shafting can be reversed in direction under the power unit, which could then sit towards the stern, making for a weight distribution similar to the outdrive unit and suitable for boats designed to take the weight aft.

Generally speaking, it is a highly reliable unit, but costs more to install than outboards and is more complex to install than outdrive, outboard or saildrive units. This is because the alignment of the shafting, and the inboard and outboard glands to carry the shafting, have to be carefully engineered.

One advantage is that with certain power categories involving multi-cylinder engines, there is a considerable range of gear-boxes to enable the designer to match the power requirements to the hull form. There are reduction gear-boxes which will gear down high engine revolutions to those that match the propeller. This gives the greatest efficiency in certain hull forms. Also available are 'down-angle' gear-boxes that enable the engine to be installed at a lower angle which, in turn, means lower floors above the engine. There are drives through constant velocity joints and coupling shafting which do the same using the engine's conventional gear-box. The more complex you make the drive, though, the higher the cost. Designs from the better manufacturers tend to stabilise over the years. This helps keep depreciation low but, more important, means spares are available over a long period.

### The Outboard Engine
Depending on the horsepower it produces, the outboard is a mobile unit, easily lifted on and off the boat — by thieves as well as owners — or it is a great lump of machinery that has to be wheeled about on a special trolley. Don't be fooled into thinking that all outboard engines are easy to take home; some of the large power units are, in essence, as much a part of the boat as an inboard. However, they are compact and only have to be bolted on to a properly prepared transom that is of sufficient strength to take their weight and carry their thrust. They can be connected to cable or hydraulic steering systems and, when anything goes wrong, they can be removed and sent for servicing more easily than an inboard.

The majority of outbound engines are two stroke but the more efficient four stroke is now appearing. Petrol consumption is generally high, especially in two-stroke versions. Put in its simplest terms: power = torque × rpm. In other words, you can get get power from an internal combustion engine by either high torque, low rpm or low torque, high rpm. To keep cylinder and engine size compact, power these days is usually from high rpm engines. This applies to other engines as well as outboards. Fuel costs will loom large in your calculations of running costs and when you consider capital outlay for the larger power units you should bear in mind their rapid depreciation in value. Many manufacturers change models every five minutes and the result is that spares can become a problem.

### The Saildrive
Of all inboard engine installations, the saildrive is the easiest for the amateur to install. The power unit is usually a conventional inboard design adapted to the drive leg which takes the drive through two 90° bevel drives from the output shaft of the engine down to the propeller. Both petrol and diesel versions are available and running costs and servicing commitments will be similar to the equivalent inboard. The saildrive is a fixed unit so you need conventional rudder gear. Some outdrives have a double-seal diaphragm to give extra safety and these can incorporate a sender connected to a warning device to let you know if water penetrates the first diaphragm membrane.

Saildrive is ideal for fast modern fin-keel design sailing boats where it fits between the fin keel and the rudder skeg or, on bilge-keel designs, where the drive leg can get protection from grounding and yet have a good flow of water to the propeller. These units have also enjoyed success on inland waterways craft. I see no reason why they could not be an attractive alternative to a traditional inboard installation for twin-engined sea-going craft, as power units up to 45kw (61hp) are offered. What has to be borne in mind is that when power units are too big to be lifted easily from the bed, the seal will be a major job to replace and, therefore, expensive. With the low-powered end of the range, the lesser weight means that the owner can do the job reasonably easily.

Two special attractions for the home boatbuilder are the excellent drawings provided for dimensioning the installation and the stage-by-stage instructions covering the fitting of the engine bed right through to the completed installation. On the hardware side, Volvo offer a complete range of equipment covering fuel, exhaust, electrical and instrument systems, that

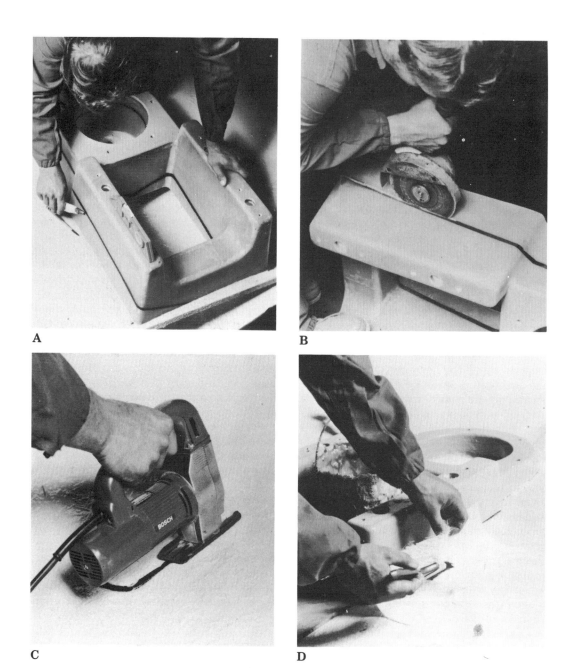

**Fig 59** Saildrive installation

**A** Scribing off the engine base moulding to conform to the shape of the hull

**B** A cutting disc removes surplus GRP from the engine mounting just marked

**C** The hole in the hull is jig-sawed out where the engine leg drops through

**D** The engine mounting is glassed into the hull

**E** The saildrive power unit is dropped through the mounting later to be fully secured in position

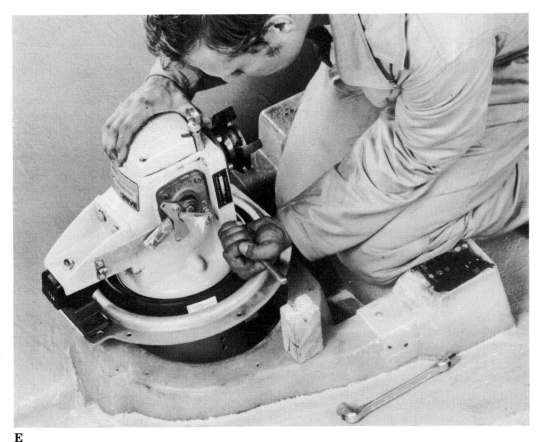

E

will save the user of their products much time and frustration. Their publications and range of hardware can be thoroughly recommended. Fig 59 indicates some of the basic stages of marking out and fitting the engine bed in a saildrive installation. After this it is a matter of following the installation recommendations.

Parameters for the necessary measurements for the correct immersion of the drive leg are minimal and the setting out of the engine bed and the glassing in takes much less time than for a conventional engine bed or an outdrive.

### The Outdrive

These are available in both diesel and petrol versions. Although the installation of the power unit is very much on conventional lines, requiring engine beds and other details similar to an inboard, the final drive is taken through the transom of the boat, down a leg via two sets of bevel gears to the propeller. The whole leg

moves to give steering control and many units have trim and lifting control to give the best planing angles in different kinds of seas. The whole drive leg can be lifted for beaching or to keep fouling to a minimum.

This type of power unit has made enormous strides into the market and its popularity seems unbounding. The development of high power/weight ratio diesel engines running at high speeds will no doubt add to this popularity.

Like the saildrive, outdrives obtain efficiency by having propeller thrust in the same plane in which the hull is proceeding. The down angle of a conventional propeller loses some efficiency.

The shortcomings to be considered are the need to keep rubber bellows (usually two or three depending on the make) watertight. Severe damage can be done to the drive gears if bellows leak and, in certain circumstances, the boat could sink. I am not so worried about the possibility of the boat sinking, as there is only a minimal risk if proper maintenance is carried out, but of the high cost of replacement of bellows each season as recommended by the manufacturers. This can add considerably to running costs, though one manufacturer says that the bellows on his engines only need replacing when visual inspection indicates deterioration. He goes on to say that if there is a need it should be done by a factory-trained mechanic — a costly way of doing things. Again, outdrive gears, clutches, etc are not the province of the amateur mechanic. They are extremely reliable or they would not be so popular, but once they need mechanical attention, expect a hefty repair bill. Outdrives are made of light alloys and must have cathodic protection, renewed as necessary. This does add to the cost, but no more than with cathodic protection on any boat. The conventional engine coupled to the drive leg needs similar attention and creates running costs similar to a package outdrive and engine from a single source.

Although at first sight the installation of an outdrive might seem to consist merely of sawing a suitable hole in the transom and bolting the outdrive leg to it, the process is more complex than this.

Propeller immersion parameters are exacting. Set too deep, the bellows would be constantly under water and water could get into the drive unit; set too high, severe cavitation and loss of performance will result. The provision of a flat surface on the transom on which to bolt the outdrive housing is another factor and the correct angle and thickness of the transom itself is important.

Templates for cutting and drilling the transom to take the outboard leg of the outdrive are usually supplied by the manufacturer. Procedures consist of marking out cutting holes and drilling for bolts, then edge finishing with resin and mat to the specifications given.

On Volvo Penta installations, except the AQ 130 and AQ 115 where it is an optional accessory, a front mounting is standard. It requires precise positioning and installation to get the alignment correct. The height and position of the engine support can be determined with the aid of a special tool. This is located and fixed in the main collar, now bolted in the transom, and, by means of a rod projecting forward with an inverted 'T' plate the position is found. You will probably have to make a cross-member glassed to the bottom of the hull on which to fix the Volvo engine support. It could be made of wood glassed over with the support secured by coach bolts. To make a stronger job of it, I would suggest making the section of the support beam like a normal engine bed with a galvanised-steel reinforcing that can be drilled and tapped. The support is then bolted in place.

A fire-and-flood bulkhead is usually fitted in front of the engine. It prevents noise and fumes from seeping into accommodation space as well as providing extra safety. Volvo give minimum distances but, wherever possible, increase this space to make for easy servicing.

One advantage of the outdrive is that there is generally a good deal of space forward of this bulkhead for a fuel compartment, storage or a fishing well. It is preferable to have fuel, especially petrol, in its own separate compartment but if it is to be an effective safety feature it must not be cross-ventilated with the engine compartment and should have its own ventilation system. Vapour-proofing takes time, but there is some consolation that the sealed space will be another barrier to engine noise.

The installation of the hardware once the main building items are glassed and bolted in is a matter of following the procedures outlined in the maker's handbook.

The weight of many outdrives is borne by the transom and two engine mountings; hence the need for a transom built strongly to take the engine's weight and thrust. If the hull is specially designed for an outdrive, you need have no concern on this score, but you should, nevertheless, check all details of installation with the manufacturer and study the literature.

For heavier and more powerful engines you should reinforce the transom with extra GRP webs to take the thrust load forward over the aft section of the hull, and put in an extra pair of mountings.

## Hydraulic Drive

The big advantage of this type of installation for the amateur is that the engine can be positioned anywhere, even athwartships, and the hydraulic motor is the only relatively small and light part of the drive that has to be connected and lined up with the propeller shafting. The snag is that hydraulic transmission of power is relatively inefficient. You pay a price for the ease of installation. However, for inland waterway boats and for yachts as an auxiliary engine, it is worth considering.

## The Water Jet

This is ideal for shallow-draught operation as there are no underwater appendages such as propellers or 'p' brackets to be knocked off. They are especially safe when used to pick people out of the water. Reverse thrust and steering may be offered as part of the design. The engine needs conventional beds and there may be special requirements for connecting the engine to the water jet unit. This will add to the expense, although once the design is worked out they can be reasonably easy to install.

## Petrol versus Diesel

Whether you are considering a petrol or diesel engine installation there are six financial considerations:

1  Initial purchase price of the engine. Petrol engines are less expensive than the equivalent power diesel engine. This price differential allows a great deal of fuel to be purchased for the more thirsty petrol engine before the initial price of the diesel engine is reached.

2  Depreciation is difficult to estimate, but is probably marginally greater for a higher cost engine than the lower cost engine. So, if you compare a petrol engine with a diesel engine of the same power, the diesel will probably have a greater depreciation value. Much will depend on how long you are keeping the boat, but where finance is a critical consideration and you don't mind the extra safety precautions involved with a petrol engine, then the lower initial cost and depreciation value could be the deciding factors.

3  Running costs. It is not realised how few running hours the average pleasure-yacht engine gets each season. It could be many years before the higher cost of petrol caught up with the cost differential of the diesel engine. However, this is sometimes forgotten when the boat is on the water. It can hit the pocket hard when the fuel tank has to be constantly replenished. Fuel costs must be considered. The conventional diesel engine uses about 0.4pt (0.2 litres) fuel per brake horsepower per hour. This is a rough figure. Specific fuel consumption figures at different engine revolutions are available from the manufacturer. Consumption will also vary with the quality of engineering in the diesel injection pump and with the combustion space design. It can be as little as 0.33pt/(0.18 litres)bhp/hr. You can make a rough check of an engine as in the following example of a 40bhp unit: $0.4 \times 40 = 16$pt or 2gal (9 litres) per hour. The carburettor-fed petrol engine will consume about 0.6/bhp/hr: $0.6 \times 40 = 24$pt or 3gal (13.6 litres) per hour. Even if diesel fuel was as expensive as petrol (which it is not) you would, from these figures, expect to pay one-third more for petrol than for diesel fuel. Although the energy crisis gunned the internal-combustion-engine designers into producing more efficient units, you must check the relevant power range if you are not to be out of pocket. At one time the diesel was at a big disadvantage as regards its power/weight ratio. It was very heavy for the power it put out and was totally out of the question for use in planing boats. Gradually, its power/weight has improved and today there are units which have the same power/weight ratio as petrol engines of equivalent power. Petrol-engine designers are trying to design more efficient engines and the mpg figures are increasing to ever more attractive levels for the motorist. In time, automotive developments will spread to the marine field. No doubt as petrol-injection equipment becomes more common and cheap, computer-controlled ignition and fuel-injection systems that squeeze the last ounce of power from every drop of fuel will come on the market. Petrol

engines tend to develop power at higher rpm even though the modern diesel is usually a relatively high rpm unit. Planing boats are best served by a high-speed direct-drive power unit, while displacement boats are best driven with relatively low propeller speeds. Reduction gear-boxes lower the rpm of the engine.

4   Will the safety aspect of diesel fuel compared to petrol be a worth-while advantage?

5   Will the higher cost of a diesel engine, set against its greater reliability because of fewer electrical components, outweigh the lower cost of the petrol unit which always has potentially greater problems, depending as it does on electrical ignition, fuel pumping and, sometimes, electrically operated functions on the carburettor? Marine electrical components become more reliable all the time, but are still a most common source of trouble. Diesel-injection equipment is expensive but modern petrol-injection equipment can be just as costly. The expense of some electronic ignition components may well sway the balance in favour of the diesel engine.

6   Costing spares and checking reliability of supply is the final requirement. An oil filter, say, if it is sold in a cardboard box with the engine-maker's logo displayed, may be far more expensive than a similar item from a manufacturer not so concerned about his image. It is not uncommon, either, to find counterfeit printed boxes exactly like the genuine article, but containing an inferior product. The service offered by the manufacturer should be considered in context with the cost of spares. You may be able to get cheap spares, but if they take a couple of months to arrive or the engine-maker goes broke and ceases trading, it's hardly to your advantage. I recommend you to talk to the engine-makers before you make up your mind. Find the ones who can back up their sales talk with first-class service.

The owner's handbook indicates the quality of the manufacturer's back up. Some handbooks leave much to be desired, giving only the minimum of information. Others may give more information but mention little about fault-finding and give no details of often-used spare parts. The best publications are comprehensive and detailed, and if a full spare-parts catalogue is included it makes the yachtsman's life that much easier. Some manufacturers offer the services of their applications engineer. This usually, though not always, has to be paid for, but it does ensure that the installation is in accordance with the manufacturer's specifications, and that the product guarantees — which depend on correct installation — are accepted. If your boat won't be finished until after the normal one-year engine guarantee period has expired, check with the manufacturer to see if an extension can be given until the boat is launched and the engines have been proved.

### Single- or Twin-engine Installation?
Usually the boat is designed for either twin or single engines, but not always. My own boat had originally been designed for a single engine of 50–70hp, but I thought it would benefit from a twin installation. This would give greater reliability and safety, the boat would have better manoeuvrability — and I would have double the work at fitting-out time.

For fast planing craft needing plenty of power, there is little or no option. I have even come across a sailing boat with a twin-engine installation, but it was neither a proper sailing boat nor a motor boat. Compromises of this kind have little or nothing to recommend them.

Manoeuvrability is greatly improved with twin engines; in most good designs a boat can be turned almost in her own length, which makes it less harassing to get in and out of narrow marina berths. For long sea passages, twin engines are a great comfort.

### Power Selection
If you have already decided on the powering for your boat, there is no need to read this section. If powering has not been finalised, or you are installing an alternative engine to the one recommended, or you are installing two engines instead of one, then there are problems to be sorted out.

## Table 4: SPEED AND POWER TABLES FOR MOTOR YACHTS AND BOATS
### Assuming suitable form for the speed in question

| Type of stern / Length (L.W.L.) | Tons disp. | Canoe | | Transom and flat stern | | | | | Transom and very flat stern or chine | | | | V chine or step | |
|---|---|---|---|---|---|---|---|---|---|---|---|---|---|---|
| | | 5 | 6 | 7 | 8 | 9 | 10 | 11 | 12 | 13 | 14 | 15 | 16 | 17 |
| 20 ft. | 0·5 | 1·0 | 1·7 | 2·9 | 4·7 | 7·2 | 10 | 12 | 14 | 17 | 19 | 22 | | |
| | 1·0 | 1·8 | 3·6 | 6·6 | 10·8 | 16 | 20 | 24 | 28 | 33 | 39 | 44 | | |
| | 1·5 | 2·6 | 5·7 | 11 | 17 | 24 | 30 | 36 | 43 | 50 | 58 | 67 | | |
| | 2·0 | 3·1 | 8·0 | 15 | 22 | 32 | 40 | 48 | 57 | 67 | 77 | 89 | | |
| | 3·0 | 3·7 | 12 | 24 | 33 | 48 | 59 | 72 | 85 | 100 | 116 | 134 | | |
| 25ft. | 2·0 | 2·4 | 5 | 10 | 17 | 25 | 34 | 42 | 50 | 59 | 68 | 78 | | |
| | 3·0 | 3·0 | 6·5 | 15 | 26 | 37 | 48 | 61 | 74 | 88 | 102 | 115 | | |
| | 4·0 | 4·0 | 8·7 | 22 | 36 | 50 | 64 | 84 | 100 | 117 | 136 | 155 | | |
| | 5·0 | 5·0 | 12 | 28 | 46 | 65 | 85 | 105 | 125 | 146 | 170 | 196 | | |
| 30 ft. | 1·5 | 1·6 | 2·9 | 4·9 | 7·4 | 11 | 15 | 23 | 31 | 37 | 43 | 50 | 57 | |
| | 2·0 | 1·9 | 3·6 | 6·4 | 10·4 | 15 | 22 | 32 | 42 | 50 | 58 | 67 | 76 | |
| | 3·0 | 2·5 | 5·0 | 9·7 | 17 | 26 | 36 | 48 | 62 | 75 | 87 | 100 | 114 | |
| | 4·0 | 3·0 | 6·4 | 13 | 26 | 37 | 51 | 64 | 83 | 100 | 116 | 133 | 152 | |
| | 5·0 | 3·3 | 7·7 | 16 | 32 | 46 | 66 | 80 | 104 | 125 | 145 | 167 | 190 | |
| | 6·0 | 3·5 | 8·8 | 19 | 39 | 56 | 79 | 96 | 125 | 150 | 174 | 200 | 227 | |
| | 8·0 | 4·0 | 11 | 26 | 51 | 74 | 105 | 128 | 166 | 200 | 232 | 267 | 303 | |
| 40 ft. | 4·0 | 2·8 | 5·2 | 8·5 | 13 | 20 | 28 | 39 | 53 | 67 | 84 | 97 | 110 | 124 |
| | 6·0 | 3·5 | 7·0 | 12 | 20 | 34 | 50 | 65 | 89 | 105 | 126 | 144 | 164 | 186 |
| | 8·0 | 4·0 | 8·4 | 15 | 26 | 47 | 73 | 94 | 119 | 145 | 168 | 193 | 219 | 248 |
| | 10·0 | 4·4 | 9·9 | 18 | 33 | 61 | 92 | 122 | 149 | 180 | 210 | 242 | 274 | 310 |
| | 12·0 | 4·6 | 11 | 21 | 40 | 75 | 110 | 146 | 179 | 217 | 252 | 290 | 329 | 372 |
| | 14·0 | 5·0 | 12 | 24 | 46 | 87 | 128 | 170 | 208 | 253 | 294 | 338 | 384 | 434 |
| | 16·0 | 5·2 | 13 | 27 | 53 | 100 | 147 | 195 | 238 | 289 | 336 | 387 | 439 | 495 |
| | 18·0 | 5·6 | 14 | 30 | 59 | 112 | 165 | 219 | 268 | 325 | 378 | 435 | 494 | 558 |
| | 20·0 | 5·9 | 15 | 33 | 66 | 125 | 183 | 244 | 298 | 361 | 420 | 484 | 548 | 620 |
| 50 ft. | 8 | 4·1 | 7·2 | 13 | 19 | 28 | 39 | 55 | 74 | 99 | 124 | 150 | 177 | 205 |
| | 10 | 4·6 | 7·9 | 15 | 23 | 35 | 53 | 76 | 100 | 130 | 162 | 193 | 228 | 257 |
| | 12 | 5·0 | 8·8 | 17 | 27 | 42 | 66 | 96 | 122 | 164 | 199 | 243 | 283 | 309 |
| | 14 | 5·3 | 9·6 | 20 | 30 | 49 | 82 | 116 | 155 | 198 | 243 | 286 | 330 | 360 |
| | 16 | 5·6 | 10 | 21 | 34 | 56 | 98 | 137 | 183 | 234 | 278 | 327 | 376 | 412 |
| | 18 | 5·8 | 11 | 23 | 38 | 63 | 112 | 168 | 212 | 270 | 313 | 368 | 423 | 463 |
| | 20 | 6·0 | 12 | 25 | 41 | 70 | 128 | 192 | 248 | 300 | 348 | 408 | 470 | 515 |
| | 25 | 6·5 | 13 | 30 | 50 | 87 | 164 | 240 | 312 | 375 | 435 | 510 | 588 | 643 |
| | 30 | 7·0 | 14 | 34 | 57 | 105 | 197 | 288 | 374 | 450 | 522 | 612 | 705 | 775 |
| | 35 | 8·0 | 15 | 37 | 66 | 123 | 230 | 336 | 437 | 525 | 609 | 715 | 823 | 900 |

I took heart when an eminent yacht designer confessed to me that power/speed calculations for small craft were not easy or too accurate, so the most often used rule was 'rule of thumb'! But as amateurs without experience it is reassuring to have something more logical to go on. Table 4 is Barnaby's 'Speed and Powering' table. We also use the 'K' formula which is the starting point for designers before application of the experienced thumb. Very few small-craft designers are able or willing, because of costs, to tank test and develop hull forms. If this happened we would know a great deal more about economical powering of craft.

Fig 60 shows graphs which will help determine safe 'rule of thumb' powering for different types of craft, provided they are applied to hull forms suitable for the speed in question. As we saw earlier, at and below a speed/length ratio of 1:34 a hull has one or more waves to support it within its length. It displaces the water and though speed is low it gives, in a displacement hull form, a comfortable ride. A speed/length ratio of 1:34 on the four graphs would produce a speed of 6 knots for a 20ft (6m) water-line length, 6.7 knots for a 25ft (7.6m) length, 7.3 knots for a 30ft (9.1m) length and 7.9 for a 35ft (10.6m) length — all very modest speeds but above

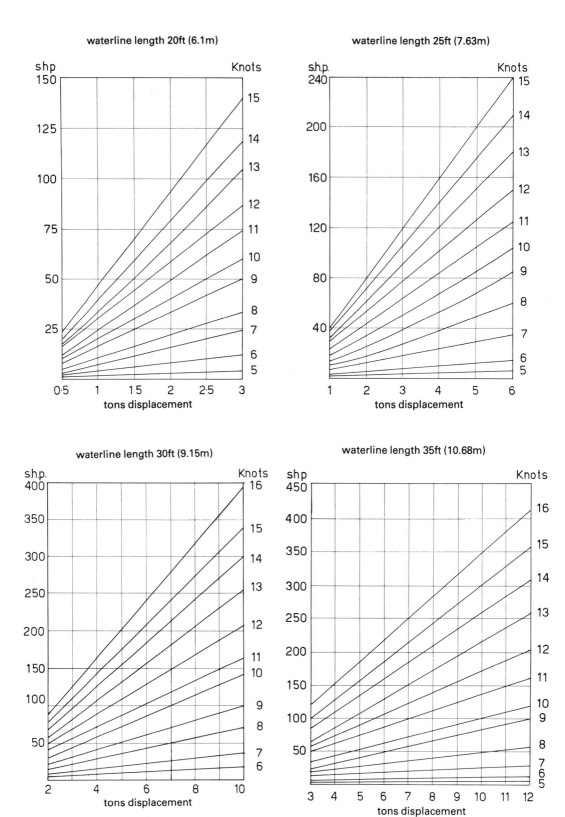

**Fig 60** Power and speed estimation graphs

these the displacement hull would have the wave moving away from the transom and it would begin to squat at the stern. Driving it harder by applying more power only makes the resistance caused by squatting increase. By merely digging a hole in the water at the stern, you are getting little value for the cost of the extra fuel used. So, for the first part of the graph at the bottom where speeds are modest, you would be best selecting a displacement hull with either a narrow transom or canoe stern. From a speed/length ratio of 1:34 upwards, the designer will try to get some dynamic lift out of the after sections. This will help to lift the boat out of the hole at the stern. By flattening the run aft and having a wide transom this would produce a large underwater area that would begin to generate dynamic lift. There is no sudden change from a displacement to a semi-planing hull. In fact, *Sea Hound* is a good example in my opinion of a hull that is economically driven at just over the speed/length ratio of 1:34.

LWL = 27½ft (8.3m)    $V\sqrt{L} = 1.45$
Designed speed: $5.24 \times 1.45 = 7.6$ knots

As $V\sqrt{L}$ increases, the designer has to flatten the stern sections still more or use a chine to get even more dynamic lift as the hull configuration moves from semi-displacement towards a fully planing form. The speeds in the four graphs are mainly to cover displacement amd semi-displacement hulls run at modest speeds but from a study of them, the potential owner of any hull can learn some valuable lessons. Notice, for example, how for quite small increases in speed the power requirements have to shoot up. An example would be a boat of about 28ft (8.5m) overall length, with a water-line length of 25ft (7.6m) and a displacement of 4 tons:

At 8 knots power required = 38shp
At 12 knots (33⅓ per cent increase) = 105shp (276 per cent increase)

In terms of fuel consumption at full throttle, allowing 0.36pt (0.2 litres)/shp/hr, the figures are:

At 8 knots 38shp consumes approx 13.68pt/hr (1.71gal, 7.62 litres or 2.06 US gal)
At 12 knots 105shp consumes approx 37.8pt/hr (4.73gal, 21.5 litres or 5.7 US gal)

In other words, for a small increase in speed, running costs would be over 2½ times as much. Most displacement and semi-displacement boats cruise at much less than full throttle — more like 50 per cent full power — but the ratio is much the same. It costs less to go slow.

It is interesting to see from these graphs how a sailing boat can use very low engine power over a great range of displacement weights. The low speeds, below 7 knots, have almost flat power needs over the full range of hull weights. The auxiliary sailing boat, as opposed to the motor sailer, can get away with very modest power units. However, these graphs are based on sea-going boats having plenty of power in hand. This is to overcome extra resistance when they go through large waves. It has been shown that an increase in power of up to 400 per cent might be called for, but it would be ridiculous to design pleasure boats for this kind of situation. However, for the auxiliary sailing yacht, there is no harm in providing a little extra power for when she encounters strong tidal streams or currents. Motor sailers nowadays have engine power very similar to a power cruiser, enabling them to be driven at speeds matched to hull form in most kinds of weather. The only way they differ from motor boats is that care must be taken to see that the engine will run at high angles of heel.

**Displacement**
Before you can use any tables or work out powering calculations, you need to know the displacement of your boat. First approach the designer as he will have the calculations to determine displacement and he may well have checked these figures on a completed, floating boat. He will probably have used Simpson's First Rule or, less accurately, Tchebycheff's Rule to calculate displacement. Basically, these calcula-

tions determine the volume of water that is displaced when a boat is floated. 35cu ft (0.98m³) of salt water weighs a ton (2,240lb (1,016kg)) while 36cu ft (1m³) of fresh water is the same weight.

A simple but less accurate method, if figures are not forthcoming, is to use the block coefficient method set out in Fig 61. This is less ominous than it sounds. It is the ratio between the underwater volume of the hull and a rectangular shaped block bounded by the extremes of beam and length at the water-line and the moulded depth. The depth of the keel must be left out of the moulded depth figure. The calculation shown will be useful for both displacement and planing boats, provided the right block coefficient value is obtained or

**Fig 61** Calculating displacement from block-coefficient

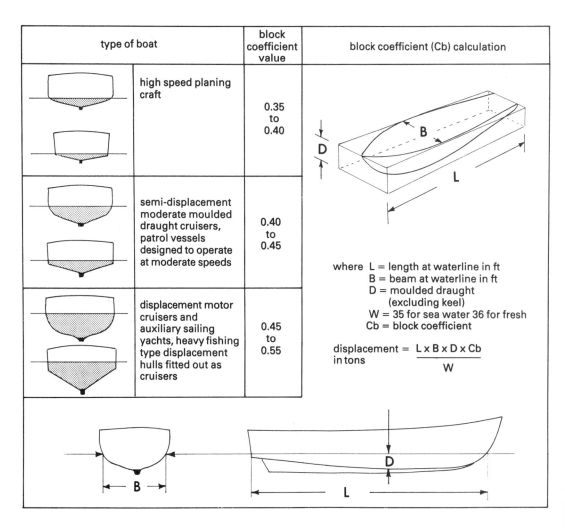

| type of boat | | block coefficient value | block coefficient (Cb) calculation |
|---|---|---|---|
| | high speed planing craft | 0.35 to 0.40 | |
| | semi-displacement moderate moulded draught cruisers, patrol vessels designed to operate at moderate speeds | 0.40 to 0.45 | where  L = length at waterline in ft |
| | displacement motor cruisers and auxiliary sailing yachts, heavy fishing type displacement hulls fitted out as cruisers | 0.45 to 0.55 | |

where  L = length at waterline in ft
B = beam at waterline in ft
D = moulded draught
   (excluding keel)
W = 35 for sea water 36 for fresh
Cb = block coefficient

$$\text{displacement in tons} = \frac{L \times B \times D \times Cb}{W}$$

guessed at, so, unless the actual figure is known, this method must still be regarded as rule of thumb. As previously stated, with displacement boats the power required does not vary excessively over a large range displacement weight if they are to travel at modest speeds. However, if fuel economy is a design target, or the boat begins to get some dynamic lift from its hull form, then you must be more accurate in estimating power requirements. You have to know something about the mystery ingredient 'K'. I will write of this further on.

Another important fact learned from the graphs is that with a displacement boat or

**Fig 62** Determination of 'K' values for semi-displacement and planing craft

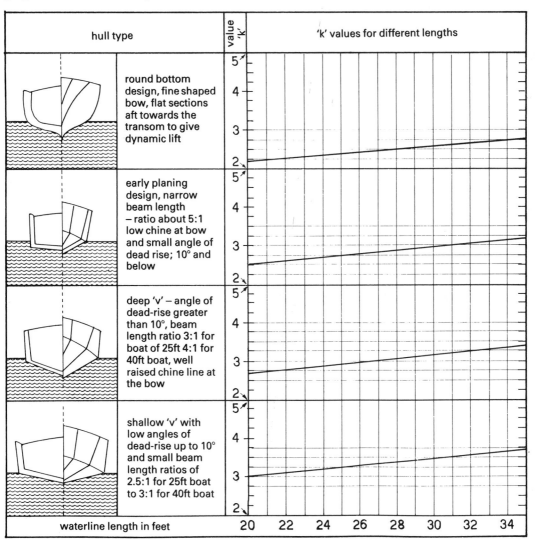

a semi-displacement boat running near $V\sqrt{L}$ just above 1:34, the weight of the boat does not have the effect of increasing power needs alarmingly. For example, a boat of 30ft (9.1m) LWL, 6 or 8 tons displacement running at a $V\sqrt{L} = 1.45$ (8 knots):

Power for 6 ton boat = approx 44shp
Power for 8 ton boat = approx 55shp
Increase of 25 per cent for an extra 2 tons of weight at the same speed.

The same boat driven at $V\sqrt{L} = 2$ (10.96 knots (approx 11)):

Power for 6 ton boat = 100 shp
Power for 8 ton boat = 130shp
Increase of 30 per cent at the same speed

By the time you have increased the speed to $V\sqrt{L} = 2.5$ (approx 14 knots):

Power for 6 ton boat = approx 175shp
Power for 8 ton boat = approx 235 shp
Increase of 34 per cent at the same speed.

Overall, the 6 ton boat needs over four times the power to less than double its speed from 8 knots to 14 knots.

Long before you buy the hull these powering requirements are worth mulling over so that you can decide if the extra speed justifies the higher costs in power and running the engine. Equally important for a fast boat is to keep weight within design limits. Really heavy traditional cabinet work using plenty of teak does not matter much in a displacement boat, neither does carrying tons of water, fuel and, perhaps, effluent in a holding tank. Do the same on a planing or semi-displacement boat and you literally burn money in fuel. Fast boats should be treated like aircraft, with interiors that are lightly but strongly constructed.

## The 'K' Method of Powering

The 'K' method of calculating power requirements is used on semi-displacement and fast planing craft. The tables just laid out are fine for modest speeds, but plenty of cruising boats are designed for more than the 15–16 knots that the tables cover.

The easiest way to find this 'K' factor is to ask the designer for its value. If this cannot be obtained, Fig 62 sets out a method that should enable you to identify the hull type from your own plans and, when you have measured the water-line length, to determine a value for 'K' from the graphs. You can now find the speed from a given horsepower:

$$V = K \times \sqrt{\frac{shp}{\triangle}} \qquad \triangle = \text{Displacement in tons}$$

or determine the power:

$$shp = \triangle \times \frac{V^2}{K^2}$$

You can get truer figures for the 'K' value once the boat is afloat, determining speed from running trials and the true shp from the engine manufacturer's power graphs related to engine rpm. Before the boat is built your calculations can serve as a useful guide to check if there is power in hand and that it will be delivered at the rpm which will not put a strain on the boat, your ear-drums or your pocket.

## Engine-maker's Power Curves

Engine power is usually given three ratings. In Fig 63 the curve at (a) is continuous operation, the curve at (b) for a one-hour maximum rating and the same curve at (c) for a short fifteen-minute rating. Except for quick bursts of speed, the fifteen-minute rating is not likely to be of much interest to a cruising enthusiast. You may be glad of the one-hour rating which could be the power in hand to get through difficult water. Of greatest interest is the continuous rating and even with that you should have some power in hand and be able to run at both economic fuel-consumption rates and at about half throttle to achieve reasonable quietness. Planing boats should have sufficient power to get them over the hump of resistance as they climb on to the plane. Once there, they can usually throttle back. This kind of boat needs the extra power for the hump and to cope with cruising gear that will not have been included in the designer's calculations.

Using *Sea Hound* as an example of how to relate these curves to the powering of a boat, to find the expected shp:

When $V\sqrt{L} = 1.45$ and $LWL = 27.5$
Designed speed $= V\sqrt{L} \times \sqrt{LWL} =$
$1.45 \times 5.24 = 7.6$ knots

From the 'K' method shp is found:

$$shp = 5.7 \text{ tons} \times \frac{7.6 \times 7.6}{2.5 \times 2.5} \quad \frac{speed^2}{K^2}$$

(from Fig 67)
$=5.7 \times 9.24$
$= 52.67$shp or approx 26shp for each of the twin engines installed

From the Perkins curves it will be seen that at the continuous rating I could expect 26shp to be delivered at about

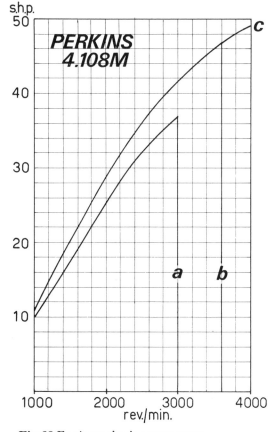

s.h.p.

Fig 63 Enginemaker's power curve

2,000rpm, provided the propeller design were right. From the speed calculation I could anticipate:

$$V = 2.5 \times \sqrt{\frac{2 \times 37}{5.7}} \quad \begin{array}{l}\text{(maximum power from}\\ \text{both engines)}\\ \text{(displacement tons)}\end{array}$$

$= 9$ knots

In actual trials the speed at 2,000rpm was 7.75 knots and a fraction over 9 knots at full throttle. In the section on noise suppression the effect of rpm on noise aboard the boat will be considered.

**Schooling in Engines**
If the amateur is to make a first-class job of the engine installation he needs to know as much as he can about it. Not all engine manufacturers are as forthcoming as Perkins of Peterborough or Volvo Penta who run schools for prospective and actual owners of their engines. The Perkins engine familiarisation course was ideal for me (Fig 64). The course lasted two days, but there were longer courses for mechanics training to do complete overhauls. With a class of only four students to one instructor and a series of classrooms devoted to the 4.108 engine, it was hardly surprising how enjoyable and far-ranging the instruction became. In no time after handling many exhibits as well as the engines, we felt we could cope with basic maintenance. With this kind of back up, anyone with even modest mechanical abilities can learn to cope.

**Physical Installation Requirements**
I admit I have definite views about the provision of sturdy engine beds on any type of boat. In World War I some superb coastal motor boats were built. These had engine beds nearly the whole length of the hull from transom almost to the bow, which were capable of transmitting power from the huge engine thrust over the whole area of the hull bottom. Compare this to the couple of matchsticks that some builders use. The engines shake themselves to bits and transmit noise all over the boat. No wonder that the sailing man is prejudiced against the iron topsail.

**Fig 64** The major engine manufacturers like Volvo Penta and Perkins run owner training courses which are highly recommended

It is not a question of glassing in two pieces of thick plank at the right angle, but the first stage of what should be a precision piece of engineering. The beds have to take a hefty weight, transfer thrust to the hull and be perfectly aligned so that when the engine is in position, shafting from the propellers joins up correctly with the output flange of the engine. For anyone determined to do all this himself, I will explain the procedures in more detail, but I would not tackle this work myself. I believe it to be the job of the professional moulder. Bear in mind the following:

1　For perfect alignment of beds the hull must be completely supported with no sag or hog in the keel and no twist in the lateral alignment.

2　The bonding of beds is best done at a time when maximum adhesion between hull and engine bed can be achieved. If the bonding is done early before total cure of the resins, perfect integrity is assured. The best moulding practice is to mould in the beds before the hull is removed from the mould, at the time bulkheads are put into position.

Except for small power units that are light enough to be manhandled aboard, the amateur will have to hire expensive lifting gear. In my opinion, this money is better spent in having the beds professionally installed.

Fig 65 shows *Sea Hound*'s twin-engine installation with conventional beds. Certain design features described in the caption are just as relevant to single and outdrive engines. Wherever possible, top-hat sections (A) should form a continuation of the main engine bed to spread thrust as well as give strength to the bottom of the boat. These longitudinal members pass through both forward and aft bulkheads, but in many yacht designs the forward end of the engine bed ends abruptly at the main bulkhead (C). Lateral strengthening (D) minimises shake from the engine, especially the diesel. At least two complete sets of webs across the hull — more for larger power units — reduce the free panel area and add enormous strength to the part that bears the greatest weight. The inset (G) shows a suggested cross-section of the actual bearer. A hardwood core is fitted along the length of its top with a steel reinforcing plate. The whole lot is then moulded over with GRP. Provided generous scantlings are given, pine is a perfectly feasible material to use in exposed bearers for small marine engines. For enclosed wood reinforcing, teak

is superior. Oak can be used but must on no account come into contact with steel or iron reinforcement or bolts, because of gallic acid in the timber. You can leave the wood exposed, merely glassing in the webs along the bottom edges, but this does not give anything like the strength. I have shown bolt holes for fastening engine feet or flexible mountings to the bed. If the reinforcing metal strip is galvanised and ¾in (9mm) or more in thickness, you could dispense with the lower holes, simply drilling and tapping the metal to take bolts.

In most installations the design will have been worked out for a standard engine, but should you be substituting another make, check that the angle of the engine bearers is within the design parameters of the new engine. Installation angle must allow the engine to get full lubrication and, in sailing boats, the maximum angle of heel for safe working

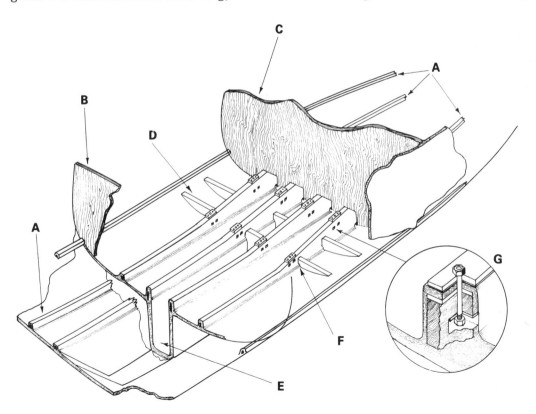

**Fig 65** Engine bed design features

must also be considered. If you do wish to glass in the engine bearers then you must make a mock-up of the engine base as a pattern. A pattern is a precision piece of woodwork made from the dimensions given on the engine manufacturer's installation arrangement drawing. Check that the drawing shows the same gear-box that you will be having. Sometimes the engine is offered with a number of alternatives. Build a mock sump on to the pattern to ensure that the engine sump will clear the bottom of the boat. In the pattern, temporary distance pieces that allow for the thickness of the GRP and the height of the engine mounting feet or flexible mountings can be used as shown in Fig 66. If you

**Fig 66** Propeller shaft installation on hull with and without skeg

have the actual mounts to hand, use them along with the GRP thickness distance pieces. Ensure that the four mounts have the same adjustment, starting with minimum height, so that eventually you will only have to adjust them upwards to get perfect alignment.

Now, taking a closer look at Fig 66, I have shown two distinct types of installation: the upper one is for a boat with a skeg, the lower for a shaft emerging through the bottom of the boat, as in a twin-engine installation, certain forms of fast power boats and some modern fin-keel sailing yachts.

**A** There is some appalling rudder design in certain modern craft, making it impossible to get the shaft in or out of an installation without first doing severe damage to the rudder by getting at bolts and nuts em-

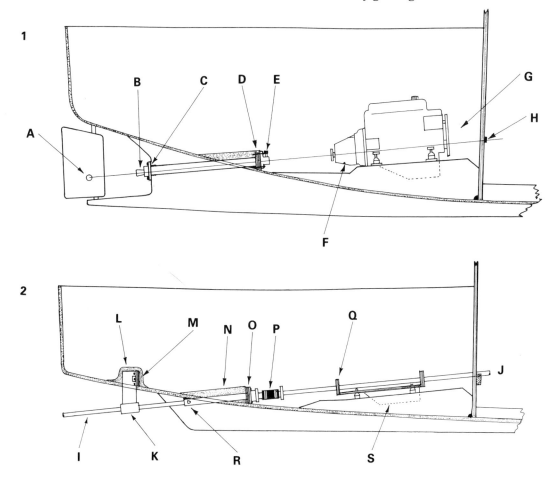

bedded in GRP to remove it. The drawing shows the old-fashioned idea of a hole in the rudder through which the shaft can be taken without dismantling or removing the rudder.

**B** The traditional method of getting the shaft line is to use taut piano wire. A pilot hole is bored through the skeg and the outer shaft bearing (C) is lightly bolted in place. A wooden plug is inserted in the bearing with a perfectly centralised hole to run the wire through. The other end of the wire is drawn tight at the bulkhead (H) to produce the correct shaft angle. The surface of the skeg behind the outer bearing may well have to be ground away slightly to get perfect alignment. The bolts that locate the bearing should have holes drilled into the GRP of the skeg, although some hulls will allow through-bolting. At this stage only fit things 'dry' so that fine adjustments can be made before finally bolting or glassing into place. Next, fit the pattern (Q) bolted to engine mountings, spacers and engine bearers as a complete unit. Check how this structure lines up with the wire. The centre-line of the engine and the lateral alignment are then checked. For precise alignment where wire is being used, metal plates on edge with small 'V' notches can be attached to the centre-line on the engine pattern block. When this gives satisfactory alignment of the main engine beds, undo the wire and slip over web (D) which will have the stern tube and the inboard end of the stern tube gland bolted to it. Now a mix containing a high proportion of glass mat is used under the engine beds and with these lowered back into position, the wire is restretched and accurate alignment obtained. While the bedding resin is going off, the stern tube is screwed into the outer bearing and the inner one, the latter bolted to the web which should be of stout marine plywood at least 1½in (38mm) thick. The web, bearing the full stern tube and glands, is now matted into place, checking that the wire is still perfectly centralised on the outside of the boat at the outer gland, and at the inner gland on the inside. Now full matting in of all parts can begin. When the bedding resin to the main

bearers has gone off and there is no chance of disturbing other parts as they set, the engine pattern can be removed and full glassing in of the engine beds with their reinforcement can be completed.

On Fig 66, (1F) shows that the gear-box drain plug can be reached. On many sailing yachts the access for draining the gear-box or sump is often difficult. Careful design and slight angling of the bed does much to make these jobs easier. Down-angle gear-box drives can alleviate this problem. Similarly (G), the distance between main bulkhead and front end of the engine, which can be arranged to give reasonable access to water pumps and belts to be serviced. Bearings for shafting are either a white metal or fluted rubber water-lubricated type. The former (E) is lubricated with grease. A simple hand-greaser is fine on small craft where the greaser is easily reached. Larger craft, or where there is difficult access, should have remote greasers as shown in Fig 51.

Completely solidly mounted engines with a reasonable distance of shafting between gear-box drive flange and inner drive can have a solid inner bearing. Flexibly mounted engines must have a flexible shaft log. To isolate engine vibration transmitted through the shafting to the hull via the shaft log gland, flexible couplings are used. I like to see flexible couplings in any installation without a flexible inboard shaft log, as in most types of boat there is some degree of flexion between hull and engine. The flexible coupling absorbs some of this. In my own boat, I used a solid inboard gland with a double flexible coupling on each shaft to increase absorption of possible movement. Because the initial design brought the output flange quite close to the inboard bearing and the engines were flexibly mounted, the double flexible coupling also eliminates the possibility of excessive shaft wear, although it does cost more than a flexible inboard gland.

On part 2 of Fig 66, I have shown the alternative method of aligning shafting components. This time, a perfectly straight length of steel rod, the same diameter as the shaft, is used instead of wire. This method is excellent, provided you can get a perfectly straight piece of metal. An engineering shop will check this, but it is surprising how difficult it is to keep it straight. Without support over its length it will provide its own permanent sag which you might well build into the alignment of the engine shafting. However, in this figure I also show the arrangement for installing shafting using the 'P' bracket (K). This bracket is the first part of the system built in by cutting a slot in the hull at the appropriate station and slipping the bracket up through it. A thick plywood web is then bolted by means of an angle bracket to the 'P' bracket to support it. An elliptical slot is cut where the shafting is to pass through the hull forward of the bracket. The plywood web (O) and inboard shaft log and tube are threaded on the shafting along with the engine bed template. The end of the steel rod is supported by the main bulkhead to give the correct alignment. The engine beds can then be fitted by tacking in place. Now, starting again at the 'P' bracket, glassing in can begin. On twin-engine installations the web across the hull can support both brackets and spread the load over a much larger area of the bottom. The stern tube (R) as it emerges from the GRP hull may or may not have a water-lubricated bearing. Fairing in the bearing is important, especially when a full flow of water is needed on the intake to lubricate a cutless bearing. The procedure for the inboard gland web and engine beds is as previously described. In any installation check that the sump (S) of the engine will clear the hull bottom comfortably.

## Universal Couplings

If, at the design stage, the use of universal couplings is anticipated, these can have some advantage in simplifying the installation. Engine beds can be mounted parallel to the water-line. This in itself can save some height above the engine — important when a low wheel-house floor is called for.

The GKN Aquadrive system is one of the most attractive couplings. It is easy for the amateur to install and gives freedom of any angle drive up to 16° through two constant velocity joints. Each joint can absorb 8° of down angle. With engines and shafting in place, then the rest of the installation is comparatively simple.

## The Fuel System

Fuel = fire. Fire must burn — but only in the cylinder-head space. You must constantly bear in mind the dangers that fuel presents if it burns outside the cylinder of the engine. The amateur builder should acquaint himself with the local regulations in the area where his boat is to be used. These rules do vary from country to country as well as within each country. In small craft the spread of fire is generally so rapid that once it gets hold, the position of fuel tanks is of relatively little importance. If the fuel tanks do not burn, there is plenty of other material in a GRP boat that will. The only policy is to avoid fire at all costs by creating a well-engineered system that will keep the fuel where it belongs and having aboard a system that deals adequately with any small fire that does develop.

## Materials for Fuel Tanks

Although glass-reinforced plastic will burn, it is still an excellent material for diesel fuel tanks. It is easily fire retarded with fire-retardant paints or fire-retardant resins used in the outer part of the lay-up. I would suggest that this is a job for the moulder as calculations have to be carefully made so that the right strength properties are developed. Have the GRP tanks built into the boat when it is moulded. This ensures complete integrity of strength with the rest of the hull and you can specify the internal gel coat which is resistant to fuel oil. Let me warn you. I have seen GRP fuel tanks which were so badly moulded that glass fibres regularly came away in the fuel to block the fuel filters of the engine. The internal gel coat should have a heavy application reinforced with glass tissue. Only metal should be used for petrol tanks.

Metal tanks for both fuels should be of stainless steel, lead-coated steel or light alloy. Lloyd's quote a minimum thickness of ⅛in (3mm) except for small tanks. When you realise that two or three 'g' might be applied to the tank and its weight of fuel when the boat falls off a wave, you will understand the need for strength. Ordinary steel can be used for tanks provided it is given corrosion protection with a suitable paint.

Tanks should be tested hydraulically to 5lb per sq in of pressure (0.35kg per cm²). Reputable tank-makers will offer this service for any tank you order.

There are other plastic materials available for fuel tanks. Some are offered as being fire resistant; others could be a severe fire hazard.

I am not happy about the use of flexible plastic fuel tanks. Though strong, they are a fire hazard and all tanks of this type, whether for fuel, water or sewage, can suffer seriously from chafe. If you do decide to use tanks of this type, they are best installed in smooth lined boxes which will stop them rolling about, even when partially full. Boxes must be firmly located.

In the second chapter I mentioned RNLI rescue statistics. Fuel shortage and machinery failure were seen as the major contributing factors to disaster. I do not apologise for drawing your attention to these figures again. In the majority of rescues, if the boat has not run out of fuel, it is some other fault in the fuel system that has contributed to the disaster. Water in fuel — from dirty shore tanks, condensation, or badly placed breather pipes — is a major hazard. Leave one weakness in the whole fuel system, either diesel or petrol, and it will catch you out. As a pre-engine filter unit, I use a Lucas/CAV Filtrap 100 on each engine. This consists of a filter element and a sedimenter bowl. The element has a dual function: filtering solids and water separation. As fuel flows down through the element, fine pores retain solid particles. The water particles that are forced through the filter element, coalesce into larger droplets and are then deposited by sedimentation in the base of the filter, where they can be drained off. If you are in any doubt as to the correct type of filter, the engine manufacturer will be able to advise.

## Size of Fuel Tanks

Earlier, when I wrote about petrol versus diesel engines, I gave rough ways of working out fuel consumption. These figures should be used to determine fuel tank size and the boat's cruising range. Sea-going boats should have fuel in hand for an emergency and, when calculating range, you must allow for the fact that you are not going to drain the last gallon or so out of the tank bottom.

To check the range, divide gallonage of fuel tank by engine consumption and multiply by speed in knots.

$$\frac{\text{Tank size 25gal (114 litres)}}{\text{consumption 2gal (9 litres) per hr}} = \frac{12.5\text{hr}}{\text{cruising}}$$

At 8 knots, range would be 8 × 12.5 = 100 nautical miles minus 10 per cent = 90 nautical miles

It would be quite reasonable to deduct 10 per cent from this figure to allow for the fuel in the bottom of the tank that cannot be used, plus a higher consumption figure to allow for bad sea and weather conditions.

In most cases, maximum range is only theoretical. Fuel consumption increases dramatically if the boat maintains speed in a rough sea. The extra power is necessary to overcome wave resistance. However, even with an approximate calculation, you do know the weight of the fuel and this is important in a planing craft. Weight is going to affect performance and there is no need to carry more fuel than is necessary on any boat, for a range that will never be used. Even on inland waterways extra weight is a waste of energy and gives the boat a deeper draught — not a good idea in shallow waters.

If you decide to have special tanks made or moulded, it is useful to know that 1 gal (4.5 litres) of fuel occupies a space of approximately 0.161cu ft (0.004m³, US gal 0.13ft³).

## Installing the System

Fig 67 shows a diesel installation. Where there are differences from a petrol installation I will point this out. The figure can be considered as for a single engine, pro-

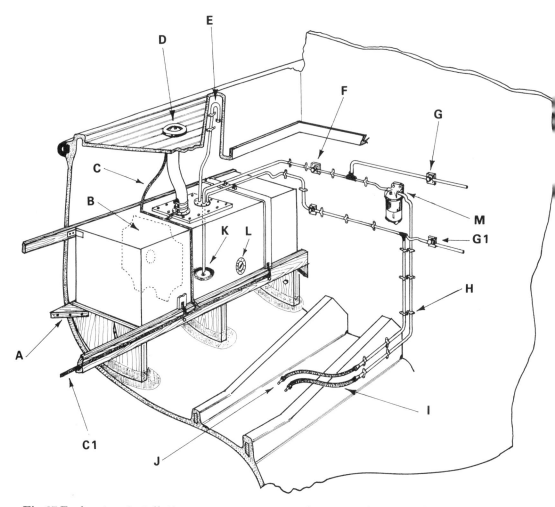

**Fig 67** Fuel system installation

vided the link pipe and valve 'V' is omitted. The link pipe leads to a mirror image plan of the system shown as being installed on the port-hand side of a twin-engined installation. Petrol tanks would not be fitted in the same compartment as the engine, but separated by a vapour-proof bulkhead in a well-ventilated space. Parts of the figure applicable generally, are:

**A** Any fuel tank must be properly cradled and strongly secured in position. Brackets welded on to metal tanks, steel or wire rope bands over the top of tanks, heavily secured, and strengthening braces are all part of ensuring that the greatest 'g' forces encountered will not cause it to break free. Provided good anchorage

points are given, steel strip or wire rope can be used to hold down a loose tank.

**B** Baffles must be fitted to prevent surge which could affect the stability of a boat carrying a large amount of fuel or, more likely, allow the engine to draw in air when contents are low. For every 11gal (50 litres or 13.25 US gal) of fuel, a baffle should be provided.

**C** Bonding, especially between separated metal components of the system in a GRP tank installation, must always be provided. The danger is of static electricity igniting fuel vapour. Static is more likely to be present in hot dry conditions, but must always be guarded against. Copper braid or copper strip is a good earth path to a ground plate or sacrificial anode on the hull. It takes time to provide proper terminals for each end of the ground wire or strip, but if the system is to work well over a period of time, these terminals must be installed. Crimped terminals are probably the quickest. A neat way is to lead all bonding round the tank to one common strip (C1) which leads to the ground plate.

**D** Fuel filler. A simple fitting that can be a source of trouble if badly designed and installed. In these circumstances, it could let water into the fuel tank with disastrous results. For safety reasons it must be installed outside the coaming so that spilt fuel will go overboard. However, in this position, it is vulnerable to weather and water that is detrimental to the fuel supply. Check that you have a deck filler which has proper seals and is raised slightly above deck level so that it never lies in a puddle of water. This is especially important when the boat is laid up for the winter and water may accumulate on deck. Multiple tanks may be connected with a balance-pipe system which enables all tanks to be filled from one deck filler position. The balance pipe, not used in my drawing, would have to be run low down in each tank. This gives a possible source of leakage and for a twin-tank installation I prefer two fillers. For a multiple-tank installation, especially when tanks are sited away from the side of the boat, a balance-pipe system would be more practical. An arrangement of several tanks gives far safer weight distribution in high-speed craft where long range necessitates that large quantities of fuel must be carried. They are usually separated from the main supply tanks by a system of valves and balance-supply pipes. Gravity supply is by far the best if it can be arranged. Otherwise, have hand or electrical fuel pumping to top up the main tank. Simplicity is the key word. In complex valve-opening sessions, part of the procedure might well be forgotten. There are devices available which warn you that the main tank is running out of fuel. This ensures that, in a diesel system in particular, air is not drawn into the fuel system to stop the engine, which might happen at a critical moment. Hand valves needing quick and easy access often complicate out-of-sight pipework. Electrical solenoid valves make the job easier, but there is a slightly higher risk of failure if the electrical supply goes wrong.

**E** All tanks must be fitted with a breather pipe that allows air to escape from the empty tank as it is filled. The breather must on no account let water down into the fuel tank. Petrol-tank breathers must not be vented so that explosive vapours could get back inboard and they must be kept away from any possible source of ignition — gas-heater flues, exhausts, etc. The terminal fitting must have a metal gauze flame trap. On the drawing I have shown how it is possible to allow a diesel-fuel breather to be led high into the space of the coaming, provided this coaming is ventilated by means of a small ventilator to the outside air. The shell should face to the rear of the boat to create a vacuum to suck out fumes. The higher the breather pipe can be installed above the level of the deck-filler plate the better. A minimum of 15in (381mm) should be achieved. In circumstances where the design prevents this, when breathers must be installed at or below the level of the deck, they must always be sited so that fuel expelled when accidentally overfilling the tank will be vented from the hull topside or transom in a relatively safe place. The US Coast Guard states that overflow should be restricted by such a pipe to less than 2 gal (9 litres) per minute. I do not believe any overflow is safe for, if it does not explode, it does pollute the waters. My answer is to have a large deck filler, 1½in (38mm) minimum size, which allows air to escape as well as at the breather pipe and gives room for 'blow back' at the filler plate should it be overfilled, rather than through the breather pipe. Minimum size for a breather pipe on small tanks should be ²/₅–⁴/₇in (10–14mm) — ½in (13mm) pipe is a good size. For large tank installations where full-flow high-capacity filling may be needed, both deck filler and breather dimensions should be increased accordingly. On sailing yachts, due consideration must be given to preventing ingress of water through the breather when the boat is heeled.

**F** Fuel shut-off valves must be provided on fuel lines to isolate the tank if there is a fire. Manual valves are fine for small craft where they can be easily reached, but classification societies require remotely operated valves that can be turned off without having to gain dangerous access to the tank space. These can be automatic types like the Beasley fire valve, or electrically operated solenoid valves.

**G**   Alternative fuel supply should be considered as a safety measure. The figure shows only one tank on the port-hand side of the boat. If you produce a mirror image for the starboard side, this shows the system I have in *Sea Hound*. The two tanks are linked by two 'T' pieces and one pipe with a central valve (G). This is normally kept closed so that each engine draws from its own fuel tank. Should one tank become contaminated, its normal supply line valve (F for the port engine) is closed and the central one (G) opened. Both engines could draw fuel from the starboard tank or vice versa, if the valve on the other supply line was shut down.

Where twin diesel installations are concerned, a similar cross-pipe system must be employed in the fuel return line (J) so that when one tank only is being used that tank alone has fuel returned to it and not to the tank that has been shut down. The central valve (G1) is connected into the mirror image of the installation so that each fuel return line has a shut-down valve like (F).

**H**   Piping must be annealed seamless copper, seamless copper nickel or stainless steel. For inland waterways boats where corrosion is not so much of a hazard, steel 'Bundy' tubing may be used. It is important to check the installation drawings so that you use the correct diameter tubing which will vary from one engine to another according to fuel consumption. Bending small diameter tubing can be a problem. It soon distorts and this will restrict capacity. Copper pipe fatigues comparatively easily. It must be fully supported and never take any weight from other fittings. I fixed pipe clips at 6in (152mm) intervals. Where pipes enter a fitting such as a fuel filter or valve, take care that the section of pipe immediately before the entry is perfectly straight, otherwise it will invite air

and fuel leakage. Compression fittings are the easiest for the amateur to use. You must finish the end of the pipe correctly to achieve a leak-free joint. Saw the pipe at an exact right angle and finish with a fine file to get rid of burrs. Never rely on sealing compounds or fibre washers to make up for poor workmanship. Overtightening compression fittings at the first attempt leaves no margin for future tightening. It is better to get the system installed with minimum tightening that will still give a leak-free system and then, when joints have bedded down, go over them as part of the whole engine check before trials. Flared pipe and hard soldered cones or nipples are probably a more professional way of jointing fuel pipework, but it takes longer and is best done by measuring the pipe on site, then removing it to a workshop for the soldering or belling out.

**I**   Flexible fuel lines must be provided to connect the engine to the solid pipe section. In past times when engines were always solidly mounted, the builder often used a simple coil in the pipe between bulkhead and engine to absorb vibration. While this could still be used for non-electric type temperature gauges which rely on a copper tube to connect engine to instrument head, it is not good enough for the fuel system. The flexible section has to be installed within specific design parameters. Sufficient length must be allowed to give a straight entry to the fitting on either end without producing sharp bends. Small radii and 'S' bends should be avoided. Plastic hose must never be used because of the potential fire hazard. Even metal hose can chafe. Give some thought to protecting it from anything it might come in contact with.

**J**   On diesel installations, a fuel-return or bleed-back pipe is necessary to return excess fuel from the injectors and fuel pump back to the tank. When this excess fuel has been through parts of the hot engine, it needs cooling down in the tank before being recirculated. Again, a flexible connection with the correct pipe is fitted between the solid engine pipe and the pipe leading back to the tank.

**K**   A fuel-tank sump is favoured by some

as it is an easy means of getting dirt out of the bottom of the fuel tank. Preferring not to have any hole in the bottom of the tank, I have one with a large access plate at the top for cleaning. The fuel-uptake pipe must not terminate at the bottom of the tank, but should be about ¾in (19mm) from the bottom.

**L** Fuel-tank contents gauge: the electric type derived from the automotive industry only gives a rough indication, somewhere between empty and full, of the fuel in the tank. Accuracy is important for safety. The dipstick is very accurate if it is calibrated properly, and by far the cheapest method. It is not always convenient to get at the tank top. On the figure I have shown a built-in glass-fronted gauge which should be of a type approved by a classification society. You do not want broken glass and fuel in the bilges. I use Unirex pneumatic gauges (Fig 68) which have the advantage of no electrical wiring near the tank, and which can be installed remotely from the tank in the position most convenient to be easily read. The makers calibrated them from the plans I sent of the shaped tanks. All I had to take care of during the installation was to see that the plastic pipe linking the dip tube in the tank to the instrument head was perfectly airtight at the joints and that it was protected from chafe. To avoid crimping it with pipe clips, I ran it inside Egatube.

**M** Pre-filtration of fuel is now recognised as essential. Water from condensation in fuel tanks and in poorly stored and contaminated fuels is the rule rather than the exception. Water in a fuel system will not only stop the engine but will seriously damage the whole of the engine fuel system. Carburettors with fine drilling in their castings soon block up with dirt. Fuel-injection systems — both petrol and diesel — will be wrecked by dirt and corrosion. The filter shown has a two-fold function: to separate water from the fuel and to remove dirt. The main engine filter sees that every last particle of dirt is separated out, but is not generally designed to deal with water. In the past, some dreadful manufacturers provided cheap glass 'jamjar' types of filter. These were not only a

**Fig 68** Unirex fuel tank gauges were simple to install and very accurate when factory calibrated; the drop-out panel provides easy access for future servicing

fire hazard but were useless since sediment falling to the bottom of the jar had to be so heavy and large that most of the water and dirt was into the engine before it could settle. Get the best water separator and fuel filtration system you can afford from a reputable manufacturer. Read all the literature on the efficiency of the system. Fit filters that require a regular drain down in positions where you can easily get at them.

## The Engine Exhaust System

The majority of pleasure craft adopt a wet exhaust system utilising raw water taken from outside the boat to cool the exhaust gases. This water, along with the gases, is then ejected overboard. This system is the quietest, although it is more complex and expensive to install compared to a dry system. The dry system has higher fire risk, danger from escaping exhaust gases due to

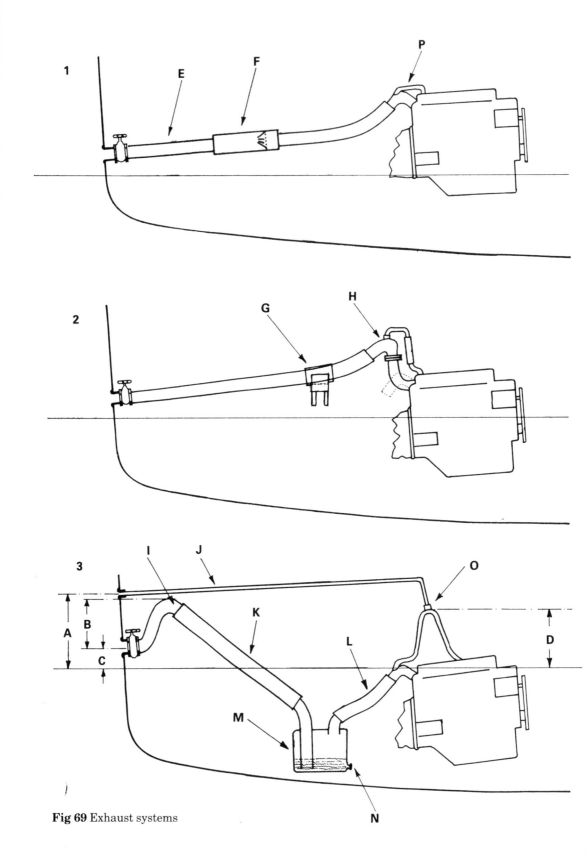

**Fig 69** Exhaust systems

greater heat expansion and cooling contraction, and must not be routed through accommodation space for obvious reasons. If you insist on having it, contact the engine manufacturer. I will confine myself here to wet systems.

Technically, a system must be provided that will allow exhaust gases and injected cooling water to flow freely from the engine exhaust and injection manifold to the outside of the boat with no danger of them getting back down the piping to flood the engine. Twists, turns, bends and any obstruction in the line produces back pressure — a resistance to the free flow of the gases and water. Manufacturers stipulate the maximum tolerated back pressure. If exhaust gases cannot escape, the incoming gases which will produce the next power stroke become polluted. This lowers the efficiency of the burn in the cylinder and you get less power. To produce a good safe design for the system, the relationship of the exhaust outlet to the water-line must be determined.

Fig 69 shows three basic installations where the engine is fixed at different heights in relation to the water-line. If you are not sure about the design, consult the engine-maker. His firm usually carries all parts for an approved exhaust system. The majority of designs do not incorporate a skin-fitting valve such as I have shown in all three drawings. Although this item adds to the cost, it does ensure that when the boat is left it is safe from accidental flooding and, if a fault develops in the system, you can shut off the sea water while repairs are carried out. On sailing craft it is usually essential to provide these valves to prevent flooding when heeled. Many power boats have a flap shutter over the skin fitting, kept closed by gravity, to prevent waves from washing up the exhaust pipe. These lift open with the pressure from the exhaust ejection but are not watertight in an emergency. Looking at the figure:

**1**   When the exhaust injection bend (P) is at least 12in (305mm) above the water-line and a constant fall to the skin fitting is possible, a simple installation can be made. If a skin fitting backed by a full-flow gate valve is not to be included, a swan neck (3I) must be provided to stop water getting back to the engine. Normally, the best type of silencer is one like the McMurdo (F) which has a reed valve to prevent back-flow. When the exhaust pipe has a long run the rubber exhaust hose has sufficient sound-absorbing properties to silence exhaust noise, so saving the cost of the silencer. The positioning of the silencer in the length between the water injection/manifold outlet and the skin fitting is important. Best results will be achieved when the muffler is positioned at two-fifths or four-fifths of the total length. The worst positions are at one-fifth and three-fifths of the total length. Lengths of rubber exhaust hose (E) should have two stainless-steel clips at each joint.

**2**   When the position of the exhaust injection bend comes within 12in (305mm) above the water-line, or closer, two alternatives are possible. First, one could treat the exhaust system as in (3) using a water-lock. Since the main injection is above the water-line an anti-syphon pipe or vacuum relief valve would not be necessary. Alternatively, Fig 70 shows a cast-iron pipe section added to the manifold to gain height before the injection bend is added. The two bends are made as identical castings from one pattern. The circular flange where they join in the middle allows variation of the angle taken at the lead off at the injection bend. This is important when twin-engine installations have exhaust pipes to one side of the boat in order to take them through accommodation space aft. The square flange ends were those from the Perkins 4.108 engines and they bolted directed on to the manifold. The Perkins injection casting in turn bolted directly to the casting I had made. The section below the injection bend was covered with heat-insulating tape as a safety measure. High temperature gaskets were used in the central flange but the standard Perkins gasket sufficed for the two ends. A word of warning: when heavy castings are to be bolted to the engine manifold, too much weight could produce a leverage and stress that could break the

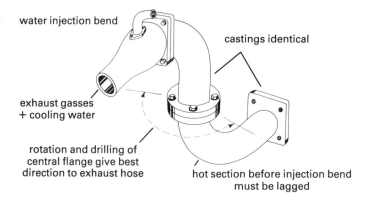

water injection bend

castings identical

exhaust gasses
+ cooling water

rotation and drilling of
central flange give best
direction to exhaust hose

hot section before injection bend
must be lagged

**Fig 70** Method of gaining height and pipe direction

manifold. I made a plywood bracket (Fig 69.2G) to take the weight of the rubber exhaust pipe near the injection bend and to relieve the weight on the castings and manifold. The hose had to move with the flexibly mounted engine but there was danger of chafe at the supporting bracket. To avoid this I wrapped the rubber hose with 18swg light alloy sheet in the area of the bracket, securing it with two stainless-steel hose clamps. This, in turn, was wrapped in rubber strip and placed in the stirrup of the bracket. Wherever rubber exhaust hose passes over or through bulkheads, chafe protection should be given.
3  When the engine injection bend is below the water-line, a water-lock system solves the problem. It is essential, I believe, to consult the engine manufacturer and the supplier of the system components first, as a number of design factors are important. First, there is the height of the lift from the water-lock (M) to the swan neck. The volume of the water-lock (M) is important as it must be capable of holding the total volume of the pipes (L) and (K). It should also have a drain (N) to empty the system for the winter. Dimensions that also need attention, are:

(A)  Bleed pipe should be ⅕– ¼in (5–6mm) bore and not less than 14in (355mm) above the water-line. The other end of the bleed pipe above the engine must be slightly higher to produce a constant fall to the skin fitting.

(B)  Height of the swan neck must be sufficient to allow water to drain down to the skin fitting and to stop small waves getting back into the water-lock when the boat is stationary and the engine not running.
(C)  A distance of 3in (76mm) from water-line to the centre-line of the exhaust skin fitting for outlets up to 2in (51mm) diameter. All skin fittings should have at least 2in (51mm) between water-line and the bottom edge of the outlet.
(D) An inverted 'U' pipe must be provided between the raw water pump and the injection bend which has its apex at least 12in (30cm) above the water-line. The bleed pipe (J) already referred to above may be replaced with an anti-syphon vacuum relief valve (O) on top of the apex at the same height.

Exhaust system materials often pose a problem. High temperature, dissolved acidic gases and impingement attack as water hits metal surfaces, all provide hostile corrosive conditions. Stainless steel and iron are the most usual materials for fabricating, although iron does not stand up too well in the wet sections of the exhaust. It suffers from impingement attack when the angle of the injected water hits the outer surface of the casting. However, it is easily bent, welded, flanged and the least expensive material. The cool sections of the exhaust for diesel engines allows diesel exhaust hose to last for years, but beware if you are unfortunate enough to forget the injection water! Plastic is now offered as an alternative to metals for such items as goose necks and water-locks. They are easy to install and stay free from corrosion. However, I do not know how they would behave if the water was forgotten or the life-span of plastic mouldings. Again, for special items in awkward installations, I would advise you to contact a local firm of engineers.

### Engine Instrumentation

An engine will run without any instruments, but if something does go wrong, you are prevented from doing anything about it before the engine wrecks itself.

Instruments are there to tell you how the engine is working and to give warning that something is failing. You must decide how complex this warning system is to be by making out a list of priorities. Many engine-makers already offer a basic engine instrument kit which is easy to connect to engine and instrument panel by means of a wiring loom. Following the maker's diagram, connect the correct colour-coded wire terminals to the matching senders on the engine or the instrument panel. The loom is usually connected with a multi-point connector near the engine so that once wiring is in place the engine section can easily be disconnected for removal. While it is speedy and convenient to use the made-up instrument panel, for the more ambitious installation it is probably better to get uniformity of design into the instrument layout by buying individual instruments and designing the panel around them.

Both engine- and instrument-makers will advise on what can and cannot be fitted on to a particular power unit. No instruments, switches or wiring are waterproof and it is essential that they are given weather protection. Do not try to save a few pounds by using automotive units which are not marinised and will probably fail in a short time. I have listed some of the principal makers in Appendix C.

### Starter Switch

A key switch or starter button are the alternatives. The key switch offers greater security since it cannot be accidentally pushed. On diesel engines the key starter often has multi-function

use–to activate the electrical circuit and cold starting aid; perhaps parallel the batteries through a solenoid switch, as well as providing starter and running positions. It may not have an automatic shut down, but another solenoid may operate the diesel injection pump shut-off. A pull-stop control can shut down the pump to stop the engine. When activating the stop control always ensure that the alternator is shut down in the correct sequence. I use cable-stop controls by Morse because they are simpler and more reliable than a solenoid.

### Generator Warning Light

The generator warning light is essential to all engines. It warns that the electrical system is switched on to the engine starting circuit and, as the generator starts charging, the light is extinguished to show everything is working correctly. It is more than a generator warning light as it can indicate a broken drive belt to the generator and, if that is broken, on most engines with indirect cooling you will lose the fresh-water pump which shares the belt. Overheating will result. The warning light must be be treated seriously.

### Lubricating Oil Gauge or Warning Light

Both are there to indicate if you have neglected to replace oil to the proper level in the engine sump, or if you have lost oil through some other fault. The oil-pressure gauge can give better warning that things are beginning to go wrong by indicating falling pressure over a period of time. This is not true in the case of sudden loss of oil, but I would always recommend an oil-pressure gauge, provided you make regular checks on all the engine instruments throughout a voyage. No doubt we will soon have talking instruments like the ones in computerised cars. The trouble with these gadgets is that you need a warning light to indicate that the voice has failed to tell you the warning light has failed! Simplicity is best — who wants to go to sea to be nagged by an anonymous voice!

### Engine Coolant Temperature Gauge or Warning Light

An essential constituent of the water-cooled engine, whether directly or indirectly cooled. Overheating damages the engine and could be a source of fire. This gauge tells you if you have forgotten to turn on the sea-cocks — usually too late because by the time overheating is shown you will have chewed the raw-water impeller to pieces. Nevertheless, you will be in time to save the engine. It can indicate an air-lock when the engines are put into service at the beginning of the season when, although you know the cooling system is fully operational, excessive temperature rise is shown. It can also indicate a failing thermostat. When the engine is running cold it may be jammed open and when jammed closed, too hot. Thermostats usually fail in the open position. Again, the warning light is a help. Engines without a proper threaded hole to take a sender unit can have a temperature gauge mounted in an appropriate water-hose by using one of the available adapters. Temperature gauges can be purchased calibrated for both raw, sea and fresh water.

### Engine-speed Tachometer

I regard this as an essential instrument for two reasons. First, it allows accurate operation of the engine at its most economical speed. Second, if properly calibrated on a measured mile, it can be an excellent navigation aid for deducing speed and distance run. The accuracy can be judged from the excellent results achieved by winners of Predicted Log events. In twin-engine installations the tachometer allows reasonable synchronisation but a well-turned ear is the best aid to final adjustment of throttles unless an engine synchroniser or differential tachometer is not to be added.

Petrol-engine tachometers may run either from the ignition system or from alternator impulses. Manufacturers or agents should be consulted as to the best one for a particular engine, especially these days when electronic ignition systems are becoming so common. Instruments must be matched to ignition characteristics.

While I regard these instruments as having a high priority, the following certainly give extra peace of mind.

### Ammeters

These indicate the charge available being generated for battery charging. They are an extra indication if the generator drive-belt is in one piece or if something has gone wrong in the charging circuit. Along with volt-meters, they must not be mounted near the compass as they will contribute to deviation via the electrical field they generate. A safe distance is 6ft (1.8m), but in a small boat this usually means having them mounted well away from the main engine instrument and steering console.

### Volt-meters

These show the voltage available from the starter and service batteries. They show when charging is needed to sustain the voltage aboard at a level that will not damage equipment. They must always be fitted with a switch so that when the boat is left, they will not drain down the battery. Battery master switches solve this problem.

### Engine-hour Meters

Although low on the priority list, an engine-hour meter is a useful aid. The counting of engine running hours is a hit-and-miss affair. Without this instrument, running hours can only be guessed at — and the consequent wear and tear on the engines over the seasons. Anyone buying a second-hand boat will have no idea at all. On work boats these instruments give excellent indication when a major service is due. With pleasure craft, big 'top overhauls' and major 'bottom end' refits might be needed at much more frequent intervals due to corrosion rather than wear. Ten thousand running hours before a major overhaul is more than the average pleasure boat engine ever gets before rust eats it up. If a marine engine runs for five hundred hours a year — and this is a generous figure for most craft — a major overhaul would be twenty years away.

### Engine Synchroniser

For anyone hard of hearing or unable to tell from the rhythm of the exhaust that the engines are synchronised, the differential tachometer is a worth-while instrument. It is more important for high-speed craft than for slower boats. Small differences in engine speed can make big differences to the handling of a fast boat. True, you can trim with auxiliary trim tabs but these are best used for fine trim, rather than adding a lot of drag to badly synchronised motors.

## Warning Devices

If you wanted, you could have the cockpit looking like Concorde with instruments that monitor just about everything aboard. In diesel installations with rubber exhaust hose, warning of the failure of the water injection for cooling the hose could save a lot of trouble. In petrol-engine installations where it is vital, for fire-hazard reasons, to keep engine exhaust temperatures within strict limits, this type of device might be even more important. Many warning devices can also be connected into the automatic shut-down, but I do not think these are particularly good to have on a boat. It would be intolerable to have an engine suddenly shut down just near a weir or when docking in a tricky current. In these situations, warning lights offer the best compromise, while for those of a less nervous disposition, a warning alarm can also be incorporated.

When your instrument list is complete, work out the layout plan for the console. Throttle and stop control should be sited immediately to hand with no chance of fumbling or accidentally shifting them. Important instruments need to be in front of the helmsman at an angle that does not stop them being read because of reflected light. Some instruments must be sited away from the compass. Other instruments that are not so important can be tucked away where they can be glanced at occasionally.

Since it is usual for boat-engine instrumentation to follow in the wake of that developed for the automotive industry, computer-controlled instrumentation with digital and cathode-ray display will be coming on to the market. Provided that these new developments are marinised for the hostile marine environment, they could eventually monitor engine functions efficiently.

## Noise Attenuation

GRP hulls tend to accentuate noise transmitted from shafting, bearings and the engine. Large free panel areas resonate or reflect sound; holes in bulkheads leak sound to accommodation spaces. Inadequate engine beds create much of this vibration. Noise can be tackled in four ways:

1 *Isolation* Separate the noise source from the surrounding structure of the boat. Rubber flexible mountings under the engine isolate it from the hull. Rubber mounting for pumps and other small mechanical items serves the same purpose. Every connection made to the engine — fuel and cooling water pipes, cables (stop, control and electrical) — must accommodate movement without becoming fatigued.

2 *Insulation* materials absorb the acoustic energy before it reaches surfaces that will propagate it. The greater the thickness of insulating material the better, but 1in (25mm) should be regarded as a minimum. All holes in bulkheads and ways up to cable-control points should be blocked off as sound will escape through any small aperture.

3 *Absorption* of sound is also achieved by these materials. Instead of noise being reflected and increased as it bounces off surfaces, it is absorbed by the insulating material.

4 *Damping* alters the vibration period of free panel areas that would normally pick up vibration and resonate with sympathetic frequencies to that of the engine noise. Free panel areas are detuned by the application of bituminous membranes which, though thin, damp out the sound that would otherwise be produced.

## Materials for Noise Attenuation

When *Sea Hound* was originally built, noise pollution was only just being recognised as a problem in small craft. We did, however, give serious consideration to it; the hatches were made noise-tight by the use of neoprene strips on the edges, whilst the undersides were fitted with sound deadening materials.

Where sound deadening materials were beginning to appear on boats they were often not only a serious fire hazard but gave off lethal fumes if they caught fire. Foam sheet materials were based on cyanurates and these gave off deadly carbon monoxide and hydrogen cyanide.

Since the mid 1980s both Lloyds and the DTI have become much more specific about acoustic materials that are safe to use in engine spaces, although many of the regulations and standards are applicable only to commercial and sail training vessels. There is, then, still a danger that the wrong type of acoustic cladding will be used in small craft engine spaces. Polyurethane foamed in situ gives off lethal products of combustion and should never be used. There are some foams still available made only to British Standard 4735; a specification which limits fire spread on the surface of the material. The danger of using this specification is that fire will still spread and it will go on burning until the source of ignition is removed. BS 476 is the specification to look for.

The following points should be considered in any material you are contemplating using for acoustic cladding in an engine space:

**1** It should not be of open cell structure that will allow wicking of fuel or oil to take place. If the surface wicks then it will provide a wall of flame if a fire starts. Closed cell foams are preferable but a fire resistant open cell with factory sealed surface and edges is acceptable.

**2** Noise attenuating materials need to be of considerable thickness to absorb sound energy. Variation in density of a multi-layer material will absorb more frequencies than a single density material. There should be either a lead or plastic barrier material interleaved between the sound absorbing layer and the layer that will isolate the acoustic barrier from the structure. Foam materials without a lead or plastic barrier are less expensive but they usually need at least two inches of thickness before they begin to be efficient.

**3** The adhesives, tapes and fixing materials should be non-flammable and suited to the marine environment. They must not affect the structural properties of GRP or any material with which they come into contact during the construction nor should they lose adhesive properties in a damp atmosphere.

**4** Non-flammable mineral, wool and glassfibre barriers have excellent fire resistance, but they are expensive and tend to be biased towards fire resistance rather than noise attenuation. In any installation it is nonsense to install a noise absorbing barrier and then, in order to prevent the wicking or spread of fuel that would produce a fire wall, cover it with a metal (steel or light alloy) sheet. The metal sheet in fact reflects noise, and vastly reduces the ability of the material underneath it to do its job. It may make an engine room look smart and may help as a fire barrier, but in small craft will reduce the efficiency of the material as a noise barrier.

**5** If you are technically minded, examine the manufacturers' graphs showing the coefficient of acoustic absorption which should show a consistently high level over the range 200 to 4000 hz.

At the outset, Perkins were most helpful in sending their acoustic engineers to take the measurements shown in Table 5 and Halyard Marine added to our knowledge when the engine room cladding was updated in 1992.

Several pointers can be deduced from the Table which might help other builders. On the Perkins' trials under column A we found the frequency analysis of noise in the wheelhouse showed a high level at the engine firing frequency, which on marine installations, is characteristic of air intake noise. This was dealt with by modifying the air intakes and replacing the standard marine version with AC Delco automotiveair filters. This problem is now commonly dealt with on modern engines right from the start. Note that the 3dbA reduction actually represents about a 50% reduction as we are dealing with a logarithmic scale; an apparently small reduction is actually a large one.

Gear box rattle on the TMP1200 boxes accounted for a disturbing amount of noise before they took up the slack and became fully engaged. It is worth checking before you buy any gearbox to see how quietly it functions. However, the original 4db reduction overall to 75dbA made the boat comfortable for the crew at the cruising speed of 2000 rpm.

Neither the forward nor the aft engine room bulkheads were lined as they were used to house the fuel system and electrical system runs. Undoubtedly, if a complete acoustic box could be built round the engine, results would be wonderful but you would then have the problem of ventilation and servicing access. Neoprene flat section sealing tapes were used to seal engine hatches. Noise escapes from the smallest hole, so pay attention to holes in bulkheads.

Air intakes and outlets must have either baffle boxes to absorb noise or, as I fitted, sound absorbing ducting. Flexible Ducting of Glasgow advised the use of their Thermaflex-KA, a lightweight ducting which is constructed with an inner mesh of fire-retarded vinyl vapour barrier reinforced with fibreglass, a fibre-glass sound and insulating layer over the reinforcing wire helix, and yet another outer cover vapour barrier of fibre-glass reinforced vinyl covered fabric to give a flameproof finish. Despite the awesome specification, it was light and does an excellent job. As this company supply ducting to the aircraft industry, the specifications of their products are excellent. From Table 5 you can compare the old material with the new.

*Table 5:* ENGINE NOISE LEVELS *(Sea Hound of Dart)*

Column   A Levels, cabin doors closed, no modification other than flexible engine
mountings and single flexible shaft coupling.

B As A but cabin doors open.

C AC Delco air cleaners fitted to the engines.

D Additional flexible shaft coupling fitted. Harrison and Jones Ranwal acoustic materials fitted under wheelhouse floors. All hatches sealed with $1^1/_4$ x $^1/_4$inch (32mm x 6mm) neoprene strip.

E Cabin doors open, aged deteriorated cladding, seals still intact, readings by Halyard Marine.

F After new acoustic materials and seals installed by Halyard Marine 1992.

| Engine Speed r/min | Wheelhouse | | | | | | Aft Cabin | | | | | | Forward Cabin | | | | | |
|---|---|---|---|---|---|---|---|---|---|---|---|---|---|---|---|---|---|---|
| Out of Gear | A | B | C | D | E | F | A | B | C | D | E | F | A | B | C | D | E | F |
| 500 | 66.5 | 66.5 | 67 | 66 | 70* | 68* | 69 | 65 | 64 | 66 | 70* | 68* | 66 | 62 | 63 | 63 | 77* | 73* |
| 1000 | 71 | 70.5 | 69 | 69 | 76** | 74** | 72 | 69 | 68 | 67 | 75** | 75** | 65 | 65.5 | 65.5 | 66 | 73** | 70** |
| 2000 | 84.5 | 81 | 78 | 74 | 77 | 76 | 78.5 | 78 | 76.5 | 70 | 79 | 78 | 73.5 | 75 | 74 | 72 | 75 | 73 |
| 2600 | 93 | 90 | 85.5 | 80 | 86 | 84 | 87.5 | 85.5 | 82.5 | 79 | 85 | 81 | 81 | 85.5 | 82.5 | 77 | 82 | 79 |
| *In Gear Underway* | | | | | | | | | | | | | | | | | | |
| 1000 | - | 74 | 72 | 73 | 76** | 75 | - | 77.5 | 79 | 83 | 85** | 86 | - | 70 | 69 | 71 | 76** | 74 |
| 2000 | - | 82 | 80 | 75 | 78 | 77 | - | 82 | 79.5 | 77 | 88 | 85 | - | 76.5 | 75.5 | 73 | 76 | 75 |

(normal cruising speed)

  * = Reading taken at 700 r/min by Halyard
** = Reading taken at 1500 r/min by Halyard

# 6   THE ELECTRICAL SYSTEM

The design of the marine electrical system is the province of the expert. A boat is a hostile environment for electricity and serious problems will be created by poor design. Some yachtsmen are happy to live with a paraffin lamp for light which is inexpensive and does work. However, most of us are now acclimatised to modern comforts.

**The Design of the Electrical System**
Fig 71 shows a method of designing an electrical installation. Understanding it will allow you to sensibly brief the electrician to your exact requirements if you do not feel secure in doing the work yourself. The great weakness of marine electrical systems is the lack of vision as to future needs and development. Electrical and electronic goodies stretch old wiring, batteries and generating systems to the point of failure as they are bolted on year after year. You must have enough excess capacity in the design to accommodate future needs. This is much less expensive to do now than to bodge things in later years.

**Determining Total Electrical Loading**
At this stage, you need technical literature (see Telesonic Marine Ltd (Appendix C)) and select equipment you think you will build into the boat. Many chandlers' catalogues do not give sufficient important information, especially about consumption. Table 6 shows how this is used to determine electrical load. With this wattage figure, you estimate the number of hours' use each day, multiply the two figures together and you get the maximum daily load in watt/hours. The total load is then divided by the system's voltage (in *Sea Hound*'s case 12v) and you arrive at a rough indication of the service battery or ship load on the battery in amp/hours. I

ended with a pretty hefty 2,117 amp/hours figure which, when divided by 12, gave 176 amp/hours for the service battery. As I did not want to run the main engine every day when in port, this figure was reduced to the nearest Lucas battery size and then doubled. As things have worked out, we find we can get three full days in port without having to charge batteries. In extremely hot weather when the refrigerator is going full tilt and the ventilation fans are working, we find we are down to what the system was designed for, two days' capacity.

Not all small craft need a double-battery system such as I have. The single-battery system is less costly and quite sufficient for small sailing boats with a simple marine engine, especially if that engine has alternative hand-starting. Hand-starting might be considered old-fashioned but it does mean that if the battery is run down you can still start the engine and get a new charge into the battery immediately. This kind of ship's load will only consist of, say, navigation lights and one or two cabin lights, with no pretence of a full electrical system or future plans to have one. It is bad practice to have a marine engine that relies on electrical starting and then proceed to load the system with gadgets until it fails.

**Planning and Siting Electrical Equipment**
In Fig 72 I show the siting of the equipment that is listed in Table 6. If you draw up a plan of your own boat and select the position for each unit listed on the load calculation, you will be able to give some thought to the run of the cables. You should keep cable runs to a minimum length to minimise voltage drop, and cables must not run where they will get damaged or look ugly.

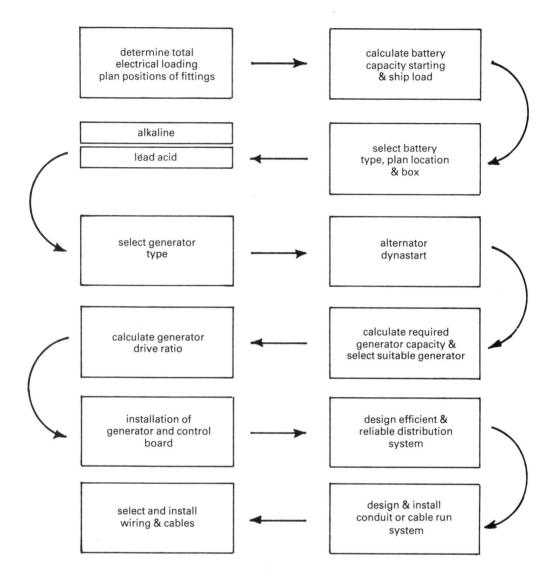

| determine total electrical loading plan positions of fittings | → | calculate battery capacity starting & ship load |

| alkaline | | |
| lead acid | ← | select battery type, plan location & box |

| select generator type | → | alternator dynastart |

| calculate generator drive ratio | ← | calculate required generator capacity & select suitable generator |

| installation of generator and control board | → | design efficient & reliable distribution system |

| select and install wiring & cables | ← | design & install conduit or cable run system |

Voltage drop is caused by excessive line losses in the cable itself. The cross-section of the conductor and its length affect the loss. Voltage drop affects the efficiency of electronic equipment, pumps and motors. At worst, it will reduce the starting capability of the starter motor and produce heat in any conductor. If incorrect section starter cables are fitted they might make it impossible for the engine to be turned over when the battery is only just below its nominal voltage. If voltage drop has to be tolerated at all, under no circumstances must it exceed 4 per cent of the battery voltage. Thus, in a 12v system, the drop

**Fig 71** Method of designing the electrical system

*Table 6:*   ELECTRICAL LOAD CALCULATIONS

| MCB | Electrical Item | Load (W) | Time (hr) | Daily Watt/ Hr Load |
|---|---|---|---|---|
| | *Forward Accommodation* | | | |
| 3 | Engel refrigerator | 50 | 12 | 600 |
| 2 | Inverter | 40 | 2 | 80 |
| 4 | AK fans | 108 | 1 | 108 |
| 1 | Lavac toilet | 36 | 1 | 36 |
| 3 | Remotron cabin heater | 25 | 2 | 50 |
| 1 | Stuart Turner water-pump | 210 | 1 | 210 |
| 2 | Cabin lights: | | | |
| | 1 halogen 20w ⎫ | | | |
| | 1 (1,2,3) 30w ⎬ | 90 | 3 | 270 |
| | 2 lights 20w ⎭ | | | |
| 2 | Sharp auto-pilot | 50 | 6 | 300 |
| 1 | Demek RS 8000 VHF | 50 | 1 | 50 |
| | CB1 = 300w − 30 amp | | | 1,704 |
| | CB2 = 180w − 15 amp | | | |
| | CB3 =  75w − 10 amp | | | |
| | CB4 = 108w − 10 amp | | | |
| | *Wheel-house* | | | |
| 5 | Wynn wipers | 100 | 1½ | 150 |
| 7 | Compass light | 6 | 2 | 12 |
| 6 | Engine-room input fan | 90 ⎫ | | ⎧ Engines |
| 6 | Engine-room extraction fan | 42 ⎬ | 182 | ⎨ running — no |
| 6 | Gas extraction fan | 50 ⎭ | | ⎩ drain |
| 5 | Rule automatic bilge pump | 60 | 1 | 60 |
| 8 | Stuart Turner bilge pump | 70 | 30 min | 35 |
| 7 | Engine-room lights | 20 | | − |
| 7 | Spotlight | 20 | | − |
| 7 | Horn | 30 | | − |
| 7 | B & G log and repeater | − | | − |
| 7 | B & G depth and repeater | − | | − |
| 8 | Navigation lights | 110 | | Engine running |
| 6 | Anchor light | 10 | 8 | 80 |
| | CB5 = 160w − 15 amp | | | 337 |
| | CB6 = 180w − 20 amp | | | |
| | CB7 =  70w −  7.5 amp | | | |
| | CB8 = 110w − 10 amp | | | |
| | *Aft Cabin* | | | |
| 9 | Bunk lights × 2 | 20 | 2 | 40 |
| | Exhaust fan | 36 | 1 | 36 |
| | Navigation light aft | 25 | − | Engine running |
| | CB9 = 76w 7.5 amp | | | 76 |

Total at 12v $\dfrac{2117}{12}$ w/hr

=   176 amp/hr

Approx 175 amp/hr

12v ship service batteries 2 ×175 amp/hr in parallel = 350 amp/hr

12v engine starter battery 1 × 140 amp/hr                     140

                Total battery capacity                 490 amp/hr

*Original equipment in Perkins 4.108*
>Lucas 11AC 12v × 45 amp × 2 (engines) = 90 amps 14v charge

*Later*
>As 11AC alternators are not suppressed
>Lucas 17ACR (M) 12v × 36 amp = 72 amps 14v

*Lupus Miniature Circuit Breakers (MCBs)*
>In a 12-way enclosure (4- to 16-way available)
>1 × 30 amp
>1 × 20 amp
>2 × 15 amp
>3 × 10 amp
>2 × 7.5 amp
>2 × 10 amp spares
>1 × master (radar?)

*Table 7:*   VOLTAGE DROP FACTOR AND CABLE SIZE

Table for PVC Cable

| Voltage Drop Factor | Cable Size (mm²)* |
|---|---|
| 0.082 | 0.5 |
| 0.040 | 1.0 |
| 0.027 | 1.5 |
| 0.016 | 2.5 |
| 0.010 | 4.0 |
| 0.0068 | 6.0 |
| 0.0040 | 10.0 |
| 0.0026 | 16.0 |
| 0.0016 | 25.0 |
| 0.0012 | 35.0 |
| 0.00091 | 50 |

\* See Table 9 for other equivalent sizes.

*Example*
What wires should be used for an exhaust fan 36w, 12v system in aft cabin 9m from distribution board?

1  Amps = $\dfrac{36}{12}$ = 3 amps
2  Distance = 9m × 2 = 18m
3  Volt drop factor = $\dfrac{0.6}{18 \times 3}$ = 0.011
4  From Table 7 cross-section cable should be 4mm²
5  From Table 9 specification of cable should be 56/0.30

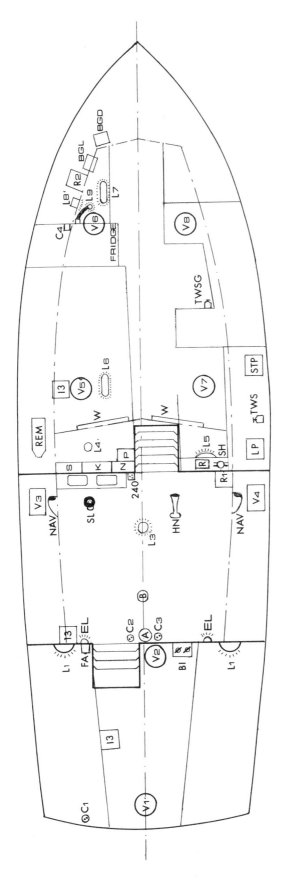

**Fig 72** Planning positions for electrical fittings

**Fig 72** Planning positions for electrical fittings

*After Cabin*
**13** 13amp 240v switched MK socket
**FA** Pyrene fire warning indicator box with test switch
**BI** Battery isolating switches and Allbright Relay Type SW.62A-54
**LI** Hella berth light with two switches for 1, 2 or 3 bulbs
**C1** Clang weatherproof deck socket for aft navigation light
**V1** Ventilation fan A.K.VI-Y3802
**V2** Engine space extraction fan A.K. VI-X3716

*Engine Space*
**A** Rule Master automatic bilge pump 1300gph
**B** Stuart Turner bilge pump 220gph manual switching
**13** 13amp 240v MK socket to plug in battery charger or light
**C2** Clang 2 pin socket for mast-head navigation lights
**V3** Ventilation fan A. K. Type MI-X3804 input to engine space
**V4** Gas extraction fan A.K. Type CF-X4360, engine plus forward bilges
**EL** Hella cabin light with switch

*Wheel-house*
**C3** Spare weatherproof Clang socket for 12v power and riding light
**L3** Hella cabin light switched by rotating lens
**240** Clang 3 pin 240v socket inlet for shore supply connection
**NAV** Channel Marine Aqua Signal port and starboard navigation lights
**SL** Hellamarine searchlight, 410yd range
**HN** Klaxon Seatone Double horn
**R1** Demek RS8000 VHF Marine Radio — cruising position plus power socket
**L4** Compass light socket

**W** Wynn Type B straight line wipers

*Forward Cabin*
**S** Wylex 240v fused distribution box
**K** Lupus MCB Ltd circuit breaker distribution box
**N** Forward cabin light and fan switches
**P** Sharp Autopilot MJ amplifier MD1 motor on other side of bulkhead
**TWSG** Aqua-marine tap water switch for hot, cold and filtered water
**L6** Hella halogen cabin light
**V5** A.K. Type H4-X5184 air supply fan
**13** Twin MK socket switched for 240v supply
**C4** Clang sockets, one for fridge and other for spare 12v supply
**V6** A.K. Type H4-X5184 supply fan to forward area
**V8** A.K. Extraction fan type H4-X5192 with finger guard
**L8** Hella shielded map-reading light
**L9** Hella flexible chart lamp
**R2** Demek RS8000 VHF radio safety position with emergency aerial
**BGL** Brooks & Gatehouse log
**BGD** Brooks & Gatehouse depth-sounder
**Fridge** Engel 1.6cu ft refrigerator 12v
**REM** Remotron cabin heater 12v plus LPG gas
**L7** Hella halogen cabin light

*Toilet Compartment*
**R** A.K. Inverter Type FC12/230/30B 12v DC to 230v single phase 50Hz to drive Boxer fan or electric shaver
**SH** Shaver socket 230v
**V7** Super Boxer fan A.K. Type WS2107F110
**LP** Blakes Lavac electric toilet pump
**STP** Stuart Turner No 12 freshwater pump
**TWS** Tap water switch to STP for hot and cold water
**L5** Hella bulkhead light with 2 switches for 1, 2 or 3 lights

should not let the circuit fall below 11½v or, in a 24v system, 23v. Basically, the longer the cable run, the bigger the cross-section of the conductor to minimise voltage drop. Cross-section of the cables is also related to the current it will safely carry. Try to put too much electricity along a small conductor and it will get hot enough to cause fire. Have a look at an electric fire to understand the principle. In designing the charging, generating and starting circuits it is imperative that hefty cables are used to handle the high power and that the designer takes into account every possible risk. I must admit that I nearly had a fire on board once when the starting battery failed to charge because of a broken wire in the loom. It was not the wire that caused the problem, but the fact that it allowed the starting battery to discharge. When the engine was started to try and trace the fault, a cable we had installed (normally only carrying a small current) had to cope with the starting current as the service batteries tried to boost the flat starter batteries. Always be aware of the smell of burning PVC and make sure that even the most unexpected situations cannot foul up the original design.

To select the right cables you need to know about Ohm's Law:

$E = I \times R.$

$E$ = voltage drop,

$I$ = the current in amps

$R$ = total resistance of the cable.

$$\text{Amps} = \frac{\text{watts}}{\text{volts}}$$

Going back to the electrical load calculations, it is advisable to make out another list, as in Table 8, to list and calculate the three columns, and, from plans, estimate column 4. It is in column 4 that the most mistakes are made and cable lengths badly underestimated. In fact, Lloyd's allow a rather high voltage drop of 0.72v, but this is for the professional installation where every factor is precisely calculated. Lucas are far more conservative, knowing that amateurs often make mistakes and suggest only 0.5v voltage drop, while 0.6v can be regarded as a safe working norm for the careful amateur.

Column 5 is computed from:

$$\text{Permissible voltage drop factor} = \frac{0.6v}{\text{Distance (metres)} \times \text{amps}}$$

Remember that you are using a negative return wiring system, so distance measured from the plan between the distribution board and the electrical item must be doubled.

The final column of Table 7 is taken by looking at the permissible drop factor and finding the value that is the *next lower* drop factor in the table.

Remember, this is an amateur installation and to come up to Lloyd's 100 A1 is a great deal more complex. However, provided you have done the sums correctly, using the above method, you should have a safe and reliable installation. It is quite safe to have cables slightly oversize when you have done the calculations. For example, in Table 8 the Remotron heater being very near the distribution board only had 0.5mm² cable and, as it was just about the only item requiring this size, I put in the next size bigger (1mm²) as I had this in stock for other wiring. In fact, when the cable calculation table is complete, you will be able to rationalise it so that you do not need to stock too wide a variety of cables.

## Electrical Distribution

Accepting that electrical failure is a serious, if not disastrous, situation, you should give very careful thought to safety at the design stage.

Two precautions are needed: mechanical protection to ensure that wiring is not cut, chafed or fatigue damaged, and environmental protection. This ensures that wires are protected from water, fuel/oil or other liquids and the damp atmospheres that will cause corrosive deterioration and breakdown.

Looking over the average yacht — including those professionally built — you will see some horrors.

**A**  Cables not properly supported and clipped so that vibration sets up fatigue, so

*Table 8:*   CABLE CALCULATIONS

| 1 | 2 | 3 | 4 | 5 | 6 |
|---|---|---|---|---|---|
| *Electrical Item* | *Load (Watts)* | *Amps Watts Volts* | *Total Lengths of Cable (Out and Return)* | *Permissible Drop Factor* | *Cable Size (mm²)\** |
| *Forward Accommodation* | | | | | |
| Engel refrigerator | 50 | 4.16 | 9m | 0.016 | 2.5 |
| AK fan (single) | 36 | 3 | 6m | 0.033 | 1.5 |
| Remotron cabin heater | 25 | 2.08 | 4m | 0.072 | 0.5 |
| Inverter | 40 | 3.33 | 6m | 0.030 | 1.5 |
| Lavac toilet | 36 | 3 | 8m | 0.25 | 1.5 |

*See Table 9 for other equivalent sizes.

breaking conductors.

**B**   Wiring hanging over the alternator drive belt on the engine. This could sag and be cut to pieces.

**C**   Wiring trapped between panels in cabin tops. This may suffer from chafe, even if that particular panel only moves fractionally from time to time.

**D**   Wiring run in exposed positions inside steering boxes, into exposed instrument panels, out to poor quality deck fittings that were not designed to be waterproof.

I wanted none of this and so determined to experiment with a plastic conduit system made by Egatube Ltd of St Asaph, North Wales, who will handle both home and export enquiries.

Basically, the Egatube system consists of lengths of PVC tubing of various cross-sections — round, square, oblong and oval — which can be joined into junction-box outlets and provide a highly protective covering for the distribution cables run through them. Big ships, of course, have steel conduit, but a small craft needs the same protection that is lighter and a great deal easier to install.

For the general wiring I used light gauge conduit in ⅝in and ¾in sizes. The nearest metric now available is 16mm round and 20mm oval. For most work the standard 90° bends sufficed but for special angles the round tube could be easily bent with the bending springs available. The oval system has side and forward type 90° bends and although it is extremely flexible in the flat plane, I think that generally I prefer the round section except where space is at a premium. In fact, when the installation was complete, I realised all the conduit should have been in the 20mm size so that some of the runs would have been less full of cable.

Except when building to Lloyd's rules, electricians seldom seem to take note of the fact that even a cable that is working within its capacity produces some heat. So, when Lloyd's state that a two-core cable should only carry something like 80 per cent of the amperage that is carried by a single-core cable, they are making allowance for the proximity of the two cores compared to the air space that is created when two single-core wires are run. From this it is obvious that should there be a lot of cables in the confined space of a conduit, less ventilation will be available and some care should be taken to ensure that overheating does not occur.

My answer was not to increase conductor sizes to cope with a temperature rise in the conduit but to allow each section of the system its own conduit, so reducing the number of wires carried and leaving breathing space. I had another good reason for

Table 9:   CABLE SIZES AND RATING FOR BOATS

| Nominal Cross-section of Stranded Conductor (mm²) | Cable Size (Metric) (Approx) | Number and Diameter of Strands Comprising Conductor (Imperial) | Cable Size B & S SAE American (Approx) | Nominal Resistance* per Ampere per Metre | Outside Diameter (Approx) | Typical Uses (but check for Specific Application Voltage drop) | Amp Capacity |
|---|---|---|---|---|---|---|---|
| 1.0 | 32/0.20 | 14/012 | 18 | 40mv | 3mm | Interior and navigation lights. Light-duty searchlights, mast lights, longer runs, electric horn | 8 |
| 1.5 | 21/0.30 | | | 27mv | 3mm | | 12 |
| 2.0 | 28/0.30 | 28/012 | 14 | 21mv | 3.5mm | | 16 |
| 2.5 | 35/0.30 | 35/012 | | 16mv | 4mm | | 19 |
| 3.0 | 44/0.30 | 44/012 | 12 | 13mv | 4mm | | 27 |
| 4.0 | 56/0.30 | | | 10mv | 5mm | | 31 |
| 4.5 | 65/0.30 | 65/012 | 10 | 8.6mv | 5mm | Dynamo, ammeter | 35 |
| 6.0 | 84/0.30 | | | 6.8mv | 6mm | | 42 |
| 7.0 | 97/0.30 | 97/012 | | 6.1mv | 6mm | Alternator | 50 |
| 8.5 | 120/0.30 | 120/012 | | 5.2mv | 7mm | | 60 |
| 10.0 | 80/0.40 | | 8 | 4.0mv | 7.5mm | | 70 |
| 25.0 | 37/0.90 | | | 1.6mv | 10mm | Heavy duties, battery starter cable. Cable to distribution board. Winches | 170 |
| 40.0 | 61/0.90 | 61/036 | | 1.1mv | 12mm | | 300 |
| 50.0 | 396/0.40 | | | 0.91mv | 13mm | | 345 |
| 60.0 | 61/1.13 | 61/044 | | 0.76mv | 14mm | | 415 |
| 70.0 | 999/0.30 | | | 0.63mv | 16mm | | 485 |

*Based on continuous current ratings for groups of circuits (up to six cables bunched) for single-core PVC-insulated cable run open or enclosed in conduit.

running sets of parallel conduit. If a circuit should fail or be damaged mechanically or by fire, other circuits would have a better chance of survival. Egatube is made of a self-extinguishing PVC.

In my design, the main part of the conduit system was run on the port side fore and aft through forward accommodation, engine space and aft cabin. For services on the starboard side, the conduit was run across the forward accommodation side on the main bulkhead. This left the engine space bulkhead free to carry the fuel-system piping and gave some fire protection to the conduit by separating it from the engine space. True, with this design and the positioning of the fuel tanks, I had to run the conduit over the fuel tanks, but the risk was countered with the fire system, which I will describe in the relevant chapter.

Anyone who has known the childhood delights of Meccano will revel in using Egatube. You need a junior hack-saw to cut the lengths and an ample supply of Egaweld No 1, a vinyl solvent which you paint over the joint before pushing it together. You then have a completely watertight joint which sticks in a few seconds.

Part of the Egatube system is the provision of moulded boxes with lids which are fixed to the box with screws at each corner. The system was designed for land-based installations, but I adapted them for the boat. The boxes have knock-outs so that adapters to join them to the conduit runs could soon be fixed. They were used as junction boxes, for light switches (12v), and for the AK fan control boxes. Even better, Ega now have the MEU range of boxes which have a gasket lid to keep out water and dust more efficiently than the flush-lidded ones I used.

Taking care to select low speeds on the electric drill, hole-saws of appropriate sizes ensured that exit and entry holes were easily cut in boxes needing extra holes.

One other Ega product I used was their industrial cable trunking size 50 × 50mm. This hefty cross-section trunking with its simple clip-on lid was used for taking the engine-manufacturer's wiring looms from the bulkhead ahead of the engines up to the instrument panel, thus affording them equal protection to the ordinary wiring. Swept-angle units ensured that no chafe could occur and 'T' units allowed the trunking to be dropped to the correct height so that the looms could be led in without creating a fatigue point. On the engineering side, I wanted to give some protection from chafe to the various engine-control cables as they dropped down from the steering console to the engines. I used the same size trunking for this. On these cables I used a household glass-fibre roof insulation material to prevent the transmission of noise from the engine space up to the console and wheel-house. Noise escapes through the smallest holes.

Fig 73 shows me working at the main bulkhead distribution centre. Some of the Egatube is in place and you will notice marine-ply boards or struts fixed on to the GRP to fix the clips or saddles. With a great number of conduit tubes, I chose the broad piece of ply shown. When running the conduit fore and aft, I found that blocks of iroko fixed at 10in (250mm) intervals with epoxy resin glue and then glassed in with 4in (100mm) wide glass tape did an excellent job. Intervals could have been longer with one of the heavy-gauge tubes, but I did not want sag in the lighter gauge I was using.

## Starting and Service Batteries

*Design and Installation*
To avoid explosion on boats carrying batteries (which give off hydrogen gas when charging) certain design consideration points must be applied (Appendix D):

1  Batteries are best installed outside the engine compartment in a space free from the possibility of arcing sparks igniting the explosive hydrogen. Sparks and static electricity can be generated in electric motors, switches and relays.
2  Ventilation is of prime importance. The compartment must provide natural ventilation immediately above the battery so that hydrogen gas can escape. Spaces, especially in moulded coamings, that

Fig 73 The main bulkhead is the focal point of many yachts' electrical distribution systems; Lupus miniature circuit breakers, Egatube conduit and proper size cables ensure safety and efficiency in the circuits

could contain the gas above batteries, must be ventilated.

3  Natural ventilation must always be provided at high level in a battery space so that hydrogen, a light gas, can escape. Shell ventilators and any other types that create suction flow rather than ram effect, are ideal.

4  Mechanical ventilation fans must be of a safe type (British Department of Trade and Industry or Lloyd's certified) for ventilating battery space which might become contaminated or charged with explosive gas mixtures (see section on ventilation, p171).

5  Since many small craft have no room outside the engine space for battery installation and since it is a prerogative of good design to keep starter and other battery cables of high capacity to the minimum lengths, it is essential that the foregoing points are rigorously observed when bat-

teries are installed in the engine space. Batteries do not like high ambient temperatures, therefore proper ventilation of the engine space becomes essential if they are to have a reasonable service life.

6  Batteries must be thoroughly secured so that the worst rolling of the boat cannot move them. Their compartment must have protection against spillage of electrolyte.

7  The batteries must be provided with a cover which will allow gas to escape but at the same time prevent cables and tools from dropping on to terminals, so short-circuiting them to cause a fire.

**Battery Box Construction**
Marine plywood painted with an epoxide resin paint system and the appropriate lining material for the type of battery make a competent job. Saturated wood is an excellent conductor of electricity. Leakage of current through wet wood can be a serious source of corrosion. The box corners should be reinforced with steel or light-alloy angle to prevent the weight of a moving battery from bursting the box corners. Boxes are best bolted to a main structural item, such as a bulkhead, and be equally well fastened at the base. Finally, at appropriately strengthened parts, battens, hinged at one end and bolted at the other, prevent upward movement of the battery on rough seas. Fig 74 summarises the important points.

**Battery Type: Lead/Acid or Alkaline**
The life of the alkaline battery is considerably greater than the lead/acid type, familiar in cars and most boats. The former type has a number of advantages in specific applications. It does not suffer if neglected during the lay-up period when left discharged; it does not mind vibration and tilting; it is easily installed and just as easily kept in good condition. However, the majority of boat owners, especially of smaller craft, are quite happy with the more familiar lead/acid type of battery. It is heavy and spillage of acid has to be guarded against; it does not like being left partially discharged for long periods, especially when the boat is laid up; its life is limited, especially if it is not looked after

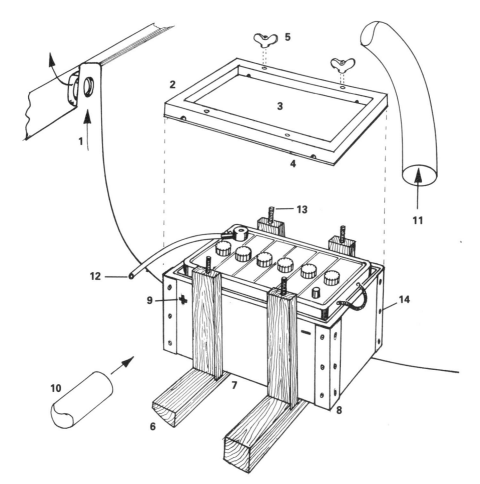

properly and it can be damaged in several ways, such as overcharging, being left discharged or by constant deep discharge use. Automotive 'no maintenance' batteries do not have characteristics best suited to marine use.

## Battery Isolating Switches

To prevent damage from accidental electrical fires or leakage of current that could set off corrosive attack, batteries must always be provided with isolating switches. It is sound practice to locate such switches as near to the batteries as possible yet in such a position that they can afford the boat some protection against intruders. Often switches are located so that the boat engines can be started up within minutes of a thief boarding.

On my own boat I located both starter and service battery switches just the other side of the engine bulkhead to the batteries, so that should an engine-room fire

**Fig 74** Battery box construction and installation

1 Coamings where hydrogen could collect should be ventilated
2 Battery cover with Celuform edges
3 Tray acts as tool shelf
4 Drain holes
5 Wing nuts secure tray and prevent upward movement of battery
6 Beds to battery box for levelling glassed to hull
7 Housing joint to stop forward movement of battery
8 Corners reinforced to stop weight bursting them
9 Positive and negative terminals marked on case to aid correct battery charging connections
10 Fresh air, mechanically blown, should be introduced at low level
11 Extracted air must be removed by approved gas extraction fan at high level above battery
12 Correct battery cables essential
13 Studs epoxide resined into top of posts
14 Back of battery box secured to bulkhead or other main member for strength

| vessel length less than | | | requirements | |
|---|---|---|---|---|
| | | | minimum | optional |
| vessel underway power driven (including auxiliary powered sailing vessel) | 7m (23ft) | maximum speed below 7 knots | all-round white | also if practicable sidelights (or bi-colour light) |
| | | maximum speed above 7 knots | masthead and sternlight  sidelights or bi-colour light | masthead all round white light  sidelights or bi-colour light |
| | 12m (39.5ft) | | | |
| | 20m (65.8ft) | | | |
| vessel underway sailing | 7m | | torch or lantern showing a white light | but if practicable sidelights or bi-colour and sternlight or tri-colour light |
| | 12m | | sidelights (or bi-color light) sternlight | on vessels less than 12m a tri-colour light may be fitted in place of sidelights and sternlight, in addition to sidelights and sternlight an all round red above an all round green may be fitted at or near the mast top |
| | 20m | | | |
| vessel at anchor power & sail | 7m | | none required when not in or near a narrow channel, fairway or anchorage | |
| | 20m | | all round white where it can best be seen | |
| customs clearance at night power & sail | all vessels HM customs request for clearance on arrival at night from foreign locations | | all round red no more than 2m above an all round white light | |

**Note** the above applications of IMCO rules are a brief guide only, refer to full rules for correct lights for other situations

| minimum range of lights | position in vessel | |
|---|---|---|
| all round white 2 miles sidelights as 12m | w | g r w 1m min |
| masthead 2 miles sidelights or 1mile bi-colour sternlight 2 miles | w 1m min g r | g r w 1m min |
| masthead 3 miles sidelights or bi-colour 2 miles sternlight 2 miles | w g r w | g r w 1m min 2.5m min w |
| as for 12m | g r w r w | g r w |
| sidelights or bi-colour 1 mile sternlight 2 miles | 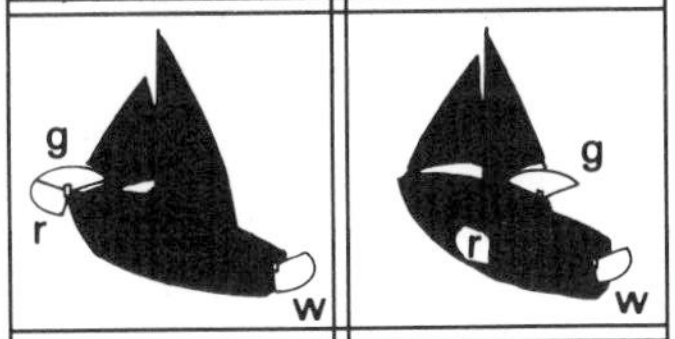 g r w | g r w |
| sidelights or bi-colour 2 miles sternlight 2 miles | as above | as above |
| 2 miles | 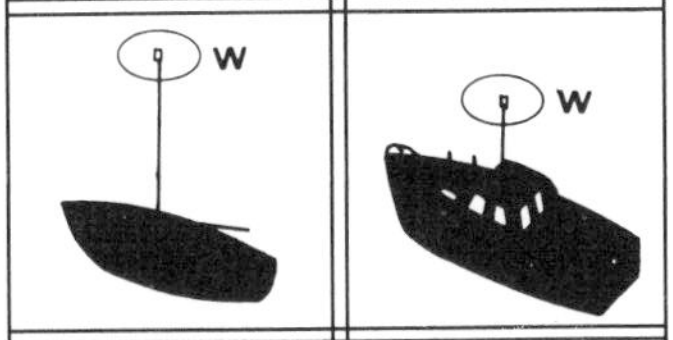 w | w |
| | | 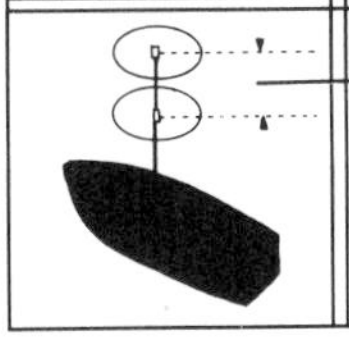 1m min 2m max |

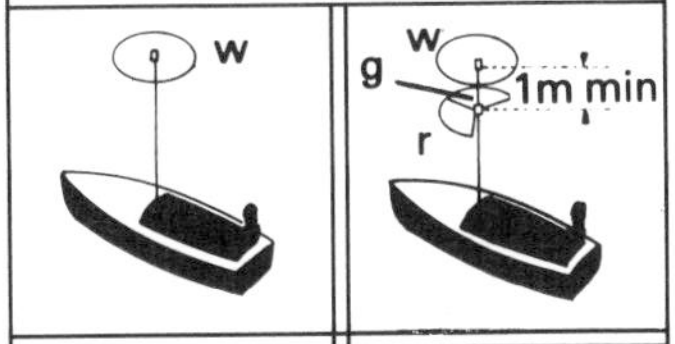

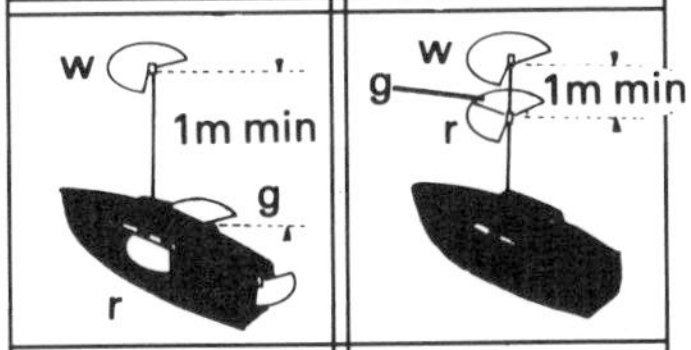

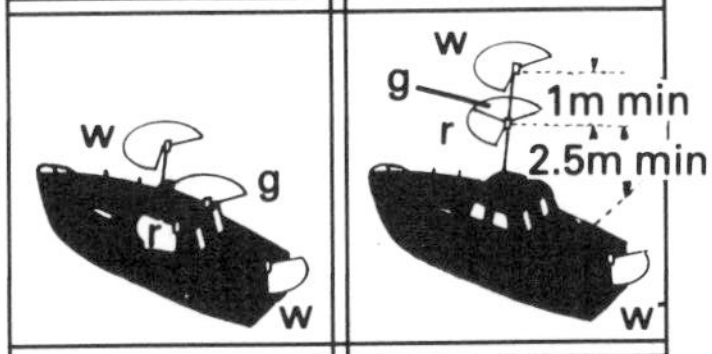

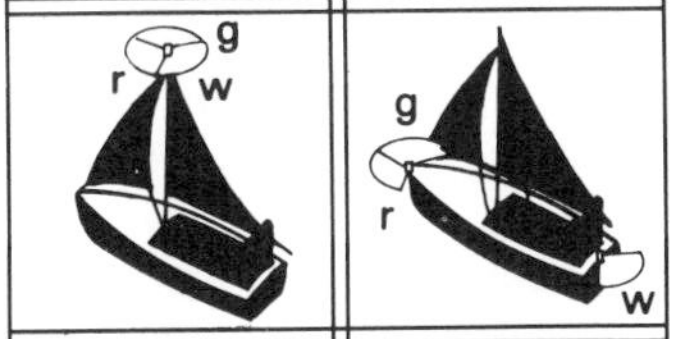

**Fig 75** Navigation light specification

occur, the batteries could be switched off from the after cabin without having to lift the engine-room hatches. They were built into an Egatube box, along with the Albright relay, that is, an electro-mechanical device for paralleling the two banks of batteries for charging purposes. Most modern systems have blocking diodes to parallel the batteries as they are completely automatic and direct a greater amount of power from the generator to the more exhausted battery. The Albright relay has a similar function to the blocking diode but paralleling takes place when the ignition or starter switch is turned on. Although the relay does not suffer from the slight losses inherent in the blocking diode, it can have the disadvantage that the batteries are paralleled and this can pull down the starter battery if the service battery is in a low state of charge. Since it is bad for the starter motor and service battery to fight over which should get the electricity, it is good policy on single-engine installations to arrange for the relay to be triggered by the oil-pressure switch so that paralleling only takes place when the engine is running and the generator is supplying current. In Appendix D, diodes are shown that allow either engine started first to operate the relay.

With a twin-engine installation the relay is perfectly all right in the starter/ignition switch wiring, since the engine not wired to the relay can be started first and then the relay switched in as the second engine is started. Certainly, the old systems using change-over switches should be considered a thing of the past, especially as wrong use could ruin an expensive alternator or leave you with a flat battery.

**Navigation Lights**
These can be defined as 'toy' or 'proper' equipment. There are toy lights by the score. In my opinion, it is a waste of time building them into a boat. The idea of navigation lights is that you can be seen at a reasonable distance at night and that a craft some distance away can tell from the disposition of your lights which direction you are moving relative to his course. Any

old red and green lights may look all right, but because the colour of the lantern absorbs a great deal of the light produced by the bulb, they are next to useless except at a very short distance. First-class navigation lights that fully conform to the specifications in the International Collision Regulations are readily available. Most nautical almanacs reprint the regulations in full, giving requirements for mounting and, in Annex III, the technical specification for the lights.

Fig 75 sets out Inter-governmental Maritime Consultative Organisation standards which should be studied to specify the lights for your own boat. Since changes occur in specification of navigation lights and local inland waterways specification which may or may not conform to IMCO standards, you should always approach the manufacturer who should have the latest information to hand.

Waterproof deck sockets and plugs should always be used so that a defective lantern can easily be removed for repair or replacement. When assembling the lights, spring contacts should be treated with an anti-corrosive spray such as WD40 or LPS. Quartz halogen bulbs must never be handled directly and the glass of the bulb must be kept scrupulously clean, otherwise it will quickly fail. The slightest trace of grease or moisture on these high-temperature bulbs usually bursts them.

## Circuit Breakers and Fuses

If at all possible, the extra cost of circuit breakers is worth while. Miniature circuit breakers, or MCBs, are combined switches and fuses. Should a circuit overload, the switch trips and the circuit is broken. Their advantage in marine use is that no small fuses have to be replaced and fiddled with, and circuits cannot be overloaded by putting in the wrong fuse or, worse still, bridging a circuit with a bit of old wire or nail. Lupus MCBs which I used on my boat were to Lloyd's-approved specification. They are available in ratings from 0.5 to 60 amps DC or to 415v AC. In the first column of Table 6 (p142), I have indicated how the various circuits were divided up and an appropriately rated MCB given to each plus some spares for future use.

One horror that often exists on boats is the hidden fuse. Often pumps and other equipment are supplied with an in-line fuse. These are fine so long as the installing electrician does not hide them away behind panelling or other equipment. With a well-designed and installed system, especially if MCBs are used, this extra protection is not necessary.

## Marine Horn and Sound Signalling

Part 'D', Sound and Light Signals, of the International Collision Regulations (Table 10) gives guidance on sound signalling requirements. Unfortunately, different

Table 10:   SOUND SIGNAL INTENSITY AND RANGE SPECIFICATION
(To comply with International Collision Regulations)

| Length of Vessel in Metres (Feet) | 1/3 Octave Band Level at 1m in db referred to $2 \times 10^{-5} N/m^2$ | Audibility Range |
|---|---|---|
| *Whistle (Horn)* | | |
| 20m (65.6ft) but less than 75m (246ft) | 130 | 1nm |
| Less than 20m (65.6ft) | 120 | 0.5nm |
| *Bell* | | |
| 12m (39.3ft) to 20m (65.6ft) diameter of bell mouth shall not be less than 200mm (7.8in) | | |

authorities deviate from its recommendations. Do check local regulations.

Chandlers' catalogues sometimes give almost inane advice. You see horns described as having 'deep rich tones' when sound is coming from a heavily chrome-plated trumpet. At least it is useful to know about the plating since the automotive-type horns advertised by penny-pinchers do not last long in the marine environment. However, horns and sound signals in general are an important part of safety at sea, or even in the confines of a river. The one essential is that they are audible to give the prescribed warnings to other craft. The louder the noise the better, and water, being non-absorbent, is the best possible noise carrier. You will lose efficiency if you buy the wrong horn and it is badly installed. With electrical horns, the worst offence is to use inadequate wiring which gives serious voltage drop. The electro-mechanical designs that are usually featured in chandlers' catalogues are heavy on current, often rating around 11 amps on a 12v system. Even with the right cable, good connections are essential. Serious loss of efficiency is caused by high resistance joints in poor connections.

Horns should be mounted as high as possible to avoid sound distortion and blanketing from deck obstructions, and to ensure that anyone working on deck is not blasted by sound. It is good practice to connect the electric horn at deck level with a watertight deck plug and socket. This enables servicing to be carried out and the winter cover to lie snugly when the horn is removed to safe storage. When you are designing, consider all the projections on deck that could rip the winter cover.

Larger craft requiring a horn with greater range would use the electric compressor type. Air pressure is created within the compressor and fed by tube to the horn to produce the sound. It has the advantage that the compressor can be mounted inside the boat and the electric parts are not exposed to the weather. Electric leads can therefore be shorter and run within the boat. This type usually has the greater range specified in the collision regulations for larger craft.

'Toy' bells are often seen on small craft but when you look at the regulation size of 200mm it is a large piece of bronze-work to keep clean. Sailing craft may find the portable aerosol compressed-gas horns adequate, but they must meet the regulations.

### Radio Interference Suppression

At a time when electronic equipment is flooding the market, it is important to know the basic problems created by energy generated in the boat by its electrical system, rigging, propellers and electric motors. Radio suppression is, essentially, the province of the expert. I would only recommend that you take basic avoiding action to minimise interference. Perfection can hardly ever be achieved, but the expert will reduce it to acceptable levels. Even if you do not intend having a lot of electronic gadgetry aboard, you should think ahead to the time when you might change your mind, only to find that the cost of installing suppression is much more than the gadget you want to install. Electric motors in fan-ventilation units and windscreen-wipers can be purchased suppressed to BS 1597 Class 1. It is far less costly to buy units made to this standard in the first place than to modify them in the future (if this is possible) or have to replace them. On the other hand, you may not consider it worthwhile suppressing an electric pump that operates a marine toilet when it only causes interference for a few seconds at intervals during the day.

Sources of interference are shown in Fig 76. Here are some of the ways to ensure that equipment is built correctly into the boat, rather than ways to modify it after running into trouble.

Buy the right generating system. Most engine manufacturers of inboard units offer some choice of generating equipment with the engine. When you come to purchase check if the generator (usually an alternator) has sufficient capacity to run the ship load and charge the batteries and if it can be used with a suppression box. Petrol engines, whether inboard or outboard, can be a source of trouble if the manufacturer has not fully anticipated the need for suppression of the ignition system. Generally,

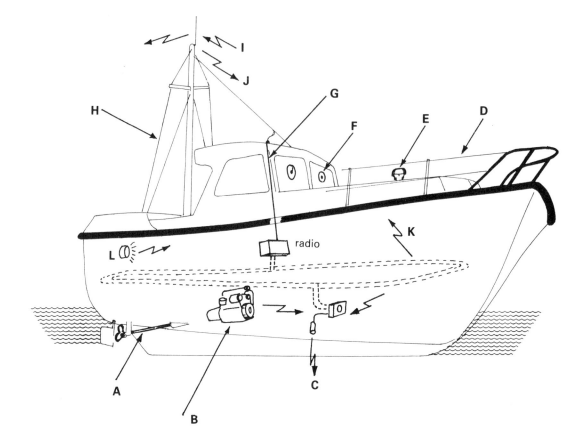

**Fig 76** Sources of electrical radio interference

when a yachtsman is buying a motor, this is the one question he forgets to ask and not many manufacturers bother to specify in their literature the suppression offered as standard, or which is available as an extra. It really is time they did this.

Looking at Fig 76, you can see where the problems of radio interference lie. Understanding the source will enable you to buy items that do not cause interference or to take the appropriate steps to forestall them.

**A** Rotating propeller shafts sometimes generate interference. A phosphor-bronze spring just contacting the shaft and properly earthed can reduce this. When flexible couplings are employed, it is necessary to bond both sides of the coupling to provide a continuous path to earth.

**B** Engines can be a prime source of inter-

ference. Suppressed ignition systems and suppression boxes for generating systems soon sort out the problems.

**C** Echo-sounders propagate and receive signals which can be interfered with by spurious emissions from other sources. Spark interference causes fluctuations on the depth reading and if the transducer cables are run near ignition switches or leads it can pick up unwanted interference. An absolute minimum distance between the transducer lead and ignition wiring should be 28in (70cm).

**D** Lifelines should have an insulated break so that closed loops are not formed.

**E** Electric motors for ventilation, bilge and fresh-water pumping may need to be fully suppressed types, especially when they might be operated for long periods; for example, in an emergency when you might be sending a distress call by radio, it would not be acceptable to run an unsuppressed bilge pump.

**F** Electric windscreen-wiper motors should be installed in such a way that they do not interfere with the boat compass or be sited close to the radio aerial lead. Do not site the aerial or D/F loop immediately above the motor on the other side of the wheel-house roof.

**G** Coaxial cable from aerial to radio set needs careful siting (see section on radio installation, Chapter 8).

**H** Rigging can be a serious source of interference and should be treated in the same way as the safety rail.

**I** Coaxial cable and the main antenna receive any spurious emissions from the sources under discussion. Correct siting is important for both (see Chapter 8).

**J** You may think that interference with radio signals is the major problem, but radio signals themselves can interfere with electronic gear. Admittedly, the majority of electronic equipment is fitted with screening which rejects radio interference in the MF, HF and VHF bands. However, there are at the present time no agreed standards and some auto-pilots, logs, computers and the like are affected when the radio is transmitting. When you buy equipment that could be affected by radio transmissions, check with the maker to see that it is built with adequate screening.

**K** Electrical wiring can form 'closed loops' just the same as rigging and safety rails. Ring circuits can be a menace and I prefer to have each electrical component served by its own wiring. Some sources say that radio sets should be directly wired to the battery, but I would suggest that this is only needed in extreme cases. Screening the wiring with screening braid, then bonding this to ship's ground plate is something that might be needed, but provided you have made wiring and conduit reasonably accessible, it is better to do this at a later stage when it has been proved to be needed.

**L** Although fluorescent lights are more economical on electricity than filament bulbs, they can be a source of radio interference. With the modern quartz halogen bulbs available for cabin lighting, the use of fluorescent lights is hardly worth while.

True, an 8w fluorescent gives as much light as a 40w bulb, but the halogen bulb gives excellent light and operates without any radio interference.

## Bonding

As already mentioned, machinery, metal fuel fillers and metal tanks must be bonded to a common ground to avoid radio interference and the chance of electrostatic discharge setting off an explosion or fire. Copper strip is often used for the main conductor while bonding cables and woven metal braiding are joined on by bolted tags, circlips and saddles as appropriate. Often the boat's cathodic system is used as the ground plate, but in bigger installations a larger area ground plate is called for. This is separate from the zinc anodes which give the cathodic protection. Although this is common practice, it can be dangerous if a leakage of current eats the anode away and leaves the metals it was protecting open to attack. On no account should bonding be solely connected to skin fittings, shafting or plumbing. Should a leakage of current occur, such fittings would be rapidly corroded away.

## Providing a Shore Connection Power Supply

For a cruising boat that is likely to call regularly at marinas, or which is berthed at a marina, the shore-side power connection is well worth considering. Large yachts and ships have always had the most complex shore-side-powered electrical systems to save running their own generators, but even the smallest cruiser can plug in alongside a marina and benefit from a 110v or, in the UK, a 240v AC supply. This kind of power, incorrectly used, will kill and is not to be fooled about with. For the amateur, I would certainly advise consulting an expert in this kind of design so that you end with a safe system. Shore-side charging of your batteries can be arranged and you can utilise electric kettles and other small domestic appliances to make life that bit more comfortable, as well as using a fan-heater to keep things dry below, as I did on *Sea Hound*.

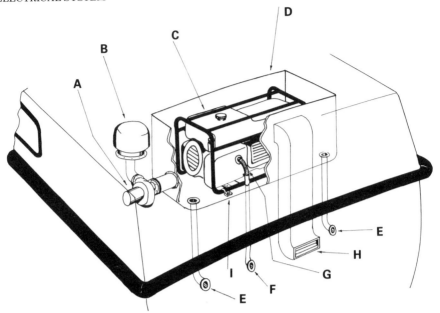

**Fig 77** Design criteria for installation of semi-portable AC generator
**A** Spark and gas-tight fan outside compartment to prevent explosion yet provide vital ventilation
**B** Weatherproof deck cowl
**C** Generator installation level and engineered to standards recommended for the main engine
**D** Installation space watertight from above and well drained with no possibility of flooding from below
**E** 1½in minimum size drains for water and heavy vapour at either end of the compartment
**F** Dry exhaust line to minimise back-pressure and be fully insulated from surrounding material
**G** Flexible section to exhaust line to deal with vibration
**H** Transom outlet for hot air which will not let water flood into the engine compartment

A Wylex fuse-box was installed near the main 12v distribution board and 13 amp cable was run from it to three socket outlets.

## Auxiliary Generating Systems

For wider use of domestic 240v appliances, consider the installation of auxiliary generating equipment. Many small generators are available which can be used on even the smallest yacht just to charge batteries or in semi-portable size to drive most small domestic appliances. Both engine and electrical engineering must conform to the highest standards or it will be lethal. Fig 77 shows some of the points that might be considered as part of a small auxiliary generating system using a semi-portable unit. In the age of the microwave oven such sets could well make the cook happier.

# 7   MECHANICAL INSTALLATIONS

## Steering

If a boat will float, move and go in the right direction, you are safe. Lose any one of these priorities and you are in real trouble. Since the steering gear rates so highly, consider its design and installation most carefully.

Small motor boats and yachts are comfortably steered by a tiller attached to the top of the rudder. On small boats this is safe and low in cost. Even in sailing boats of considerable size, the yachtsman may prefer tiller steering to give him a better feel of the balance of the yacht. By the feel of the helm he decides when too much, or too little, sail is being carried and the noise of the water past the rudder can give a good idea of the speed.

Wheel steering can be connected to the tiller by means of pulley blocks and multi-strand wire cable (Fig 78). The wheel allows greater flexibility in the steering position, can still give good 'feel' and is next up the cost scale. Provided wires are given a good lead through the blocks and they are of sufficient diameter to take the strain, all should be well.

In motor boats and some yachts where the wires emerge through the deck on either side of the tiller, a small traveller is incorporated on the underside of the tiller so that the wires will remain fairly centralised as the rudder turns, so eliminating some of the chafe when a deck outlet is

**Fig 78** Pulley block and wire cable steering system
**A** Steering wheel
**B** Retaining nut
**C** Gypsy for chain
**D** Key
**E** Bulkhead mounting with provision for auto-pilot take-off
**F** Chain drive to auto-pilot drive unit
**G** Calibrated chain to fit gypsy
**H** Shackles to join chain to eye in cable
**I** Double pulleys
**J** Cable-tensioner bottlescrew with shackles to eyes
**K** Slide to allow for alignment of cables as tiller geometry changes
**L** Single pulley
**M** Easily disconnected tiller which can be used for emergency steering if any other part of the system fails

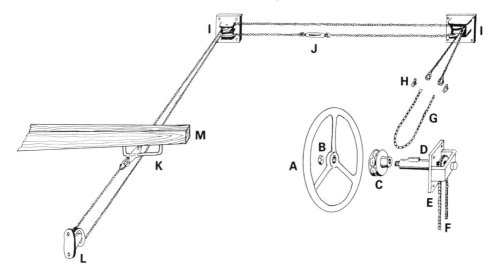

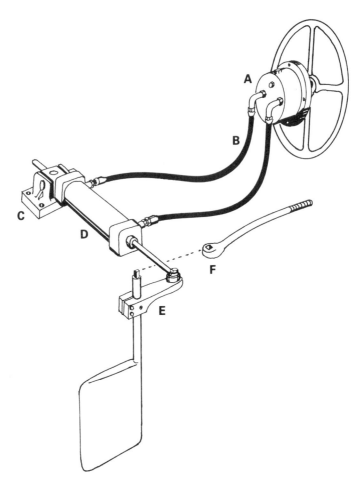

**Fig 79** Simple hydraulic steering system
**A** Hydraulic steering head with axial piston pump
**B** Special nylon flexible tubing for small applications; rigid piping must have flexible end section near the ram to take up movement
**C** Fixing plate for ram
**D** Hydraulic two-way ram
**E** Tiller arm with top engineered to take emergency steering tiller
**F** Emergency steering tiller

incorporated. When installing this type of steering gear, ensure that you get the best wire lead possible. Try to design the system so that when a steering wire needs replacing, it can be done without dismantling the stern of the boat. If a steering wire should break, this system already has the tiller arm for emergency steering. Any system you adopt should have emergency provision for steering.

Fig 79 shows an hydraulic system which is more often associated with large ships but which is now available at reasonable cost for the smallest of boats.

Hydraulic systems have the advantage that pipes which link the pump at the steering wheel, and the hydraulic ram which moves the rudder, can be placed in the most convenient positions and will not get in the way of other gear, especially as they pass through the confines of engine space. However, they must not be placed near high-temperature sources such as near the engine or exhaust system, since hydraulic fluid must not be overheated. The traditional piping was copper or brass, but nylon hose can be used in small installations. Personally, I do not like nylon since it softens in fire and will burst when it is soft.

The third type of steering system is the purely mechanical one, utilising bevel

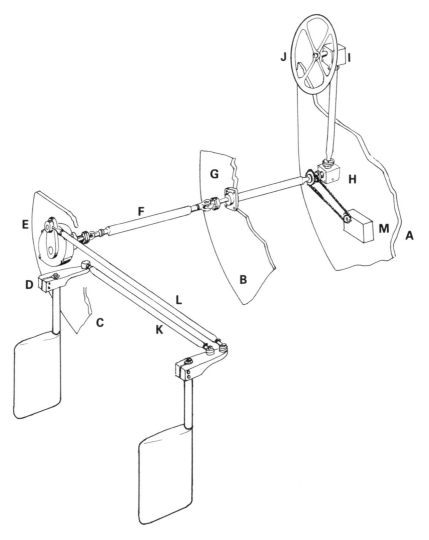

gear-boxes, reduction gears and torque tubes. Whitlock and Mathway engineer excellent systems that can be adapted for sailing and motor boats. Wheel steering can be provided at either pedestal position in a sailing boat's cockpit, or at a helm position in a motor boat. Fig 80 shows twin rudders but single rudders and dual-steering positions can just as easily be installed.

Since safety is paramount, the tiller-arm drag links and tie rods should all be secured with castle nuts and split pins (cotter pins) so they cannot fall off. The tiller arms are usually secured on a key with compression bolts. If the tiller arm was loosened, the rudder could drop out. To prevent this, the top of the rudder stock

**Fig 80** Mathway steering gear installation
**A** Main bulkhead
**B** Bulkhead aft end of engine space
**C** Semi-bulkhead aft cabin
**D** Tiller arm
**E** Aft end reduction gear-box Type XL
**F** 2in diameter torque tube, universal joint, one splined end
**G** Watertight bulkhead bearing
**H** Two-way bevel box; three-way box is used in dual steering position applications
**I** Steering bevel box
**J** Steering wheel
**K** Tie rod 1¼in diameter
**L** Drag link
**M** Auto-pilot drive unit

should be tapped and drilled so that a bolt can be used to secure a washer that is larger than the bearing below. The rudder cannot fall out with this in position.

When you are deciding on either hydraulic or mechanical steering systems, there are a number of facts you should give the manufacturer so that he can advise on the most appropriate gear for your boat:

1  The length of the boat, type and rudder configuration. These all affect the maximum torque that the steering will apply to the rudder, or rudders, without strain.
2  Whether single- or dual-steering positions are required.
3  Whether arrangements are needed in

Fig 81 The aft cabin — a vast GRP enclosed void starting to be filled with Mathway steering gear; a mock-up using old boxes and odds and ends was used to get the reduction box and the rest of the system into the correct position to ensure steering geometry was correct

the design for the accommodation of an auto-pilot. With hydraulic systems an electro-hydraulic pump might be needed. This pumps oil to the ram as required by command from the auto-pilot. It adds cost, is an extra item to go wrong in the steering system and consumes extra electrical power to drive the motor. For this reason, among others, I prefer the simplicity of a truly mechanical system such as the Mathway Series XL which I have on my boat. The only extra item needed to connect it to the Sharp auto-pilot, was a sprocket for the chain drive that linked the auto-pilot drive motor with the bevel gearbox. It is interesting that the Sharp motor consumes only about half the amount of electrical power compared to an electro-hydraulic pump of a similar sized hydraulic system.

4  The size of the head of the rudder stock for a matching tiller arm linking either a ram or drag link. Again, once you have decided on the type of system, the manufacturer will offer advice on the length of

tiller arm to match the rest of the gear. I found that Mathway issued an excellent booklet *Ordering and Installation Information* which told me all I needed to know before I actually bought the gear and what details they would need from me so that the gear was made to match my boat. The manufacturer may call for a general arrangement scale-plan so that he can offer a full design and specificiation service.

## Steering Geometry

Rudders operate most efficiently over an angle of about 35° either side of their central position. As rudder angle increases beyond this point, flow characteristics deteriorate, producing more drag than turning effect. Rudder stops are often installed to prevent rudders from turning beyond the stage where they become inefficient.

Fig 81 shows the temporary rig-up I made to check the Mathway steering gear geometry. Boxes, spirit levels and 'G' cramps were pressed into service to check the position of the steering box and the small semi-bulkhead that had eventually to be made to carry it. Fig 82 shows the aft end reduction box bolted to the semi-bulkhead, which also acts as support for the two bunk-side beams. The hands in the picture are mine, connecting grease tubes for the rudder shaft lubrication. Tecalemit screw-down greasers were used for the inboard end of the propeller shafts and for rudders. These are placed in a convenient position so that they can be reached easily each day and given one downward turn to force grease into the bearing. Nylon tube and compression fittings connect greaser to the lubrication point.

## Tufnol Bearings

These were used at the top of the rudder stock and were turned slightly oversize on the inside bearing surface so as to allow for expansion as the material absorbed water or grease. It does expand slightly and although it is easier to make it a tight outside fit, rather than using locating and securing grub screws, it is bad practice. Any bearing that might need future renewal should be made easy to remove.

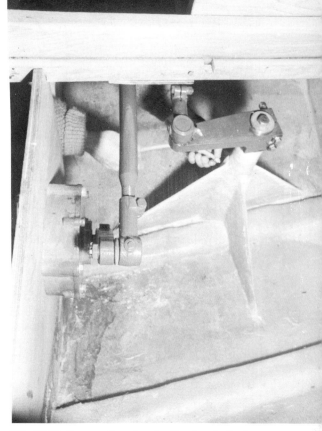

Fig 82 Mathway aft end reduction box bolted to semi-bulkhead that supports the port-hand bunk in the aft cabin; note the hefty tie rod

## Torque Tubes

These link the bevel and reduction boxes of mechanical systems. They are cut to length and their end fittings welded in place as the last job in the Mathway type of installation. I found with one end of the Mathway torque tube already fitted with a flange and the free end provided with a splined fitting, exact accuracy in length was unnecessary, the spline taking up the adjustment and providing movement for when the hull flexes in a rough sea. Universal joints ensure that the torque tubes can run sweetly and be diverted in small angles to avoid engines and other obstructions. Watertight bulkhead fittings are available. These offer extra safety, enabling compartments to be kept watertight. I enjoyed assembling the steering as it came complete down to the last nut and bolt and was just like putting together a child's construction kit.

### Rudder-position Indicator

Although small boats make do with a bit of tape on top of the steering wheel to indicate when the rudder is amidships, boats with hydraulic and mechanical steering systems are safest when a rudder-position indicator is installed. Most of these are electrically operated with a sender unit at the rudder head connected by cables to the indicator placed in the helmsman's position.

I selected the VDO hanging-needle type of recording head as this gives instant visual indication of rudder angle, rather than the ruled-bar type which you have to read off the angle on a ruled scale either side of the zero position. Installation is a matter of following instructions, although you have to be careful to work out the geometry of the sender unit arm which works from the rudder tiller arm in most cases. Slots in the sender plate will allow for adjustment to zero the instrument head when trials finally indicate that the steering geometry of the rudder is adjusted properly and the boat steers in a straight line.

### Enclosed Cable-steering Systems

These have their advocates and are simple to install, the only critical items are the length of the cable and the types of terminal ends to connect on to the rudder. Dual and single cables are available and it is suggested that motor boats up to 30ft (9.1m) length can be steered with a single-cable system. The problem with cables used for steering is that you cannot see what is happening inside them — corrosion and fatigue can take place in the best-made steering system, especially at exposed ends. If the installer puts in bends that are below those specified by the manufacturer, they will soon break. Read the literature before you start any installation.

For small lightweight boats — runabouts with outboards and the like — the enclosed cable system is adequate.

### The Fresh Hot-and-Cold-Water System

Having suffered from oxtail-soup-type fresh water on a previous boat, I determined that on my new boat I would have a good fresh-water supply, both in quantity and quality. I often wonder how many families suffering from upset stomachs can attribute them to the boat's water supply.

The quantity of water a boat can carry is limited by the size and space available for tankage. Water weighs 10lb per gallon (454g per 4.5 litres). If there is a crew of three, using 2gal (9 litres) of water each per day, the boat needs to carry 60lb (27kg) of water for one day's use. In a small performance racing cruiser or a planing power boat, large tankage would be disastrous, altering the sailing characteristic of one and the ability to get on to the plane in the other. In these cases it would be wrong to alter the original tank specifications and if the designer does not provide adequate tankage it would be best to consult him.

With a cruising boat used by the average family and where weight is not too critical, it is a good plan to have sufficient water for five days or so, avoiding the chore of constantly having to find a water supply. My calculations were for a crew of four using 5gal (23 litres) per member, per day. The extra allowance was because a fresh-water shower was to be installed and weight in water was substituted for ballast. If tankage is to be ballast, it is vital to ensure that it is confined and cannot upset the stability calculations. Fit baffles as per the fuel tank.

The sophistication of the system depends on what you want or can afford. Some people manage with a couple of jerrycans and perhaps a simple galley hand-pump. This type of system needs no explaining, but even a small craft can have a sophisticated electrical system that is easy to put together, reliable and reasonably low in cost. Fig 83 shows the Aqua-Marine Aquaflow system that is one of the few that is completely integrated.

A  *The tank,* moulded from food-grade polyethylene, can be used in any position and joined to similar tanks to give increased capacity. All tank materials should be hygienic and made of materials

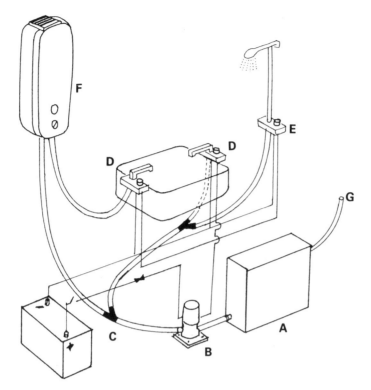

Fig 83a The Aquaflow hot and cold water system

that will not contaminate or taint the water. Plastic hoses for cold-water supply should be of food grade and similarly with the hot supply lines, but these must also be able to withstand heat without the plastic softening.

**B** *The pump* is the heart of the water system. The Aquaflow pump has a drowned suction, that is, it is not a self-priming pump and has to have a gravity-fed supply filling the pump housing before it will operate. The line to the suction side can be hand-pump primed and there is a version of the pump which is simply dropped into the water container with a feed line. When you are buying the water pump, ensure that it will operate to suit your particular design. Some pumps require a pressure accumulator tank which evens out pressure fluctuations. They add to cost, but are necessary for some systems.

**C** *'Y' branches* and other fittings to take plastic hoses should be designed into the system. Plastic piping is usually sold in 'i/d' (internal diameter) sizes. Water- and air-tight joints are easy to make and clip when the system is integrated.

**D** *The faucets* are cleverly designed so

that the electric switch operates the pump motor and, just after pressure is built up, opens the faucet valve. Many water systems depend on indirect switching of the pump by means of a pressure-drop switch. As a tap is opened, water in the line flows out, lowering the pressure and a switch, sensing this drop, turns on the pump. I am not amused by the antics of these switches. My original system had one but I got fed up with aiming three hard kicks at the panel behind which the pump lurked to get it started.

**E** *Showers* are possible, even on a small boat and are a boon if you plan to live on board for any length of time. Cabinet work should be covered with a plastic decorative surface and corners and edges sealed so that water cannot get behind them. Silicone rubber is ideal for this job.

**F** *The water-heater* uses air in combustion and must be properly ventilated so that full combustion of the gas can take place and you still have air to breathe.

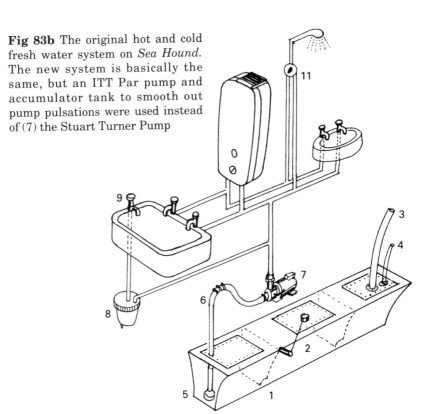

**Fig 83b** The original hot and cold fresh water system on *Sea Hound*. The new system is basically the same, but an ITT Par pump and accumulator tank to smooth out pump pulsations were used instead of (7) the Stuart Turner Pump

Fireproof lining above and behind the heater should be installed, even if you fix the heater the recommended distance from the cabin ceiling and bulkheads at either side. Modern gas heaters, working on low-pressure water automatically, are extremely efficient. If you are not sure of plumbing gas and water, engage a professional. Calor Gas will advise and there are installers whom they specially recommend for this type of work.

**G** *Tank-filler* inlets can be either 1¼in (32mm) or 1½in (38mm) diameter, while ⅜in (19mm) is adequate in small installations for the air breather.

Now I will tell you of the system I installed (Fig 83b):

**1** GRP tanks can be moulded in as an integral part of the hull. Holding 100gal (455 litres) of water (1,000lb (454kg) weight) it acts as ballast. Hatches must give access to every part of the tank for cleaning.
**2** A tank-contents gauge is useful and might merely be a graduated dipstick, or the electric type which is inaccurate, but

roughly able to show when supplies are getting low.
**3** If blow-backs are not to occur, 1½in (38mm) diameter hose, at least, is needed for filling. Deck-filler plates should be weatherproof so that contaminated deck water cannot seep on to the clean supply. Metal-to-metal joints are not good enough and a neoprene seal should be looked for.
**4** A tank-breather pipe must be led up to a coaming, where air expelled from the tank when filling, or air entering when emptying, does not bring dirt into the system. On no account must the fresh-water breather be put on the same side of the boat as the sewage-tank breather. The end should be protected with a fine mesh filter. For small installations ½in (13mm) or ¾in (19mm) pipe is sufficient; for larger installations, 1in (25mm) or 1¼in (32mm).
**5** A non-return valve was necessary to keep the prime of the Stuart Turner pump. This kept a head of water when the pump stopped. Impeller-type pumps are available and these are of course self priming. Centrifugal and impeller-type pumps will

be damaged if they are allowed to run dry. Diaphragm pumps (also self-priming) do not suffer this way but sometimes they generate a pulsating pressure which some gas water-heaters do not like as they, too, have a diaphragm where pressure opens and closes the automatic gas valve.

**6** I had to provide a break in the pipe from the tank to the pump so that I could hand-prime the swan neck to drown the pump inlet. A small section of aluminium tube was inserted and stainless-steel hose clips used to get a good seal. This must be really secure and air-tight; it is surprising how air will find its way into the pipe. A Stuart foot valve in the tank maintains the head.

**7** The Stuart Turner pump consumes 210w, but any pump should have correct wiring to minimise voltage drop. I did away with the pressure switch and had ordinary switches installed in the galley and WC compartments. A WIPAC Mixo-Mini Relay was wired to switch the hefty pump current which proved very reliable.

**8** Even when the best tank materials are used there is always some danger of water supplies becoming contaminated. Algae grows in water-supply lines in marinas and this contamination gets into even the cleanest tank. While chemical tablets can be added to water to purify it, they are bad for the Scotch. Our beagle hound refused to drink water on the boat for years until I put in an Ogden water-purifying filter! These units, made in the USA, provide sterile water in hospitals — a good enough recommendation. It also provides the lowest point in the pipework to drain down for the winter. This is essential to prevent frost damage in the system. Frozen water will burst tanks, rupture the heater diaphragm and even burst pumps as well as pipes. Design accordingly and see that filters are in a position to make servicing them easy.

**9** The pure water supplied from the Ogden filter will flow safely until the silver filter becomes so blocked that hardly anything comes from the faucet.

**10** The water-heater, a Vaillant 125/1B for LPG propane/butane, was connected to the main gas pipeline by solid drawn copper, complying with BS 2017, with compression-type fittings for joints. All equipment was purchased from the Calor Gas Company, having discussed with them beforehand the installation requirements and specifications. BS 5482 Part 3 1979 is the code of practice for butane/propane installations in boats, yachts and other vessels. On no account must the amateur attempt gas installation without knowing what he is about. There should be a minimum number of mechanical connections, as it is far safer to use a pipe bender for corners so that there are few joints to leak. Pipework must be well supported by clipping, and the weight of appliances must not be borne, or even partially borne, by the pipework. Calortite, a gas-jointing compound, is only safe on low-pressure installations. Minimal quantities of jointing material give a far better joint than one which is plastered over with gunge which could be concealing a poor joint. Gas joints are never tested with a lighted torch or match. A liquid household detergent painted around each joint with the system under gas pressure is the safe way. Bubbles in the liquid show escaping gas.

Perhaps the most important point is the need for correct ventilation when a gas appliance is in operation. Butane or propane gas are not in themselves poisonous and the products of combustion usually are harmless if properly vented outside the boat. They become deadly when there is inadequate ventilation for the cooker, space heater or water-heater. The falling level of oxygen as it is used up by humans and heating devices causes the combustion process to change, so that instead of carbon dioxide, carbon monoxide is produced. The first effect of carbon monoxide is to remove the will of anyone nearby to take any action. Long before the appliance goes out through lack of oxygen, the crew will fall asleep and die. Certain heaters now have a device which shuts them off if ventilation becomes inadequate. However, these are only just being produced and not all appliances are available with this kind of safety protection.

Ventilation of unflued appliances is given as:

1in² (6cm²) free ventilation area for each 1,000 btu/h input, divided equally between high and low level or 15in² (97cm²) whichever is the greater.

On the Vaillant 125 the input was 36,000 btu/h, therefore:

Ventilation area needed = 36 × 1in² (6cm²) = 36in²(216cm²) *for the heater.*

Additional ventilation for the crew must be added. If in doubt on any of these matters, call in a professional installer.

### Fresh-water Piping
Plastic piping is extremely easy to install and flexible and rigid grades are available. These are safe to use with fresh water and with hot and cold water. Chandlers' catalogues carry full ranges of fittings. In the UK, Acorn (Cleghorn Waring of Baldock) market integrated plastic plumbing pipe and accessories which make the job simple for the amateur. I used ordinary 1/2 in (13mm) domestic copper piping and fittings. Compression fittings are quite expensive so I resorted to soldered joints for acute bends, 'T's and fittings. Provided the precaution of thoroughly cleaning the copper pipe and fitting with steel wool is done, the job is easily accomplished. Be fully aware of the danger of fire when working near GRP and plywood bulkheads with a gas torch or blowlamp. I used scrap pieces of Heatshield behind piping to give fire protection. On any kind of pipe the best fitting is obtained when a perfect right-angle cut is made across the end of the pipe. The burrs should be removed from plastic and copper piping with a fine file. PTFE tape can be used on both gas threads and water-pipe threads of compression fittings.

### Gas Installation
Apart from the safe specification and installation already mentioned, a safe storage area for the containers of gas that will fuel the stove, water-heater and space heater should be considered.

Before starting a gas installation, make sure that it conforms to local regulations.

In the UK the source of information is Calor Gas Ltd, while in the USA the local waterway, lake or USCG, plus gas suppliers, will know what regulations are in force. For blue-water yachtsmen, Calor Gas publish an extremely useful leaflet, *LPG (Bottled Gas) for 'Blue Water' Yachtsmen* which sets out clearly the problems of the gas user operating different storage systems and using either butane or propane gas in different parts of the world. In the UK we generally use butane and the 4.5kg gas container is popular as it is just about the maximum weight and size to be carried around and can be transported in the tender. Although one cylinder will cope with the cooking needs of a small boat, it is advisable to find room for a spare. This should still be stored properly (Fig 84) and, if possible, connected into the system so that as one cylinder empties the spare can be turned on to give a continuous gas supply. 7kg or even 15kg gas cylinders might be needed on large yachts, but replacement is then more of a dockside operation.

Butane is predominant in temperate climates such as Britain, France and Mediterranean countries where it turns to gas at higher ambient temperatures. Propane has a lower boiling point, which means it turns into gas at lower temperatures. This makes it suitable for use in the colder climate of Scandinavia and parts of the USA. Both propane and butane are heavier than air (air = 1, propane = 1.5 and butane = 2). This is the danger for, if they escape from an appliance, they will fall into lower spaces, such as bilges and build up there until a source of ignition is reached and they explode. Like any other fuel, if it is installed correctly and used sensibly it is safe. No fuel is idiot-proof.

### Basic Specification and Installation for LPG Installations
Numbers refer to those on Fig 84.

1  Although gas cylinders can be placed on deck so long as escaping gas cannot get into any nearby hatch, they are best kept in a ventilated locker made of 20swg sheet metal with welded seams or made of glass-

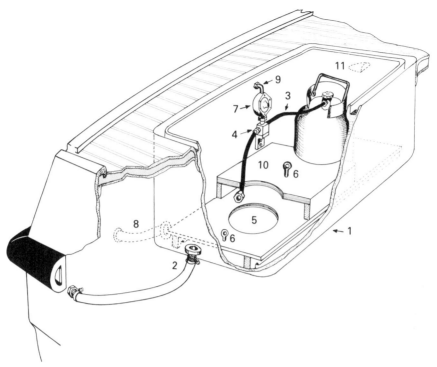

reinforced plastic with self-extinguishing resin, minimum thickness 1/8in (3mm). *Sea Hound*'s gas lockers, moulded in as part of the stern structure, are 1/2in (13mm) thick and sited at the farthest point from possible sources of ignition and above the water-line.

**2** Drains must be provided to cope with gas leakage or any water entering the locker. Minimum diameter should be 1/2in (13mm) or larger. I found that even 3/4in (19mm) drains became blocked with dirt from decks. The replacement 1in (25mm) drains have proved excellent. I led them from the bottom of the locker to the transom just below the fendering where they have some protection.

**3** Flexible gas hose must be up to specification to carry the gas supply without deterioration. Specifications are given in BS 3212/1975, but your gas dealer will recommend those that are safe to use. The cylinder-to-regulator section must be of high-pressure hose while the connections to a gimballed stove would be of the low-pressure type. Hose nozzles must be firmly clipped and not damage threads or nuts.

**4** This is a double wall block and bracket for running two gas cylinders. For a single

**Fig 84** Gas cylinder locker

cylinder a single wall block would be specified. The block must be bolted to the locker side for strength.

**5** Gas cylinders must *always* be kept upright. I fabricated the marine-plywood structure shown to keep them steady with the base of the cylinder out of drainage water.

**6** For sea-going boats the cylinders must be lashed in place so that they cannot jump out of the cradle. Rubber shock cord is not strong enough. 1/4in (6mm) rope can be led through the eye bolts for this job.

**7** The regulator is matched to the type of gas in use to reduce the high pressure from the cylinder to the low pressure needed for consumer units. It is easily fitted direct on to the wall block.

**8** An alternative position for the gas safety drain is shown on the bottom vertical side of the gas-cylinder container.

**9** The outlet for the main supply line to the appliance must be near the top of the locker. A bulkhead fitting will enable you to assemble a gas-tight outlet.

**10** The platform of the locating structure is shaped to fit the side of the bottles to prevent lateral movement.

11  Ventilation through the top of the locker cover must be provided. I used small shell ventilators which gave minimum obstruction on the aft deck. A gas locker must only open from the top.

The run of piping after it emerges from the bulkhead fitting of the gas locker must avoid hot spots like exhaust pipes, and bilges where it could rapidly corrode. Piping that has to pass through an engine space or electrical compartment should be housed in gas-proof conduit. Pipework must be supported by clipping to supporting blocks at 6in (152mm) intervals.

Pipe size is important. As electrical appliances must not suffer voltage drop in cables, so it is important not to allow pressure drop caused by long lengths of piping, bends, etc to exceed 2.5 mbar (1in wg). It is probably best to consult your dealer, or Calor Gas (UK) direct, but for most small boats 2/5in (10mm) pipework will serve cookers and single- or multi-point heaters. If both are on one supply pipe it should be increased to 1/2in (12mm) but can be 'T'd off the main line to 2/5in (10mm), as I did on *Sea Hound*. For small appliances the manufacturer may recommend 1/4in (6mm) piping. If you have a long pipe run for this small size, check that pressure drop will not be prohibitive.

## Cabin Heating

Perhaps because of the growth in marina berthing and the high expenses involved, more and more yachtsmen have tended to keep their boats afloat during the winter months. GRP, with its excellent weather resistance and comparatively low maintenance in the first years, has helped the yachtsman to get the most out of his yacht during this extended season.

There is much to be said for restricting the number of fuels carried aboard a small boat. There can be dangerous mix-ups if one fuel is accidentally substituted for another. Obviously, a diesel-fired heater is attractive on a diesel-fuelled boat, while a boat that already has a gas installation is suitable for a gas heater.

There are cabin heaters available for every size of boat and type of fuel — paraffin, diesel, propane and butane gas. Before buying an appliance, think about the installation area. Unless special care is taken with ventilation, I think it is highly advisable to have a heater which draws combustion air and vents combustion products to the outside of the boat. I also like to see fail-safe devices incorporated into the design. For these reasons I chose the Remotron ducted hot-air central-heating system. The kind of protection offered was:

1  Low-voltage sensing. The heater would stop if the voltage fell to 11v or below.
2  A photo-electric cell monitored the flame size and if this went either high or low the gas supply was cut off by a solenoid valve.
3  Thermostatically controlled fuse cut off the unit should temperature rise above a set figure at the hot-air outlet.
4  All venting was either from or to the outside.

Check all the safety features on the heater you are considering.

Heaters must obviously be installed to the maker's specification, but with inflammability of GRP, the insulation of the heater compartment or the bulkhead to which it is fastened, must be very thorough indeed. The Remotron body does not get very hot on the outside, but I nevertheless protected the surrounding surfaces with Heatshield (Fig 85). Make sure the flue is sufficiently isolated from the GRP structure. The Remotron flue only needed a 3 3/4in (95mm) hole drilled in the right position in the deck for the whole unit to be fitted in place and the heater bolted on beneath the deck. Cunning positioning ensured that the retractable chimney could be opened from the cabin window in bad weather.

The installation instruction book was excellent. Gas piping and electrical cables and connections were all installed as recommended and it worked first time — not, however, before every gas connection in the system had been tested with liquid soap.

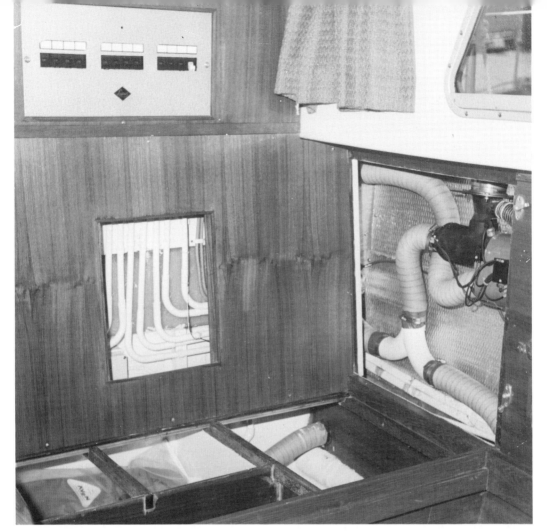

## Ventilation

Ventilation usually receives scant attention, perhaps because it is not thought necessary when so much fresh air surrounds a boat. Also, it costs money and thought and adds little to a 'boaty' appearance. A couple of deck Dorade boxes on the forward cabin, a ship-type ventilator or, on small craft, a mushroom ventilator or two, and the yacht-builder thinks he has done a good job. Unfortunately, ventilation plays such an important part in the efficiency of both boat and crew that it needs careful design and installation.

The very act of filling the GRP hull with woodwork closes off volumes of space where air cannot naturally circulate, conducive to an accumulating odour of mould and sweaty socks. The engine compartment in itself needs air for the combustion process and to keep the ambient temperature at levels where equipment can oper-

**Fig 85** The Remotron heater is installed under the side deck in a compartment lined with Heatshield; air for the heater is taken in through the engine louvred air inlet and then ducted out to the aft and forward cabin spaces; combustion air and flue gases are self-contained in the special deck outlet

ate efficiently and safely. Batteries have to be kept cool and all electrical equipment — pumps, alternators, wiring, etc — benefits from ventilation. Corrosion is kept at bay when condensation is not allowed to accumulate. But perhaps the overriding function of ventilation is to prevent the build up of explosive vapours from fuel, especially petrol, from cooking fuels, especially gas, and from the hydrogen gas given off when a lead/acid battery is charging.

The main problem is to get air in and keep rain and sea water out. You should

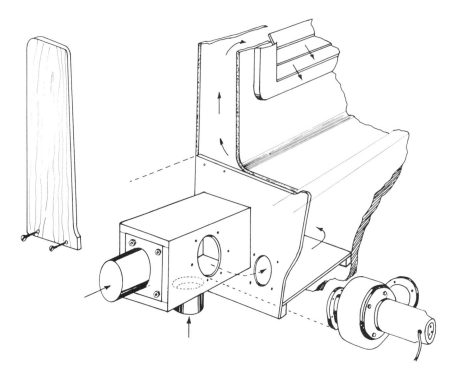

**Fig 86** Coaming ventilation system

design a system which has two basic features: passive and active ventilation units. Passive units are bell-mouth cowl, frog (a low version of the former), shell- and mushroom-type ventilators, which let in air and keep out rain. Active ventilation units incorporate an electric fan to draw in air or blow it out.

Obviously, no engine-room ventilation systems, unless they are designed for RNLI lifeboats with one-way ball-valve inlet compartments, can be watertight if submerged. All deck intakes, however, must have some form of water/air separation so that the fan does not get ruined by the constant ingress of rain or sea water. Fig 86 is the drawing of the system I designed. The moulding for the wheel-house provided a space above the deck to cut out and insert a louvred ventilator to port and starboard. This led down to a watertight box fabricated from marine ply and glassed in. Any water entering the box is removed via a 1½in (38mm) drain in the bottom and a plastic bottle trap (Terrain) and plastic piping to the engine-room bilge. The bottle trap, when filled with water, prevents air circulation through

the drain hole. The figure shows the arrangement for the starboard-hand side gas-extraction fan. The end of the box was bolted in place to provide access for servicing. Fig 87 shows the unit under construction in the workshop. Gaskets for the ventilation units were cut from sheet rubber, ⅙in (4mm) thick.

**Ventilation Calculations**
Mechanical ventilation, electrically driven, should be designed so that the correct size fan is chosen.

**Engine-room Supply and Exhaust**
Engine manufacturers will advise on combustion air consumed. You will then have to measure the rough volume of the compartment. The following calculation is for *Sea Hound*:

A   2 × Perkins 4.108 @ 110cfm
     =   220cfm for combustion
B   Cubic capacity of engine-room = 190cfm
     272cu ft less 30 per cent volume
     taken by equipment, engines, etc
C   Total air requirement
     =   410 cubic feet per minute
       (cfm)

From the fan-manufacturer's catalogue (in my case AK of London) you can choose the fan to deliver this volume. One warning. If you are putting air into a compartment you can build up pressure which will lead to fumes and oily smells leaking out into accommodation spaces. The specification for *Sea Hound* included an extraction fan for the engine compartment that would extract volume (B). A fan of 190cfm was chosen to give slight under-pressure and therefore hold smells in the compartment. You must not under-pressurise and remove the engine's combustion air.

US Coast Guard rules give another simple method of determining volumes of air for the engine compartment (Table 11).

This gives a slightly more generous supply of air than the first calculation, which is not a bad thing, except that costs go up for larger fans as does the difficulty of installing larger ducting.

**Fig 87** The Airmax gas extraction fan and its housing being fabricated; an important criteria in good design is that components which might need servicing can be easily removed

*Table 11*    USCG: VENTILATION OF ENGINE AND FUEL TANK SPACES ON
SMALL PASSENGER VESSELS

| *Sizes of Space in Cubic Feet* | | *Minutes per air change* |
|---|---|---|
| — | Not over 500 | 2 |
| Over 500 | Not over 1,000 | 3 |
| Over 1,000 | Not over 1,000 | 4 |
| Over 1,500 | | 5 |

*Calculation*

Engine space = 6 × 4 × 10ft =
240cu ft × 2 = 480cfm

## Accommodation Space

In fine weather when no cooking is being done, open ports, hatches and passive ventilation units are adequate. In bad weather, some mechanical ventilation is needed to change the air about fifteen times an hour. The galley, even on a small boat, should be fitted with a fan to extract cooking smells. All ventilators into accommodation space should have some form of insect filter.

Calculation for the forward cabin of my boat:

12.8 × 9.5 × 6.25ft = 760cu ft
Less approximately 25 per cent volume of furniture = 570cu ft
At fifteen changes an hour 570 × 15 = 8,550cu ft
Divide by 60 to get cfm = 142cfm
Conversion factors: cubic feet to cubic metres multiply by 0.0283
cubic metres to cubic feet multiply by 35.31

I decided to have two supply fans, one over the dinette and the other over the navigation table, each supplying 75cfm.

## Galley

The extraction of steam and cooking smells is important, particularly in bad weather when the saloon is crowded, or when it is cold and condensation from steam would be a nuisance. It is a simple matter to balance the extraction fan in the galley with the volume of the input fans.

Another way is to put two-speed controls on the fan switches so that input and output can be balanced that way.

## Toilet Compartment

Where the toilet compartment is close to living space the need for an extraction fan is obvious. A high-extraction rate is valuable from 50 to 75cfm. I used a Super Boxer fan, a 230v unit adaptable with an inverter to change the 12v system to a 230v 40hz supply. This doubles as a shaver socket provided the fan is off. There is no need for a small boat to lack comforts these days. Fig 88 shows the fan installed.

## Sleeping Cabins

The volume of air needed is governed by the number of people sleeping in the cabin. Each should be given 50cfm when windows cannot be opened. Extraction is not necessary as the space becomes slightly pressurised and only a means of egress is needed. This is why I used louvred doors to the compartments. Even when making washboard doors for sailing yachts, some provision for ventilation louvres should be incorporated.

## Bilge Ventilation

Ventilation fans to extract air from bilges must be spark-proof and installed in such a way that even switching will not induce a spark to ignite any explosive vapours that might collect there. I think it is better to remove air constantly, along with any potentially dangerous gases, by means of a

**Fig 88** Boxer 240v electric fan in the WC compartment has inverter which also powers a shaver socket; linings are Formica on the bulkhead and Duraform for the head lining

**Fig 89** Marking out the forward ventilation position for the AK fan unit

safe fan, rather than spend money on an instrument that only tells you that the gas is there, but does not have the ability to remove it safely. Explosive vapours are dense and build up from the lowest areas in the bilge. Any gas-extraction fan should be fitted high up and, preferably, outside the compartment. I was not able to fix a gas-extraction fan outside the engine space but it was fitted high and a shell ventilator gives it natural ventilation under the side deck. Fig 87 shows how two suction ports were incorporated in the gas extraction unit to ventilate both forward and engine-room bilges.

## Fitting Ventilation Fans

If your plans already specify the positions for ventilation fans, you have nothing to worry about. If not, make sure their position on the outside does not interfere with deck operations, and on the inside that they are not likely to interfere with human activities. Nothing is worse than a badly positioned fan blowing cold air down your neck.

Fig 89 shows an AK weatherproof filter cowl being tried for position on the forward coach-roof, the gasket being used for the marking template. Check the same position from the inside and, when satisfied, use a jig-saw to do the cut out. Fig 90 shows a typical cross-section into which the ventilation fan might fit. Note that the motor unit is separate from the weather cowl, being fitted in the cabin-roof lining. This makes it easily removable for servicing. The thickness of the wood fan-mounting ring can be made to suit the height of the motor unit so that it fits properly into the cowl area. The gasket itself should have additional sealant (silicone rubber) to bed on to as it is imperative not to have any leaks through the gasket or around the securing bolt holes. I cut the mounting rings from ¾in (19mm) marine plywood and pre-finished them with two-can polyurethane. It is advisable to fit finger

**Fig 90** Ventilation fan installation

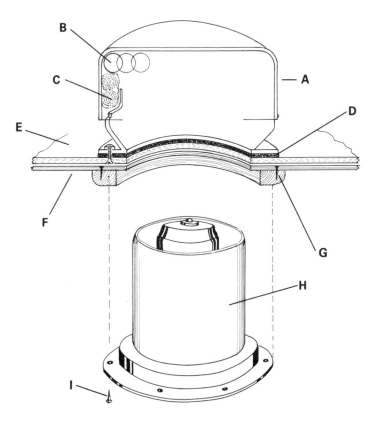

guards, especially with young children around. It is also a good plan to have the electrical cables run close to the fan and terminate in a plastic or bakelite terminal block. The flying lead from the fan motor can then be easily connected in, or disconnected for servicing.

## Ducting Ventilation Fans

There are, no doubt, commercial lightweight alloy or plastic flanges to connect ducting to fans, but I did not find any when I was building. The problem was overcome by fabricating them from sheet alloy and marine plywood. Epoxide resin glue was used to make a lap joint (Fig 91). The plywood ring was cut, sanded and had holes drilled in it to match the fan-unit flange face. The alloy ring was then pushed into the flange face, using epoxide resin glue again and, when set, the joint was smoothed off using Epophen putty. The result was inexpensive and easy to make.

The ducting itself was secured to these flanges with large circular clips. Ducting should be arranged so that full cross-ventilation is achieved from the input at the rear of the compartment to an exhaust at the forward end. Gas-extraction ducts should take from low levels, but be arranged so that bilge water does not affect them.

## The WC and Sewage Disposal System

Three basic options are open to the designer:

1  A self-contained chemical toilet which is compact and low in cost — but a nuisance to cart ashore, empty and replenish with chemicals.
2  The chemical recirculating toilet which is used in aircraft where a holding tank is charged with chemical and water and at the end of a certain length of time has to be pumped out and replenished.
3  Marine clean-water flushing WCs where the effluent is pumped directly overboard or into a holding tank for later discharge into the sea or ashore at a pumping-out station.

In the 1970s there was an outcry against

**Fig 91** Fabricating flanges for the ventilation system using marine plywood, light alloy and an epoxy resin system for bonding; protective plastic gloves are worn when using resin

pollution and we all acknowledged the disgraceful way humanity was polluting rivers and seas. Safe bathing was, and still is, impossible in some places. Many authorities, especially on inland waterways, have not tolerated sewage discharge for many years and I foresee a time when we must accept it as a duty not to foul up any waterways. In the confines of a marina it is not amusing to be enjoying a drink with friends, surrounded by sewage-laden water.

While (1) and (2) systems are fine for boats under about 24ft (7.3m) in length, larger craft can probably find room for a decent sized holding tank. Size is important for, in some areas, when there is a charge for pumping out, the advantage of a 40gal (181.8 litres) tank over a 16gal (72.7 litres) one is obvious. The problem with toilets on boats is one of smell. Chemical smells can be almost as obnoxious as effluent smells. Any holding system must

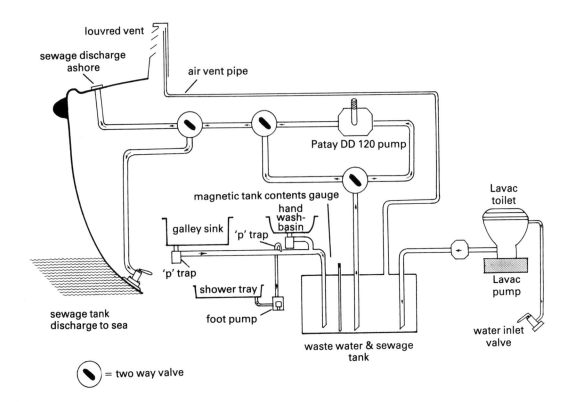

**Fig 92** Schematic of waste water and sewage system on *Sea Hound of Dart*

then be able to absorb or dissipate chemical and effluent smells safely so that the confines of the boat remain sweet.

Fig 92 shows the system on *Sea Hound*. There is a 40gal (181.8 litres) holding tank moulded into the keel section of the hull. It is arranged so that sewage could be discharged ashore via the boat's pump, via a pump at a shore-side station or via a seacock directly into the sea. Therefore, it covers all eventualities. Unfortunately, however, it costs more than a simple direct discharge-to-sea system. It has the advantage over chemical systems in that waste water from sinks, basins and showers can also be discharged into the tank. We do use a formaldehyde-based deodorant and disinfectant occasionally, but provided the tank is thoroughly flushed out with sea water after discharge of the effluent, there have been no serious problems. We did find that if the boat was left for a long time with

the tank half-full, obnoxious gases built up. But it is easy to cleanse the tank in these circumstances and we now take extra care that this never happens.

The toilet manufacturer will give full installation details. As there can be danger of flooding, these must be carefully followed. Each boat will differ in the height of the lavatory-pan water in relation to the water level outside the hull. The manufacturer will specify valve and anti-syphon arrangements to prevent water from being syphoned back into the boat.

Inlet and discharge valves should be bedded down on marine-grade plywood pads, glassed over to give a firm base and distribute the load from the bolts over a wide area of the GRP hull. I used a two-part polysulphide sealant on the bolts and under the valves to give a perfect watertight seal. Make sure all valves are readily accessible as they should always be turned off when you leave the boat.

The 1½in (38mm) plastic pipe used to link the various parts of the system can sometimes be difficult to get over spigots, especially in cold weather. Heat it in boiling water and it softens sufficiently to be slipped on. Although bends are not to be encouraged, the usual plastic pipe sold in chandlers' has very severe limitations on the minimum diameter bends that can be obtained, so I decided to experiment with the products of a firm called Flexible Ducting Ltd of Glasgow. They made a range of ducting products used in industry. Flextract is a smooth-bore lightweight PVC hose with wire helix reinforcing which enables it to be used under low positive or negative pressures. Vinyl end finishes are screwed on to the helix and stainless-steel hose clamps make the joint watertight in seconds. I used the CLD medium-duty hose. It is still in good condition. Heavy-duty grades are available.

## Design for the Holding Tank

If noxious gases are not to build up, good ventilation must be arranged, from a vent pipe.

Waste water from sinks was plumbed with Key Terrain plastic piping system and a constant fall had to be ensured. The 'p' traps under sinks are essential to prevent tank odours getting back to the living space. The shower tray is pumped by means of a small foot-pump into the main pipe falling to the holding tank. Water in the bottom of the shower-tray discharge system also acts as a trap to prevent the back-flow of odours. I fitted the holding tank with a non-mechanical magnetic gauge. This is totally isolated from the sewage. By lifting out a rod, an indicator shows how full the tank is. The system is comparatively complex (Fig 93) and costly to install, but I wanted to test a system that would provide the flexibility to cope with any anticipated legislation. I have found it works extremely well.

Make certain that important panels which give access to pipework and pumps are quickly and easily removed. From Fig 94 you can see how I situated the main holding-tank pump behind the removable cabin steps, so that the tank is pumped out from the shelter of the cabin. In the WC compartment all panels were fixed with raised-head countersunk screws.

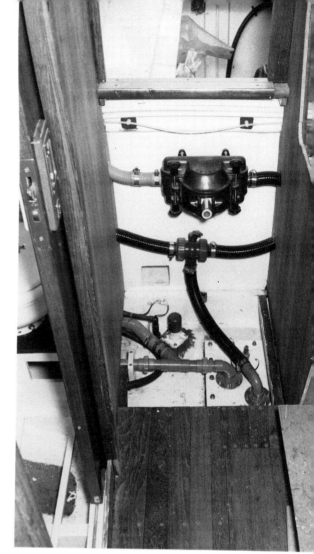

**Fig 93** Holding tank plumbing; above the Patay DD120 pump is the 'fire-wire' on its way to protect the toilet and freshwater pumps

**Fig 94** The main companion steps hide the holding tank plumbing but the tank itself can be emptied from a comfortable position

## Bilge Pumping

When wooden sailing yachts of ancient vintage made a windward passage with the garboard creaking and groaning under the strain, the need for bilge pumping was paramount. In the modern GRP boat the watertightness and integrity of the hull might tempt you to treat bilge pumping as yet another excuse to add a piece of toy equipment. For anyone who has seen how the failure of even a small skin fitting can let in a frightening amount of water in a short time, the need to provide adequate bilge pumping will be obvious.

The provision depends on the size of boat and whether it has flow-through or watertight compartments. Most small craft are open-plan in the bilge area or, at best, the boat is sub-divided by one main bulkhead which is probably not watertight. Should flooding occur, free-flowing water will quickly affect the stability. For this reason, I decided to have four semi-watertight bulkheads on my boat. I say semi-watertight because they are watertight up to a height of just over 1ft (305mm) above the water-line. Any equipment passing through them below that level was made watertight and any above, though not watertight, was made so that little water would pass. With modern sealants the job of making watertight holes for wiring or conduit, passing through bulkheads, is straightforward and helps prevent chafe on the surrounding structure.

## How Many Bilge Pumps?

Boats up to 20ft (6m) or so can have a 1in (25mm) suction pump and a bailer. Larger craft of 20–30ft (6–9.1m), will need at least a 1½in (38mm) suction. It is not worth worrying about the price difference between a 1¼in (32mm) and a 1½in (38mm) model — the bigger the better in an emergency. With watertight compartments, or those like the ones on *Sea Hound,* it is necessary to have pumping arrangements for each compartment. It does involve extra expense but there is no reason why, with two-way valves (or removal of a hose clip on my own boat), one bilge cannot pump two or more compartments. The holding-tank pump can be utilised to pump tank or bilge by means of a diverter valve. A toilet could be used as an emergency pump by inserting a spare length of pipe in the bowl outlet and leading this over the bowl side into the bilge to be cleared. The Lavac toilet system turns into an excellent high-capacity pump when used in this way.

Special considerations are necessary with hull designs that incorporate interior mouldings for furnishing (Fig 95), toilet compartments, galleys and stowage spaces. It is quite possible, and highly probable, that if water gets into this type of boat it will not always drain to one point in the bilge. Some boats are made with composite mouldings that create a single bilge on the interior moulding. Others leave these voids and create serious safety and

**Fig 95** The Sadler 29 has excellent internal mouldings which give the hull great strength; bilge pumping arrangements need to be carefully considered to cater for the many voids

servicing problems. A power boat I came across had this foam filling and all was well until the owner noticed that there was a squelching noise when he trod on the cockpit floor. Eventually, at some cost, it was established that the water in the space was not coming from outside, but was the result of a split in the water tank. The water was seeping through into the foam filling to saturate the space. This worsened when frost froze the water and caused further delamination of the tank and floor. The repair bill was horrific and, for this reason, I do not like foam filling in bilge areas, even though it might help to keep the boat afloat in an emergency. If foam is used, then I would make provision for drains that would allow all spaces trapped within the foam section to be opened up to either a bilge pump or inspection/drain hatch. A portable bilge pump is handy for emptying difficult spaces. *Sea Hound* carries a portable pump that has proved useful for small amounts of water below the suction limits of the built-in pumps.

### Bilge Pumping the Engine Compartment

This is the most vulnerable space in the boat. Inlet valves and plastic hoses to exhaust cooling water are a possible source of flooding.

Most sailing yachts have self-draining cockpits over the engine but water often finds its way below to the engine space. Other boats, especially motor boats with large open cockpits, get a lot of rain-water in the bilges. This has to be pumped out automatically by a bilge-level control switch and automatic pump, or by hand. Cockpit covers keep out a lot of this rain-water and are to be recommended. Water around the engine is bad news for electrical components. Evaporation and, later, condensation makes the worst possible environment. The outside environment, too, is not improved by pumping out bilge oil and fuel. A number of countries have strict laws about the pumping of contaminated bilge water overboard. There are mats available which will soak up oil from the surface of water. The alternative is to pump into the holding tank for shore-side dis-

charge. The best way to ensure that bilge water is reasonably clean is to provide an engine oil drip-tray and see that all seals on the engine are in good condition so that minimum amounts of fuel or oil escape.

Another consideration to be kept in mind is that water is still a good cheap medium to use for dealing with class 'A' fires. Fire also melts plastic hose. Hand bilge pumps are best placed outside the compartment they are expected to empty. This is why single pumps are often located in the cockpit. Automatic and emergency bilge pumps for the engine space should be placed so that they can be worked without opening hatches, and hoses should be kept away from hot pipes and possible fire sources.

Bearing in mind that *Sea Hound* has semi-watertight bulkheads, I used two electric pumps in the engine space: a Stuart Turner bilge pump (550gal (2,500 litres) per hour) and a Rule heavy-duty automatically switched pump with a 1,166gal (5,300 litres) per hour capacity. Two Patay DD120 hand pumps (1,800gal (8,183 litres) per hour if your energy lasts or the panic is serious), pump forward and aft compartments and holding tank (forward compartment pump) or aft and engine compartments when clips are removed or valves changed over.

All pump suctions must be provided with a strum box or water filter so that debris cannot block the pump. When you have finished building the boat, go over it with a vacuum cleaner and remove every shaving, speck of dust, plastic and other rubbish out of the bilges. Many professional builders are guilty of neglecting the areas difficult to reach. The result is blocked pumps when water swills this muck into the main bilge suction. Bilges should be kept as clean as a new pin.

When making provision for bilge-pump outlets, they are best made well above the water-line and with a swan neck that will not let water back into the pump. If they have to be near the water-line, they must be given a full way valve inside the skin fitting. I used swan necks to cut down cost, and had the discharges just below the rubber fender. Beware of plastic fittings that constrict the flow because they are made to take a variety of pipe sizes. Intake size must always match outlet size, and bronze fittings, though more expensive, last longer than plastic and are full flow in design.

**Cockpit Drains**
A self-draining cockpit should be provided on sailing craft so that on either tack, water coming in will drain to the lower side and out of the boat. An 'X' arrangement is usual and sea-cocks must be fitted at the lower skin outlets.

The size of cockpit drains depends on how serious you are about removing the water that gets in the boat. Look at the domestic bath which probably has a 1½in (38mm) drain. Half-fill the bath and see how long it takes to empty. Your bath will be about a quarter of the size of a small yacht's cockpit, so multiply the time by four. When next you go to a boat show, check the drain sizes on most boats. When you recover from the shock and realise that such small drains will probably be blocked with dirt anyway, you will understand why I suggest that four 1½in (38mm) drains — two each to port and starboard — should be considered even for a small (20–25ft (6-7.6m)) sea-going sailing boat. For larger sea-going craft, certainly for those of 30ft (10.4m) or more in length, four 2in (51mm) drains should be considered. Many boatbuilders fit screens to stop large pieces of debris blocking the outlet. The trouble with these is that they seriously restrict flow and negate the advantage of the large drains. If you only intend to go to sea in fine weather, the above recommendations might seem excessive, but it is always pleasing to know that if you do get caught out the boat will cope.

**Installation of Skin Fittings**
Fig 96 shows three skin-fitting installations:

**A** *Above the water-line* for such applications as bilge-pump outlets. Provided there is sufficient height, a swan neck is incorporated to prevent water returning. The diagram shows only a short neck, but a longer one would be more practical. There are one-way valves available to prevent water from returning down the pipe, but if the outlet is high, there should be no worry in this respect. Drains from the gas locker must have a continuous fall from locker bottom down to the skin fitting since gas, heavier than air, must escape and not be impeded. A silicone sealant is used for bedding outlets above the water-line.

**B** *Near but above the water-line* skin fittings should have a gate valve. Applications include exhaust outlets and sailing-boat cockpit drains. The valve is to prevent flooding should a fault develop and waves wash in through the skin fitting. The gate valve has locking nuts. A polysulphide rubber sealant is used when bedding on to the load-spreading marine-plywood base.

**C** *Below the water-line.* Although an engine-cooling water intake with strainer is shown, other types of valve include those for the WC water inlet, WC discharge, holding-tank discharge to sea, echo-sounder and log valves, etc. Again, though it is more expensive, a gate valve (Fig 97) is the safest way to prevent flooding. A polysulphide sealant is used in underwater applications to seal the fitting into place.

All three diagrams have certain installation points that warrant study:

**1** All hose pipe is double clipped with stainless-steel clips.
**2** In a GRP construction, whenever a hole is drilled in the main hull, a marine-grade plywood backing pad is glassed in to reinforce the area around the hole and spread the stress from the fitting-retaining nuts or bolts. The plywood is shaped to the curvature of the hull with a Surform tool which leaves it nice and scarred. Edges must be tapered so that no hard spots are created. The pads are stuck into position with epoxide resin adhesive or wet mat and a polymer resin before being glassed over with a minimum of three layers of mat.
**3** In certain cases, illustrated in Fig 96C, it is necessary to form the bed at a definite

angle to the curvature of the hull. Echo-sounder valves have to be installed within certain parameters so that the sender gives accurate results. The plywood pad has to be built up to get the correct angle for through-bolting. The GRP on the outside of the hull may well have to be ground back to accommodate the outlet flange. This can be faired in with an epoxide putty at a later stage or, if only small as in the figure, rubber sealant will do the job. When the pads are fully cured, cut the hole with a hole-saw in an electric drill. Drill a small diameter pilot hole from the inside. Now cut from the inside just through the plywood and stop before you get to the GRP. Push a piece of wire through the pilot hole so that you can locate it easily on the outside of the hull. Retreat to the outside with the hole-saw and drill in. By this method you will get a clean hole on both sides, with no danger of delaminating the

**Fig 96** Installation of skin fittings

ply/glass pad or chipping out the gel coat on the outside. Drill to get a clearance. This is because you should seal the surface of any hole cut through GRP laminate with an epoxide resin glue or polymer resin. This is to prevent the ingress of water along the fibre structure. You also need room for sealant and if you should have to remove the fitting at some future date, an overtight fit would be hard to shift.

4   Before final fitting with sealant, always do a dry run. This is to ensure that you assemble items in the correct order. In B and C the threaded skin fitting is passed from outside, the inside securing nut put on loosely and then the valve or valve strainer screwed on. This is important when the valve has to give a specific lead to the hose. The gate valve or gate-valve strainer is locked up first and while it is held in the correct position, the skin fitting nut is tightened into place. When you have the assembly procedure right, get the sea-

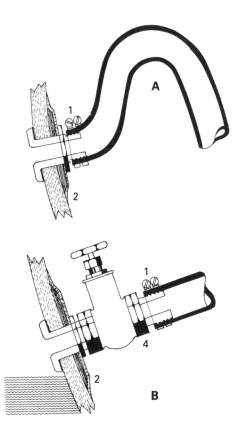

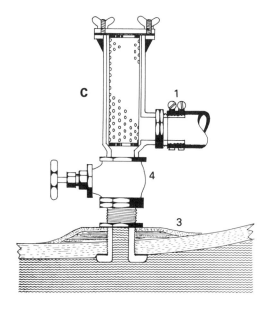

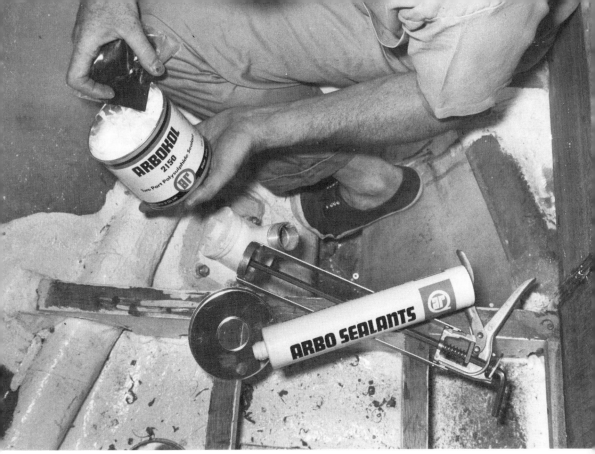

lant and do it for real.

5   Clean off spare sealant right away with the proper cleaner both inside and outside.

## Bolted Skin Fittings

Certain types of valve skin fittings, such as the heavy-duty manganese bronze rotary valves used by Brooks & Gatehouse, or WC discharge valves by Blakes, need four bolts to secure them. A washer plate or, in some cases, a cast water strainer is used on the outside of the hull. This plate is used for marking out the position of the main valve hole and the four bolt holes from the outside. The problem is to make sure the outside positioning is also correct for the inside position — not too near bulkheads or other obstructions. With clear GRP mouldings, shine an electric torch through at the exact position of the valve from the inside. With the torch held by an assistant, or taped into position, mark the outside with the plate. The most difficult part is to drill four perfectly parallel holes through the reinforced ply/GRP plate so that bolts fit properly. Again, a dry run is best before final assembly of the fitting.

**Fig 97** The gate valve safely fitted using rubber sealant ensures that the depth-sounder transducer can be removed without any water getting into the boat

## Keels

The design function of the boat's keel has no place in this book, except that you should consider its function as something on which the boat sits at a drying mooring. When selecting the hull, make sure the keel is capable of taking the bouncing about on the ground four times out of every twenty-four hours, without poking out the bottom of the boat. A cruising boat, whether power or sail, is not a joy to own if it cannot take the ground comfortably and in a position which allows normal activities to be carried on while she is dried out. Boats with long straight keels can have more reinforcing in their topsides to take legs. Many sailing yachtsmen select twin-bilge keels so that the boat remains upright on a falling tide. The home boatbuilder must be certain that there is sufficient strength in the hull and keel joint to take the enormous strains the area is subject to. There have been excellent designs which were all right when the yacht took up a normal level position on the ground and the stress and weight were shared between the supporting members, but they failed disastrously when, by accident, the excess weight was forced on to one or other of the keels.

I looked carefully at the possibility of providing bilge keels on my own boat. They do give some extra protection to the hull if you accidentally take the ground, but I was more concerned whether the very round bilge hull form would roll a lot. As this was a prototype design I had the bilge keel reinforcing areas moulded in but decided not to proceed with the keels themselves, which would be made out of wood. The final decision was not to install them as we calculated we would lose speed and the effect on such keels would probably be minimal. After trials and cruising I have found the hull form extremely stable and I am pleased that the extra touch of speed — probably only $1/4$ to $1/2$ knot — was not sacrificed.

You might have the option of a loose keel provided the hull is adequately reinforced. The complications involved need serious consideration. You can save some cost, but balance this against the cost of lifting the hull and juggling with its heavy weight, particularly if you are working alone. Once again, I would recommend the moulder as the best person to fit this item.

Whoever does fit the keel must have the best possible specification keel bolts. Yachtsmen have nightmares about keel bolt failure and the keel dropping off. Recently, when talking to a surveyor who had seen this happen to a yacht, he told me that five different metals had been used for the bolts. While battles have been lost for the want of a nail, it can equally be said that boats have been lost for want of a keel bolt. Follow the designer's specification and order from a supplier who will sell you precisely what is specified.

In many modern designs the ballast is encapsulated in a resin and is poured into the keel space. Moulders offer the option of incorporating this ballast at their moulding shop or selling the GRP hull mouldings and ballast materials for home completion.

Once *Sea Hound* was afloat, I had to adjust her trim by adding 100lb (45kg) of pig iron which I obtained from the local iron foundry. Loose ballast iron is a menace to keep rust-free, so before I put it in the bilges, it was given the full epoxy paint treatment, then wrapped and sealed in polythene sheet.

Keel bolts should be fully accessible so that they can be inspected regularly and withdrawn at proper intervals. Quite often one sees keel bolts and rudder fittings completely glassed in, which might make them waterproof, but impossible to get out without chopping away half the boat first.

## Rudder Installation

The rudder is a vital item. You should be sure that its strength and installation is nothing less than perfect.

I am assuming that the supplier of the hull will furnish you with a rudder of correct area and with fittings which are suited in dimension and strength to the hull form. If he does not supply the hardware himself, he should advise on where it can be obtained. Even though the basic rudder is supplied, you may need to buy in other parts, or have a local engineering firm make them up for you.

Transom-hung rudders have the advantage that the bearing surface at least can be easily inspected and, on most small craft, the rudder can be easily removed. They do not take up space inside the hull when there is tiller steering over the transom, and they do not have to be put through a hole in the bottom of the boat. Usually they are hung on a pair of pintles (Fig 98A) and gudgeons (B). On heavy rudders which are carried down to the level of the skeg, a fitting at the bottom of the rudder on to the skeg gives a third pivot point. The pintle (A) used to have a pair of straps on either side to secure it to a wooden rudder, but in GRP constructions an internal strap and, sometimes, a reinforcing web are fitted. This is very much more streamlined, but I do not like the idea of metal fittings which are encased to be under water. You cannot check them for corrosion and fatigue. Furthermore, when

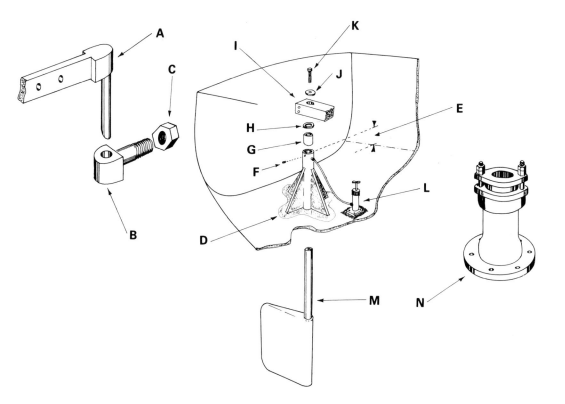

**Fig 98** Details of rudder installation

they do go wrong or you have to remove them to get at other work, it is not pleasant to have to smash off the GRP first.

When you put either pintles or gudgeons through the transom, large areas of reinforcing marine plywood should be glassed in. This might be better done at the factory, but it must be done in order to distribute stress. The nut (C) should have a large plate washer fitted under it and then locked. A pintle is usually used at the bottom of a small rudder, pointing upwards. This is the one to watch for corrosion. Silicone rubber sealants should be used on fittings passing through the transom. Monel or bronze are ideal materials provided you get most metal fittings around the stern area of the same materials and then give them cathodic protection.

The spade rudder (M) is fitted through the bottom of the boat. The central part of Fig 98 shows the arrangement used when the top of the bearing tube can be brought well above the water-line (E). The installation and reinforcing of the tube (D) should be properly carried out and on my own boat I had it done at the factory, because I

wanted maximum strength. The method, if you are doing it yourself, is to drill a pilot hole in a position taken off the plans well before any cabin fittings are built. The tube is made of glass wound on to a former covered in release agent to get a thickness of ³⁄₈in (9mm) or so. The internal diameter is large enough to allow Tufnol bearings (G) to be inserted in the tube located with grub screws (F) into holes drilled and tapped in the tube when it has cured. A Tufnol bearing to take the main wear from the weight of the rudder (H) is used under the tiller arm (I). A key way cut in the rudder stock and the tiller arm prevents lateral movement between the two. If you fear that a clamping action might loosen and let the rudder drop out of the boat, then the large diameter washer (J) (larger than the overall size of the main tube) is bolted (K) into the top of the rudder stock which has been tapped to take it.

In some designs it is impractical to carry the rudder-bearing tube well above the water-line and a different arrangement using a watertight rudder gland (N) will be used. The gland has a female thread in the bottom which takes the rudder tube.

Some accurate measuring is called for with rudders that receive extra support from a skeg since the exact positioning of the tube, so that the rudder runs parallel to the skeg, is necessary. It is almost like lining engine beds up with plumb bobs and tight wires to get perfect alignment.

After the pilot hole has been drilled and position checked, cut a hole in the hull with the hole-saw to take the rudder tube. The gland is now screwed on to the tube and if a suitable bolting platform is not provided (and it often is in the form of a platform linking the seating either side of the cockpit or the bottom of a locker) then you build a marine-ply platform and glass it in, ensuring that you have provided a hole to take the tube and that this hole is perfectly in line with the first one to give the correct angle. When cured, the rudder tube is passed up through the hull and screwed into the bottom of the gland. The gland is now temporarily bolted to its platform. Provided you have made the platform at the correct height, there should be a bit of tube outside the hull which will later need cutting off flush and finishing with epoxide resin putty or a dough mix of glass-fibre and resin. When the temporary installation has been checked, the tube can be glassed in and the gland bolted to the platform, using a silicone rubber sealant under the flange. The space around the tube should be filled gradually to prevent exothermic heat from building up as this would crack the resin. The weight of cloth to get sufficient strength should be specified in the drawing, but at least $3/8$in (9mm) thick, upwards, will be needed. On my boat the reinforcing around the rudder is $1/2$in (13mm) and the supporting web $1/2$in (13mm) thick to match general strengthening.

Many rudder installations depend on water for lubrication. Ensure that if you are using Tufnol or other plastics which expand as they absorb water, you engineer them to be a little larger than the shafting they take. For installations with tubes and glands, I really prefer to see them grease-lubricated. The rudder gland has packing material in it which will last longer if it is kept lubricated with a normal underwater grease. In the past, and perhaps even today, packing incorporating graphite was used. It is not often realised that the carbon in graphite will set up an excellent electrolytic cell to corrode metals around it with indecent haste. I use the remote greasers (L) to lubricate rudder shafts and bearings.

# 8 SAFETY AND NAVIGATION EQUIPMENT

The safety of both crew and boat is the responsibility of the skipper. The burden of responsibility can be lightened if you make sure that the boat is safe and is kept that way.

## Fire Protection
Fire is a frightening thing in the confines of a small boat; you must take every precaution to see that your boat is not a fire hazard.

## Design
When you are building to someone else's plans you must make sure that the designer has given thought to the avoidance of stowage spaces, coamings, hollow double bottoms and buoyancy chambers that could house inflammable materials or accidentally collect explosive vapours. The initial design should place gas-cylinder lockers away from heat sources, refrigerators with a gas pilot-light away from hatches, and paint lockers away from the cockpit areas where cans of varnish are dumped on top of the engine exhaust-pipe.

There nearly always has to be a compromise on a small boat. Batteries, for example, are best kept out of the engine space but might have to be housed there to keep cable runs short. To compensate for this there must be excellent mechanical and natural ventilation so that there is no possibility of a gas build-up above the batteries.

Even though you might be working to someone else's plan, it very likely does not go into the fine details of installation. This is where you can make sure all risks are minimised in the planning of electrical, gas, fuel, exhaust, heating and cooking arrangements. It is better to prevent a fire than to cure it.

## Selection of Materials
Materials can minimise fire hazard, for example, cabin head-lining materials. These are available, as already mentioned, in fire-retardant qualities. Avoid those with foam backings that could give off toxic gas in a fire. Whatever finishes you are using — upholstery, paints, varnishes, head-linings, mattresses — find out how they are likely to behave in a fire. Most manufacturers will give guidance, otherwise contact the Fire Prevention Officer of the local Fire Brigade. Do not buy anything that is doubtful. There are always alternatives, although they might be more difficult to locate.

The resin part of a glass-reinforced plastic construction is inflammable and, set alight, will burn a boat down to the waterline. I looked into the possibility of Tylers moulding my boat in a fire-retardant resin. These resins usually incorporate a chemical such as antimony which interferes with flame propagation. The process of the decomposition of a material in heat to produce flame is a complex one, but in certain applications a fire retardant is ideal. Unfortunately, these resins do not weather well in boats. They are, however, worth considering for the outside laminations of GRP fuel tanks and gas-cylinder lockers where they are not exposed to the weather.

An alternative to a loaded resin is one with an intumescent resin coating. This type of finish foams up to provide a barrier between the flame and the resin surface. It is generally self-extinguishing with a small flame spread from the original source of ignition. These surface treatments, such as Scott Bader's Crystic Fireguard, are excellent for small areas, but should not be used where items may have to be joined to treated surfaces. This may be a problem if you wish to do modifications at a later date. Fire-retardant paints can be both decorative and practical for fire-protection purposes.

## Protective Design

The next step is to provide a system to put out any fire that starts. Three things are essential to a fire:

1   Fuel. Any combustible material — bedding, engine fuel, woodwork — upon reaching the temperature for ignition, will start breaking down into chemicals which continue to create more heat, more breakdown and spread of flame.
2   High temperature to reach ignition point and continue the chemical process.
3   Oxygen from the air.

Take away any one of these three and the fire goes out. Fire-extinguishing systems are based on this precept. In some, the chemicals in the extinguisher interfere with the production of the chemicals that cause flame propagation. Others, like water, drastically lower the temperature to below ignition point and some, like carbon dioxide, displace the air and rob the flame of the oxygen it needs. Many fire-fighting systems have a combination of these properties.

Fires are classified into the following types:

A   Combustible solids: wood, textiles — curtains, bedding, upholstery.
B   Liquid fires: fuels, oils, paraffin, paint, solvents, fat, etc.
C   Gas fires: LPG, propane and butane.
D   Burning metals, such as magnesium (we need not concern ourselves with this).
E   Electrical fires which will involve all or some of the categories from A to D.

Different fire-fighting media have been developed to fight specific types of fire, but in the confines of a boat all types are so quickly involved you must think carefully about the most effective methods. Your choice will be based on:

1   *Water* There is a lot of it about and it is good for a class A fire. However, it is deadly with electrics, especially high-voltage systems, where it could conduct the power back to you and finish your fire-fighting career for good. It will cool gas cylinders but is useless for putting out a gas fire. A last resort for class A fires only. If used in quantity it will flood the boat and affect stability, so keep bilge pumps going.
2   *Carbon dioxide* is a gas which displaces oxygen. If it displaces oxygen from your lungs, you will die as well as the fire. It is good on type A, B, C and E fires. When any gas-extinguishing medium is used, give consideration to the volumes of space to be protected: 3.9cu yd (3m³) of carbon dioxide or other gas will not put out a 13cu yd (10m³) fire, especially if ventilation fans are left on, and the gas is whisked away as soon as it is pumped out. For small boats I favour the more modern fluorine compounds.
3   *Bromochlorodifluoromethane (BCF)* and *bromotrifluoromethane (BTM)* Both have big advantages over carbon dioxide in that their low toxicity and high efficiency make them ideal for fighting fires in small craft. Type A, B, C and E fires can be dealt with. Being gaseous, they are clean in use and do not leave any deposit, so that there is no powder to get into an engine air intake or carburettor. The important advantage is that they need a lower saturation level than carbon dioxide, so small extinguishers will douse a larger fire. A reputable manufacturer will advise on the correct size of extinguisher for either a fixed or portable system to protect each compartment on the boat.
4   *Dry powder* is available in two forms. The older and cheaper type was based on sodium bicarbonate, potassium bicarbonate and potassium chloride. More efficient is ICI Monnex dry powder (monoammonium phosphate). Dry powders are effective on B, C and E type fires while Monnex will deal with A, B, C and E type fires.
5   *Fire blanket* for smothering type A, B, C and E fires and also useful if a person's clothing has caught fire or to smother a pan of fat on the galley stove.

**6** *Foam* deals with type A and B fires, but is not often used on small craft. Although this is an excellent medium to fight fuel fires, it is messy afterwards and could prejudice starting the engine. If you are at sea you would have to get the boat and crew safely to harbour after the fire.

These fire-fighting media are available in portable canisters or, for all but the blanket, can be built into the boat as a fixed system.

Local authorities usually lay down minimum equipment standards for craft operating in their area. Table 12 sets out the requirements of the Thames Conservancy, but this, while satisfying the authority, should be regarded as a minimum requirement. As mentioned earlier, the effective use of BCF, BTM and $CO^2$ depends on the medium reaching specific saturation levels related to the volume of a compartment. While the figures in the table assume reasonable correlation between size of the boat and anticipated size of a compartment, they cannot always be assumed to be adequate for a specific application. In many cases, fright makes for poor aim of an extinguisher into the seat of the fire and ventilation can reduce saturation to an alarming degree, depending on the site of the fire, strength of the wind and direction in relation to the position of the boat.

If you wish to provide a first-class fire-protection system, you should really have a fixed fire-extinguisher system for high-risk areas — the engine space, electrical distribution space — backing this with hand extinguishers. Go to a reputable specialist fire-fighting firm, where you will be given sound scientific advice. Better this than buying a few hand extinguishers through a doubtful service and blithely imagining the boat is fully protected.

The fire-fighting system on *Sea Hound* was designed and supplied by Chubb Fire Security of Sunbury-on-Thames who market their products under the Pyrene label. There are two fixed systems, the first to protect the electrical distribution area on the main bulkhead, and toilet compartment electric pumps (fresh water and toilet). The unit selected was the Pyrene Kill-Fire automatic BCF system which would protect 90cu ft (2.55m³) with its 3lb (1.36kg) cylinder. The nylon tube from the cylinder softens and bursts when it is subjected to flame or temperature in excess of 300°F (150°C). The advantage is that it bursts at the seat of the fire source as well as creating an inert space around the area as saturation takes place. In Fig 99 I am pictured installing the cylinder inside the steering console in the wheel-house. It is vital *not* to install any extinguisher inside the actual compartment that it is to protect. You fight a fire from outside a compartment to avoid noxious gases from cumbustion and with a fixed cylinder containing gases under high pressure, you want them

*Table 12:* FIRE EXTINGUISHER REQUIREMENTS *(Thames Water Authority)*

| Length of Craft | Min No of Extinguishers | Types of Extinguisher and Minimum Total Capacity | | |
|---|---|---|---|---|
| | | Dry Powder or BCF | CO² | Foam |
| Up to 16ft (5m) | 1 | 3.3lb (1.5kg) | 4.96lb (2.25kg) | 2gal (9 litres) |
| 16–25ft (5–8m) | 2 | 5.5lb (2.5kg) | 9.9lb (4.5kg) | 4gal (18 litres) |
| 26–36ft (8–11m) | 2 | 7.7lb (3.5kg) | 12lb (5.5kg) | 4gal (18 litres) |
| Over 36ft (11m) | 3 | 12.1lb (5.5kg) | 20.94lb (9.5kg) | 8gal (36 litres) |
| Minimum size of extinguisher | | 2.21lb (1kg) | 4.96lb (2.25kg) | 2gal (9 litres) |

a copper pipe and fire nozzle system supplied from a 4in (102mm) diameter cylinder filled with 6lb (2.72kg) of BCF. For ventilation purposes we calculated the free volume of engine space to be 190cu ft (5.37m³); therefore if 1lb (454g) of BCF (BTM) protects 40cu ft (1.13m³), in theory 240cu ft (6.8m³) can be protected with a 6lb (2.72kg) cylinder. The excess is to allow for some loss by ventilation outlets, but we would have to switch off fans before releasing the gas. The cylinder was located in the aft cabin (Fig 55) again, outside of the engine space it was to protect and connected to a 5⁄8in (16mm) pipe system with Enots fittings. Full plans for the system were provided by Pyrene and it was easy to fit. The knuckle valve to operate the release of the gas was actuated by means of a bronze wire cable led through pulleys and Egatube plastic conduit to a hand-pull immediately inside the aft cabin door. Although it is near my head when I am occupying the bunk, it is sufficiently out of the way of children who might accidentally discharge the system.

These fixed systems are backed up by three hand extinguishers. One, a general-purpose powder extinguisher, is situated in the wheel-house, and two small 1lb (454g) BCF extinguishers are sited near the galley and in the after cabin. It has been argued that such small fire extinguishers, which would not be accepted by some authorities, are useless. My argument is that these small Pyrene units are instantly to hand and would douse a small fire if used quickly enough.

Although manufacturers have made progress in providing extinguishers that are made of metals and plastics that will stand up to the corrosive environment of a boat, this aspect should be looked into by the purchaser. A seized corroded valve is hardly efficient. Extinguishers must also be given weather protection as mechanisms are not waterproof. Some plastics are affected by strong sunlight and will deteriorate if left exposed to it, especially in tropical climates. Unfortunately, in the UK we are more likely to suffer from rain corrosion than from the ultra-violet rays in sunlight.

**Fig 99** The Kill-Fire BCF extinguisher with its nylon 'fire-wire' which protects the electrical distribution board on the other side of the bulkhead; note the strength of the Mathway steering system

to work normally and not explode as they would in a fire. The nylon fire-wire (16.4ft (5m) long) was led through the bulkhead, down to the electrical distribution board and then across the bulkhead to the toilet compartment where it wound its way round and past the pumps. Installation was very easy following the maker's instructions. It is ideal for the amateur to install. A fire-warning box with test circuit is wired on to the cylinder but, to be honest, you would certainly hear high-pressure BCF going off if you had a fire. However, as it is a pressure-drop switch it would tell you if a slow leak had developed and the cylinder had accidentally emptied when you were away from the boat.

The engine compartment was fitted with

The hand extinguishers should be one of the first items on your shopping-list when the hull is delivered. Accidents with blow-lamps and electrical misdemeanours could cause you to lose the boat before it is built. Fixed systems are built into the boat as convenient. After that, it is up to you to make sure your crew know how to use the fire-fighting equipment you have aboard when sea trials start.

**The Log**

No matter what degree of sophisticated electronic gear you are planning for the boat, the simpler it is, the safer you are likely to be. When all electronic gear fails you can still resort to log, lead and lookout. Perhaps it is cheating to employ an electronic log and depth-sounder, but for sea-going boats I would certainly advise that you get the very best log and depth-sounder that you can afford.

The log is more often than not of the impeller type. A small rotating impeller in the wake stream or flow of water past the hull produces a small magnetic impulse. This is fed to an amplifier circuit which then converts it to a display. Sometimes logs give speed only but, more usually, distance travelled and speed.

As mentioned later, when calibrating instruments it is as well to relate speed from the log to engine rpm so that should the log fail, the dead-reckoning navigator can fall back on a distance and speed table.

Apart from the type of log that is streamed from the stern, many logs need some kind of underwater housing which keeps the sender unit in close contact with the water. When you are buying, check that the manufacturer is prepared to advise on the precise location of the sender unit. Most will be pleased to give you the information as they want their units to give the accuracy and service it was designed for. I sent away plans of my boat to Brooks & Gatehouse and they marked in all the details necessary. Their publication *Underwater Housings — Selection, Siting and Installation* is well worth reading before you go out and buy or design this part of the boat. Location varies with different hull forms. In sailing and displacement boats, where pitching is the likely source of the impeller being forced into inaccuracy through being lifted out of the water, the site will be towards the forefoot, but sufficiently low to ensure that it is always immersed. It will usually be on the centre-line of sailing boats, ahead of the ballast or fin keel but, in some cases, it might be worth installing twin units and having a gravity-operated selector switch. If a single unit is used, sailing trials will assess the performance on either tack, as differences of several per cent in the readings can be created. In planing craft, the log unit must be sited aft of the point where hull meets water at the top planing speed, and near to the centre-line. This will bring the unit well aft and perhaps close to the engine installation. This introduces another factor, that of interference from electrical sources.

Logs, especially the electro-magnetic type, can be badly influenced by spurious radiation from generators and other sources indicated in the section dealing with interference. Site the unit as far from engines and shafting as is practicable in fast boats. In all craft keep cables connecting sender to control unit well away from other wiring. The siting of the control unit must be at a safe distance from the compass. What is 'safe' should be specified by the manufacturer. 18in (457mm) from the compass is the distance given by Brooks & Gatehouse for the repeater units for log and depth-sounder. I needed them slightly closer, so housed them in mu-metal housings which provide screening, so reducing the safe distance to 8in (203mm).

The sender unit must be away from water turbulence caused by other skin fittings — depth-sounder, toilet outlets and inlets and engine water inlets. These could produce inaccurate readings. If you allow weed to grow on the boat's bottom this, too, will cause deterioration of the log's accuracy during the season. With senders that are permanently in position, the whole unit can become weed-bound and necessitate slipping of the boat to clean it up. This brings me to another design consideration, the underwater housing for the sender.

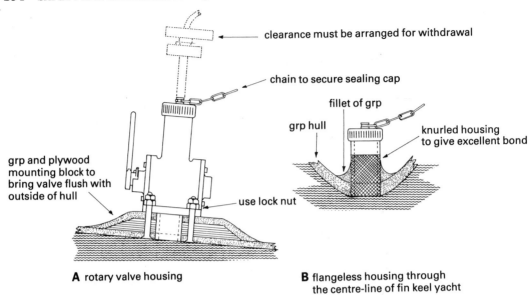

clearance must be arranged for withdrawal

chain to secure sealing cap

fillet of grp

grp hull

knurled housing
to give excellent bond

grp and plywood
mounting block to
bring valve flush with
outside of hull

use lock nut

**A** rotary valve housing

**B** flangeless housing through
the centre-line of fin keel yacht

**Fig 100** Valves for log or depth-sounder

The fixed type is the cheapest and will produce the most problems. A valveless housing should only be used up to a maximum depth of 3ft (1m) below the water-line. Below that depth a valved housing must be fitted. If it is not fouled up it will probably get knocked off when the boat hits a lump of floating debris or gets lifted out for the winter. The projection, though small, is vulnerable. Valveless housings (Fig 100B) are the next least expensive. The sender unit can be removed at the cost of letting water into the boat until you can get the cap on. This type is often designed with a retracting facility that withdraws the impeller into the housing. This does inhibit some weed growth.

The best but most expensive unit to hold the sender is the rotary valve housing (Fig 100A). This allows the sender unit to be kept perfectly clean and inboard when the boat is not in use and it is only a matter of seconds to remove the cap from the housing, insert the sender head and open the valve. The operation does not let any water into the boat and, if damage is sustained, it can easily be repaired without slipping the boat. The same considerations apply to the housing of the transducer of the depth-sounders, although some of these have no need for a hole in the bottom as they are mounted inside the hull. With valveless housings that partially retract the impeller or transducer, and for all units housed in valved housings that allow them to be fully retractable, you will have to arrange internal cabinet and flooring to give proper access. Allowance must be made for clearance heights to remove the impeller or transducer. Convenient hatchways in the cabin sole or a cupboard can be utilised. I placed the transducer in the cupboard under the sink and the log valve under the forward floor hatch.

**Fitting a VHF Radio**
In recent years there has been a huge upsurge in the fitting of VHF radio sets. What used to be a luxury has, like so much electronic gear, come down in price. It is also an important safety factor. With visual watch by coastguards decreasing each year and radio communication being the key to successful rescue at sea, the time is fast approaching when anyone who goes to sea should fit one. When you are building your boat you will find no doubt, as I did, that money is tight and a radio seems to be a luxury. If you cannot afford one initially, then you should make provision for its future fitting.

The following points should be considered:

*Cost* of the set in relation to anticipated 'down time'. This is a euphemism for the time much electronic gear spends at the repair shop. Talk to other yachtsmen about their sets and find out which are the well-made ones that function for years and those that spend a great deal of time not working at all.

*Spurious noise* rejection characteristics of the set. Fortunately, the general radio interference produced by a boat and equipment are out of the VHF reception band, unless you have a modern high performance outboard with electronic ignition or run windscreen-wipers or other non-suppressed electric motors just near the aerial cable. The better set, which is well-designed, has good component layout and balanced sophisticated circuits, will have a better rejection performance than the cheaper set.

## Aerial Selection

The most sophisticated VHF radio set will not attain its designed performance unless it has a suitable aerial and it is correctly mounted. Again, prices vary enormously but the main factor governing choice is the anticipated mounting site. Deck mounting on top of a cabin roof or wheel-house demands quite a different type of aerial from that which will perform well at the top of the mast. With VHF transmission and receiving, the higher the aerial, the longer the range, for it is essentially a 'line of sight' system governed by horizon distance. Line of sight is not quite correct; while light travels in a straight line, VHF radio waves tend to curve slightly. Thus, in the estimation of range calculations shown below, 30 per cent is added to the distance to allow for the curvature. Deck-mounted aerials are usually of the whip type — long and expensive. If a mast is available this should be utilised to get the range and save in aerial cost.

Using a nautical almanac with Distance to the Horizon tables, you can work out the anticipated working range. *Sea Hound's* mast is 16ft (4.8m) at the top above sea level, therefore:

Distance to the sea horizon at 16ft (4.8m) = 4.6 miles
Reliable range = 4.6 miles + 30 per cent = 6 miles

Add to this the range of the other VHF station, eg the local coast guard station, in my case Brixham Coast Guard, Berry Head:

Berry Head: 220ft (67m) above sea level
Distance to the horizon = 17 miles
Reliable range = 17 miles + 30 per cent = 22 miles
Total theoretical range: 28 miles

It is interesting to make this calculation and note that even by doubling the height of the mast the theoretical range would only increase from 28 miles to 30.5 miles — an increase of only 9 per cent. The matter does not end there, though, for many transmissions and receptions are from boats within your horizon and extra height is then of importance:

Distance to the horizon + 30 per cent at 16ft (4.8m) = 6 miles
Distance to the horizon + 30 per cent at 32ft (9.7m) = 8.45 miles

This shows an increase in range of 41 per cent, not counting the range of the other boat and it does give the installer some comparison to work on, so that if the site for the aerial has to be a compromise the best one can be chosen.

Vulnerability of the aerial to damage during storage of the mast in winter, or problems of space for it when so many mast heads are cluttered with wind direction and other gear, should be considered. I chose the V-Tronix Heliflex aerial which had been given a technical performance test to show that it was, at only 6in (152mm) in length, 'barely distinguishable from that of a standard full length end-fed dipole' (which would be about 4½ft (1.4m) long). I also checked the materials the V-Tronix aerials are made from and found that the manufacturer used only the best materials that would stand up to the weathering and corrosive environment of

**Fig 101** Clipping the V-Tronix emergency aerial in place in the forward cabin

the top of a sea-going boat's mast.

In addition to a main aerial which could be carried away, I fitted an emergency aerial in the main cabin in the second position for the VHF set. The second position is necessary for safe storage, as no valuable items should be left in an open wheelhouse. For the emergency aerial I chose the completely self-contained V-Tronix Flareflex, which is another helical aerial stored in a tube like a hand flare (Fig 101).

**Aerial and Power Cables**

The performance of any VHF set is dependent on it having a first-class power supply free from interference and an aerial cable linking the antenna and the set which must be totally uncompromising in both design and installation. The usual cable suggested in the UK for the aerial is type RG 58 CU, a low-cost cable, flexible and easy to run in the tight spaces found in a boat. Like all cables, it suffers from power loss related to length and this is usually specified as 3db per 20m; in other words, you lose half your transmitting power in a 20m

cable run. It sounds quite alarming when you think that your transmitter puts out 25w of transmitting power and the aerial cable immediately loses 12w of it. However, when talking of power in radio terms the loss refers to logarithmic terms, not linear. Thus, although we talk of a 50 per cent loss or thereabouts, in radio terms this loss would be barely noticeable. This is not to say that you should be unconcerned and make a slipshod installation for, in an emergency, poor workmanship could lose another chunk of transmitting power that would, in turn, lose vital range. If longer runs have to be coped with, then type RG 213 cable must be used. In short runs it only gives a marginally better performance but in the longer run, although it is difficult to install, losses are less than RG 58 CU.

Whichever type of cable is chosen as most suitable, it should still be run the shortest possible route between aerial and set. In designing the run for *Sea Hound*'s aerial cable I had two alternatives: I could either take it down the mast, through the engine space and up to the set, or down the forestay rigging from the aerial through the wheelhouse roof and down to the set. The internal run would give better weather protection but it would pass the engine's generating system on the starboard side making it vulnerable to interference. More joints would mean that if there was slight tarnishing of contacts, or soldering was not perfect on the connection, impedance would be increased. The wheelhouse route would be exposed to the weather, the cable would still need a coaxial deck plug and would pass near the starboard wiper motor. However, the Wynn wiper motor was fully suppressed and the V-Tronix deck socket was made of first-class materials and easy for the amateur to assemble. Cable loss for RG 58 CU coaxial cable is given as 0.15 db/m so the calculation to check the best cable run was:

Forestay run = 3m = 0.45db = 10 per cent loss
Through hull run = 8m = 1.2db = 24 per cent loss

The forestay run was chosen and carefully protected from chafe. It was fixed to the stainless-steel rigging at 6in (152mm) intervals with self-amalgamating rubber tape. Hard fixing, such as with plastic cable ties, must be avoided as these will dig into the cable and be a source of real problems. If a nick is created by accidental damage or chafe on the outer insulation of a coaxial cable, moisture will reach the outer conducting braid which will act like a wick throughout its length. This will dramatically increase cable loss.

You should give as much attention to the power supply to the set as to the aerial cable. Voltage drop and radio interference from other sources picked up by the cable are the problems.

Voltage drop is particularly important with radio telephones as manufacturers have a cunning way of rating their sets. For example, one manufacturer quotes a 25w output but, in small print, states that this is when the set is receiving 13.5v to power it. Voltage from any battery, even when it is in excellent condition, varies. When charging, it might well be receiving 14.5v, but if it has been left for some time this may drop to 11.5v or so. Nominally, it is about 12v. However, at 12v, this particular set will only deliver 20w output. In a poor installation losses can mount up. In Fig 102 I am pictured using a multi-meter to check that provisionally run cables had a full 12v plus and that the polarity was identified. Like so much electronic equipment, my Demek RS 8000 set is designed to blow its fuse if you connect the terminals with the incorrect polarity. For deck

**Fig 102** Checking the polarity of the electrical supply to the VHF cabin operating position with a Multi-meter; this also indicates whether there is a full 12v in the line

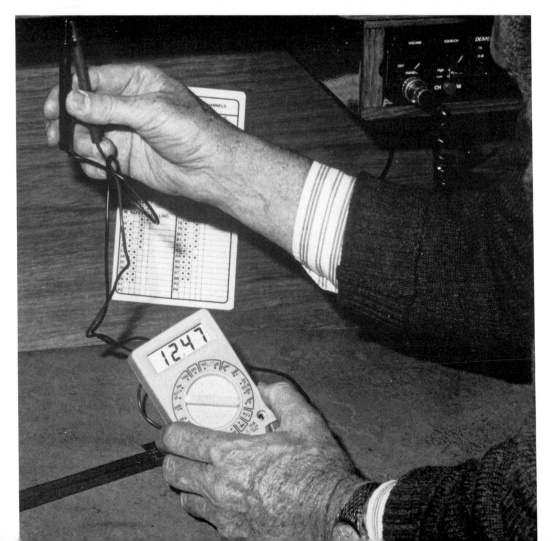

socket connections, it is wise to select unequal-size pin-plugs and sockets so that once correct polarity is identified there can be no accidental misconnection that would blow a fuse or worse.

To avoid interference from the power supply cable, some authorities suggest direct wiring to the battery. I found by tests that I could safely wire into the main distribution board, but I still gave the cable its own circuit breaker.

### Aerial Cable Deck Socket

The deck socket has to be matched to the 50 ohm cable and must be watertight with perfect connections. I first turned a mounting pad on my workshop lathe in teak. This was secured on the wheel-house roof with three screws from below and sealed on with Arbosil 1081 (Fig 49). The lower plate of the deck connector was then passed over the coaxial cable ready to be bedded down with the same sealant when the soldered connection was made. Soldering quality is important. A poor, dry joint will ruin the low impedance connection. I learned to get the solder on to the joint immediately it was off the supply coil. If you hang about, the solder oxidises and this makes for a poor joint. The system is: let solder run on to the iron and then flick it off to get a good tinning. Immediately run new solder on to the iron and then on to the joint. To be durable and efficient solder must actually run into the joints and not just sit on the surface.

### Licensing for Boat and Radio Operator

It is illegal in the UK to operate a radio transmitter without proper licensing. Full information is given in the booklet *Maritime Radio Services for Yachts and Small Craft,* published by the Post Office External Communications Executive, Union House, St Martin's-le-Grand, London EC1A 1AR. Once licensed and the boat launched, a full test programme can be undertaken. A friend with a VHF installation on his boat is needed. Telephone your local coast guard to arrange a test transmission.

Tests I made were as follows:

1   At anchor, ship to ship with all other electrics off. This tests quality of transmission and reception with minimal ship-borne interference.
2   As above, but switching on one power consumption source at a time, engine-room fans, windscreen-wipers, etc, to see if they have any interference effects.
3   Under way, all off except, of course, the engine generating system. Then, with items switched on.
4   Yacht to coastguard — long and short range.

All tests except the third section gave excellent results. I did have one problem that I had never seen mentioned in any book or yachting magazine, but once I started asking questions with electronics manufacturers it was suggested that I was stirring up an electronic hornets' nest!

The problem was that when transmitting, the signal interfered with the auto-pilot, putting the boat 10° off-course to starboard. I was into a problem area that should not put the amateur off asking questions, but perhaps we should hear more about it from manufacturers.

### Spurious Emission and Reception

Electronic equipment has circuits which can sometimes radiate signals to affect other apparatus (spurious emission) or which can be received and affect performance (spurious reception). Manufacturers are well aware of these problems and overcome them by designing circuitry that does not propagate signals of sufficient strength to interfere with other apparatus, or has built-in rejection circuits. You have to anticipate that some electronic circuits could be affected by minute amounts of transmitted power.

We are approaching a time when something will have to be done to build electronic equipment to agreed standards which will not interface with other products. Electronic interface is nothing new, the computer and hi-fi industries have been sorting out such problems for years. The clock cannot be turned back in the yachting industry and more and more electronic equipment will be used on boats.

Just suppose a radio transmission opened up the engines in a computer-controlled fuel system, or using the computer affected the satellite navigation system. I believe that manufacturers in the USA have been getting together to talk about these problems. Perhaps there could be some kind of worldwide agreement to ensure that boating electronic gear is, in future, designed to agreed standards. There should be compatible systems that will interface or some sort of warning given to the user. My problem is solved by switching off the auto-pilot when using the transmitter.

## Safety Rails

Unfortunately, the height of stanchions and the safety rails they carry is usually dictated by what looks good on a particular boat. The smaller the boat, the smaller the stanchion height is the general rule. I say unfortunately because they are meant to keep the crew on deck rather than let them fall overboard. Crew size is more standard than boat size and therefore the minimum height of rails should be 2ft (607mm). The 18in (457mm) size is just about right for legging people up. If the boat will take it, 28in (711mm) stanchions would be better, for then you are getting within the normal hand height for a standing person.

A safety rail on large craft is often made with a wooden top and hinged openings at strategic points. Boats that are to berth stern on in the Mediterranean should have provision for a stern gangway. Smaller yachts usually have wire rigging through stainless-steel or light-alloy stanchions. When there is to be a gangway the stanchion must be braced as in Fig 103. Stanchion bases must not be fixed to the deck with screws, but with bolting through a reinforced area (Fig 104). The reinforcing here was made up of two pieces of ½in (12mm) marine plywood, glued together with resorcinol glue and bonded in place with epoxide resin to fill completely the underside of the coaming moulding over a length of 3ft (914mm). The stress put on the stanchion base, when the stanchion acts as a lever for the full weight of a man falling on it, is enormous. Some stanchions are designed with bracing which will not

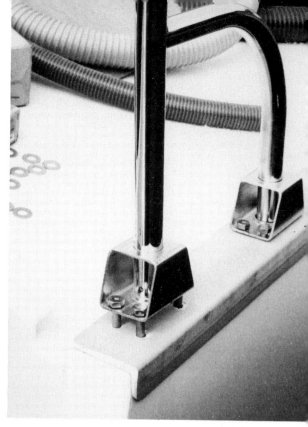

**Fig 103** Stanchion bases through-bolted to reinforcing under the deck coaming

allow a slow collapse when the stress limit is reached. A sudden failure of the bracing will put a sufficient shock load on the tube housing so that it, too, will tear off and project a person overboard. The type shown in the photograph will bend slowly outwards and resist sudden collapse. There are so many different types of stanchion bases that it pays to think how they will perform in a real test, before you make up your mind on a particular model.

The rigging is best made by the professional, perhaps the same one who makes the standing rigging for the mast. Pelican hooks at gangways and rigging screws with fork and swage terminals to connect to pulpit and push-pit ends will then be designed to make sure they do not pull out under severe strain. All you have to do is to specify which kind of ends you need and, once push-pit, pulpit and stanchions are in place, have galvanised garden wire made up into the correct lengths between terminations and send these off to the rigger. The rigging screws will give you some

**Fig 104** Bonded-in marine plywood spreads the stress from deck fittings over a large area of the GRP moulding

tolerance in length and will allow you to get the lines under reasonable tension for a safe handhold, though not too much tension as this will do the deck fittings no good.

Except on very small craft, two wires are better than a single one. As extra protection for small children, firms like Bridport Gundry or Bridport UK, supply netting that can be rigged to stanchions and wires to prevent a child falling overboard.

All stanchion bases and push-pit and pulpit bases should be fastened down on a silicone sealant which should be applied to each bolt so that there can be no leakage through the area where they sit.

## Push-pits and Pulpits

These parts are made professionally from stainless steel, usually about 1in (25mm) diameter. For small boats there are die-cast light-alloy fittings which can be made up with various angle bases and tees so that you can fabricate your own using ⅝in (16mm) diameter tube. Since bending even this small section tube accurately is not easy, unless you have the right mandrels available, it would perhaps be best to let the professional make these parts.

Many suppliers of kit boats will offer these as part of their package deal. If you are to have special ones made up you must supply accurate drawings and be specific about the angle the base has to be welded to the tubing so that when it is eventually bolted into place the base sits square on the GRP surface.

## The Liferaft

The liferaft is a necessity for any sea-going boat. It is expensive to buy and keep to full safety standards with an annual inspection and certificate. A liferaft that is not serviced each year might deteriorate so much that it would be useless in an emergency. For coastal sailors who are usually only out in good weather in daylight, it would probably be better to buy wetsuits and rely on the rubber inflatable tender for any possible short duration emergency. In really heavy weather and for emergency long-term survival, there can be no substitute for the liferaft.

Siting is important. Liferafts come in either a soft valise that can be stowed inside a compartment, or in a GRP container which can be sited on deck. The valise model is suitable for small craft with limited deck space. Sited on deck, the liferaft can be over the side and inflated in seconds rather than minutes. Build in a strong point, such as an eye-plate, to which you can fix the release lanyard. In fact, you need eye-plates to secure a liferaft to the deck so that it is not thrown about in bad weather.

## Life-jackets

Always incorporate a storage compartment for safety equipment when you are working out the interior design of your boat. All too often life-jackets get thrown into lockers where they fester and mildew, gradually deteriorating. Chafe is a big problem. The life-jackets roll around in the locker until the edges become frayed and then whole patches show signs of wear from the constant movement. Try to arrange stowage in plastic bags in a hanging or horizontal position, so that the bags take chafe. They should be stored away from any fire hazard. Inside a cockpit locker next to the fuel tank and engine is the least suitable for stowage.

# 9  MASTS, RIGGING AND DECK FITTINGS

## Masts and Rigging

The wind might be free but you have to spend a lot of money to catch it so that it drives your sailing boat efficiently. If the mast, rigging and sails are to be your prime means of moving, design and installation must be of the highest standards. The designer's specifications on the rigging and sail plans must be adhered to. To alter them might be as disastrous as moving the wings of an aeroplane to a position you liked better. There are, however, some practices that might be questioned. Methods of attaching standing rigging to a GRP hull sometimes leave much to be desired.

Stainless steel is a most commonly used material for deck and terminal fittings, as well as the wire rope for the rigging itself. It has an excellent performance above the water-line and, provided it is not constantly fatigued near its limits, will last many years. Failures seldom occur in the rope itself but are common on terminals and deck fittings. If not on the deck fittings, damage occurs in the laminate around them. A yacht will often go as fast, if not faster, under an efficient sail system than it does with its auxiliary engine. All that power, instead of being put into the hull through the engine beds, is being put in through the foot of the mast and some of the standing rigging, depending on which point the boat is sailing. When a sailing boat goes from one tack to the other, one side of the rigging loses all the strain and it is taken on the other. Several tons of stress may be transferred in this way every time a boat changes tack. The standing rigging takes this strain and at the same time stops the mast from bending, breaking and falling overboard. The mast itself takes enormous stress even when the boat is moored and carrying no sail. The rigging pulls down and, in poorly designed and constructed boats, mouldings suffer compression that soon gives way to stress cracking. Slack rigging will allow a mast to pant.

## The Mast

Most kit boats, and those that are supplied as hulls, will generally have a mast offered with them. However, once you have the mast specification there is no harm in getting a few different quotations. I found the exercise well worth while, the quote from Sailspar of Brightlingsea being 54 per cent less than some other quotes. As I wanted a prototype mast, the personal service they gave was an enormous help.

When ordering the mast, check what other fittings you are likely to put on it. Fig 105 gives rigging details to be considered. Navigation lights (I), radio aerials (H), radar reflectors (J) and radar domes may need a perch on the mast and it is less expensive to have this sorted out at the start than to do the jobs piecemeal.

You must have a scientifically designed radar reflector in which you can have confidence. A tin bucket hauled up the mast is not good enough. The higher you can get an efficient reflector the greater the range at which you will seen.

Electrical wiring for navigation lights, and a radar if you are to carry one, will be best run inside the mast, provided proper rubber grummets are fitted where the wires pass through the metal. It is never a good idea to have running steel-wire rigging and electrical wires inside the mast section where the two could meet and chafe. A compartmented mast section would keep them separate.

The mast on my own boat was not a ges-

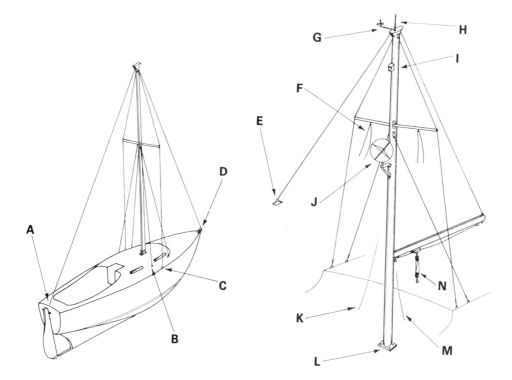

**Fig 105** Rigging details

ture to sailing friends. I had already decided that a mast with a steadying sail was more efficient than having bilge keels on the hull and it also offered features which would increase the efficiency of working the boat and safety. The boom was designed so that the heavy tender could be lifted on and off the aft deck. A double-purchase tackle was rigged to a heavy-duty traveller (N) so that the boat could be moved inboard or outboard during launching. This same tackle could be moved by undoing a single shackle to the end of the boom where it could be used for lifting a man-overboard back into the boat. It is almost impossible for a wet, inert body weighing some 250lb (113kg) or so to be hauled over the topsides of a boat by bending persons trying to get a grasp. An extremely fit person (and not many of us are) might exert a force of 150lb (68kg) provided he had a good grip with both feet and was standing in the most efficient position for lifting. It is more likely that a man might be able to lift 110–30lb (50–59kg) and a woman somewhat less. Many yachts sail short-handed and have no provision for this emergency. The double purchase

tackle reduced the power needed to haul 200lb (91kg) to just 88lb (40kg) and, allowing a loss of efficiency of 20lb (9kg), we would be able to manage with about 106lb (48kg) of effort, well within an average person's capability when hauling on a rope. The effort would be less if the tackle were rove to advantage, but the hauling part would be on the deck rather than running along the mast boom out of the way.

If you are interested in providing this kind of lifting tackle, you will need an expert to work out what is called the triangle of forces. This enables him to calculate safe working loads for mast, boom and the tackles rigged to it. The UK *Admiralty Book of Seamanship* (HMSO) gives a comprehensive explanation and simple methods of estimating stresses and reducing them to safe working loads.

The hollow mast section was used to ventilate the top of the battery compartment. The mast head provided a pitot head which induces low pressure and any explosive gases could flow up the mast to the outside air.

Flag signal halyards (F) were provided to port and starboard on the cross-trees. Flag signalling is a dying art and, in any case, the flags flown are generally so small as to be useless. However, I can fly basic signal flags as well as house and club burgees. More appropriate these days is the VHF radio aerial carried on a special bracket alongside the wind-speed anemometer head (G). Even in a motor boat it is good to know what the wind speed is.

Looking at a typical small sailing boat rig on the left-hand side of Fig 105, note the points of attachment of end fittings to the hull. The backstay takes the real weight when going down-wind and if the mast is stepped on deck it will automatically tension the forestay (D). The backstay forces must be passed right down into the transom and not into the deck/hull joint. The forestay usually terminates on the stem fitting. While most stem fittings either hold the forestay tight because they have a strap which goes over and down the bow to pass the strain where it belongs, into the hull, they fail as anchor-chain rollers. Sheaves and drop-nose pins are too small to prevent the chain from jumping out. Keeping the mast up and the anchor down in bad weather means having the strongest possible fittings, installed in such a way that they cannot rip out of the hull.

Cap shrouds (C) are usually led down from the mast head to the topsides. This is fine in wooden vessels when the strain can be led right down the topsides into the hull with long plates. On modern GRP constructions, however, the cap shrouds may terminate in a deck plate, which is hardly satisfactory. It damages the hull and badly built boats may show cracking in the plate area. The answer is to take the stress right down through the deck and on to a bulkhead designed to take it. The best designs have support for the mast which is often stepped in the deck these days, and strong brackets or chain plates bolted to the bulkhead for fastening the shrouds. Where the plate or bracket head passes through the deck there should be sufficient space to fill with a rubber sealant, (Arbosil 1081). This should be covered on deck with a small plate to protect it from ultra-violet light and the weather. This seal will work with the slight movement of the changing strain passing through it. If the lower shrouds (B) are led to the topsides they need the same treatment. However, in many yachts they are led inboard and terminate on deck with a deck plate of some kind. The stress pattern developed is even worse. By setting the plate in from the topsides, a lever is created for the upward forces to work the hull at the deck joint. This is a design fault, but if you come across it, and there is no handy bulkhead, an extra glassed-in beam will carry the strain where it should be. I had this problem with the forestay of Sea Hound's mast, but fortunately Tylers had built a 2⅓ × 1½in (60 × 40mm) beam across the wheelhouse, already glassed in, and with a little extra reinforcing work I was able to through-bolt deck plate (E).

Fig 104 shows the method adopted for reinforcing the deck plates and stanchion bases, which sit on the raised toe-rail moulding. Laminated plywood lengths were glued with epoxide resin adhesives and then glassed over to spread stress right along the moulding. True, it was above the deck-to-hull joint, but there was a vertical pull through the ½in (13mm) thick GRP and Tylers had provided mechanical fastening as well as glassing for the hull-to-deck joint.

Looking at Fig 105 (L) the mast step plate is usually designed for quick stepping of the mast on deck. It may well have variable position slots on modern racing designs to enable fine-tuning positions to be tried. The step on my boat was fabricated by the mast-maker to my design so that I could lift the mast out easily and yet have a through-way down into the engine space for electric cables and for the batteries to breathe. Just below the light-alloy mast plate I fitted electrical weatherproof sockets and with plugs on the mast cable ends, the detachment of the mast is quick. The topping lift for the boom (K) runs up to a double block on the aft side of the mast which takes the main halyard (M) for the mizzen.

## The Practical Details of Standing Rigging

Most standing rigging is of stainless-steel wire rope of either 1 × 19 (one rope with nineteen wires in it) or 7 × 7 (seven strands each comprising seven wires to make one rope). The first type is the most common in use because the fewer the wires the higher the breaking load for a given diameter. Also, it has lower stretch and is cheaper.

Standards for terminal fittings are as variable as standard threads for nuts and bolts. Many organisations recommend standards — and seem to make sure they do not conform to anyone else's. However, there are improvements as international trade in boat fittings increases. Your concern is to buy bottle screws, toggles and shackles to fit the deck fittings. Go for either imperial or metric sizes, not a mixture.

Rigging is really an expert's job, though there are several makes of hand-fitted terminals aimed at the DIY market.

Mechanical Roll or Rotary Hammer swaging is a process approved by aircraft and marine industries alike. Whenever you see a standard for an aircraft component it will be of the highest quality. True, you have to pay for this, but why is your life less important than that of an aircraft passenger? An improperly swaged fitting will not take the full strain any more than a bad splice so that even using one of these specialised machines, a novice could still make a mess of things. You will have to send precise measurements of the length of rigging overall and the terminal type — eye, fork or stud. Whichever type of terminal is used, it is put over the wire and then its body is rolled right into the wire strands. It is there for good.

The alternative to mechanical swaging is the use of hand-fitted terminals. I specified Norseman brand terminals as I believe these to be the best available in the UK (address in Appendix C). Norseman supply excellent instructions with their product and if you take great care to comply with them, you could turn out a professional job. Careless fitting will lead to failure.

I had my rigging professionally made. I sent them my rigging plan with the specification of the terminal I wanted and coils of galvanised wire cut to the exact lengths of the standing rigging and safety wires. The rigging fitted perfectly first time. It will be an expensive mistake if you measure incorrectly or specify the wrong kind of terminal, so take your time over this.

## Setting up Standing Rigging

This will be one of the last jobs before the boat goes in the water. Delay ordering until you can calculate the launching day as this is a great help with cash flow!

You must first rig the boat to check that you have given the correct specification and that items have been made up properly. You will then probably have to dismantle the lot and take the mast down for transportation to the launching site.

Once launched, the rigging is set up again and this time every single screw, clevis pin, split pin and lock nut must be checked for tightness. Any protruding split pins must be taped over and anything that might chafe sails should be suitably protected. Plastic covers are usual these days for the cap and lower shrouds, especially around the rigging screws.

Running rigging can be tried out when the standing rigging is first completed and if you get a really calm day, even the sails can be hoisted while the boat is still on the building site.

Plans will include specification and positioning of sheet winches. They are expensive items and you should go for quality and reliability. Consider, too, the cost of spares and the kind of after-sales service available. Make sure that you install them so that when they have to be serviced the job is as easy as possible.

Two makes that have had world-wide acceptance by yachtsmen come from Lewmar and Gibb. Quality, reliability and service are assured if you install them in the right way. They will have hefty loads applied to them and these loads will be transferred through the mounting base into the hull. Check that the moulder has provided the correct reinforcing in the laminate beneath the winch base. If not, you must make a workmanlike job of it.

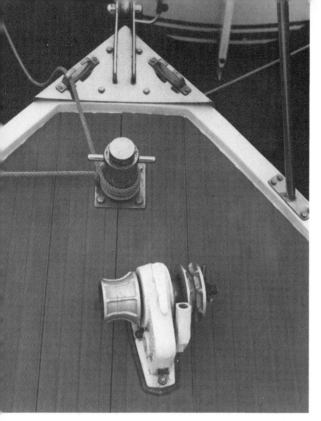

**Fig 106** Foredeck arrangement; the Moyle Tigress winch was offset to port of the bollard to give a fair lead to the anchor chain over the stem-head fitting but avoiding the bollard

When the moulder is working on an inverted deck mould he is easily able to get at the narrow coamings where main sheet winches often sit. If the reinforcing is not up to standard or has not been beefed up at all, you will probably end up upside down in some locker trying to get glass cloth and resin into place. The moulding on to which the winch will be bolted must be perfectly flat. You can bolt direct to a flat surface. If it is slightly rounded you will have problems. For preference, use a circular teak winch pad, usually available through chandlers' catalogues. This gives a flat mounting and can be replaced if damaged by chafe. The teak pad takes some of the compression strain as you through-bolt the winch. Both pad and winch can be bedded down with a small quantity of silicone rubber sealant. Go sparingly as some makes of winch have drain holes in the bottom which must not be blocked. The winch-maker will specify and probably supply the correct bolts and all you need to

do then is drill the holes to take them and, when you have the winch in place, not overtighten them. Always clean off excess rubber sealant the moment the bolt is tightened.

When choosing sheet winches for smaller boats you will have a choice of top or bottom action. Top action winches where the handle is inserted in the top are quicker in use, the winchman being able to wind the handle full circle. The bottom-handled winch is less prone to having handles lost overboard. Fixed handled winches may get in the way but they are safe from being catapulted overboard.

**Deck Fittings**
Time and time again you see toy deck-fittings put on yachts. They are worse than useless — they are downright dangerous. Boatbuilders insist on scaling down the size of fittings for smaller boats; aesthetically pleasing, perhaps, but certainly not practical. Prissy rope cleats on foredecks are expected to take the weight of the anchor, fairleads that are excellent for chafing ropes are fitted and some boats have no stem-head fitting to take the chafe and wear of the anchor chain. I have seen a boat where the stem head and much of the bow was sawn off by a chain that had jumped the stem-head fitting in a storm. The damage caused the boat to sink.

GRP may need extra chafe plates made of stainless steel over the edge of moulding where ropes would normally lie and chafe. The Ferodo mouldings on *Sea Hound* have been very practical and non-slip as well as giving the top of the toe-rail moulding some protection.

Fig 106 shows the foredeck arrangement I decided on. I had the stem-head fitting welded up from 1/4in (6mm) stainless-steel plate by Uni-tools of Brixham. They also made up the anchor bollard to my design. This acts as a waterproof ventilator, chain pipe through the threaded lid and as the main bollard. Reinforcing of 1/2in (13mm) thick marine plywood was moulded in by Tylers to disperse what could be dangerous loads right through the forward part of the boat. Any anchor bollard must have massive reinforcing if it is to be safe in bad weather.

Now that anchoring is perhaps not so much in fashion, a foredeck winch is perhaps a luxury many boats can do without. For the cruising man, it still offers much in the way of back relief when the anchor needs hauling in and anno domini is against you. I find the Moyle Tigress double-acting winch a boon. This has both a chain gypsy and rope winch drum. Some care in its siting was needed. It was placed slightly off-centre and angled so that it did not interfere with the anchor bollard but was able to provide a fair lead from the stem-head fitting for either rope or chain.

When ordering the anchor winch you should specify the size of chain you are to use so that the gypsy can be supplied to match it. The maker may ask for a sample of chain which, like so many items in yachting, comes in a bewildering range of imperial and metric sizes, plus one or two others of no definite size which would not fit any gypsy. When fitting the winch to the deck, think about putting it on a slightly raised platform to ensure the underside drains quickly and dries out. I made a shaped teak platform ½in (13mm) thick and bedded it and the winch with silicone rubber sealant. I put plenty on all the foredeck bolts so that even with the worst strain they will not let in water.

### Cleats

These should be chosen so that they hold the kinds of rope you will be using on deck. Many are too fiddly and ropes get jammed under them. When you do get decent-sized ones, position them carefully so that cleated-on fenders will be in the right positions. They need as much reinforcing under the deck as any other item.

Small deck fittings like cleats are available in a variety of metals, many of which have shortcomings. Brass, chrome-plated, looks good for a few seasons, but then it turns decidedly tatty and has to be re-plated. There are die-cast products in all sorts of rubbish metals which crystallise like sweets and then break in a random and remarkable way. Then there are excellent sea-water-resistant light alloys which retain their looks over many years. For the aft deck bollards I wanted a fairly massive pair, 13½in (343mm) long and capable of taking a weight of 5,512lb (2,500kg) — just in case I needed to tow a boat. Once again, I had had Tylers reinforce the aft deck in a wide area around where they were to be through-bolted. A local engineer cut a light-alloy plate 15 × 6in (381 × 154mm) and I bolted it up through the deck with ¾in (19mm) stainless-steel bolts.

Wherever you are jointing stainless-steel fasteners into aluminium, an inhibiting chromate jointing compound (Ministry of Aviation specification DTD 369A) gives excellent results. Instead of the white powdery product of bimetallic corrosion forming and jamming the bolt into the fitting, you will have a clean joint which can be easily taken apart in the future.

All other deck fittings — cleats, fairleads, bollards, etc — were made of stainless steel. GKN had then just developed a method of casting stainless steel and I was fortunate to get some of the first products. They have been immensely strong and still look good as new. The only problem was that they were more expensive than the general run of similar fittings. This must be set against their life and excellent strength.

# 10  THE PROOF OF THE PUDDING

As you near completion of your boat, if you are like I was, you will undoubtedly be very near to a state of exhaustion. The state of anxiety experienced will depend on how hard you have been working to achieve a definite launching date. And there are always a hundred-and-one jobs to be completed in the last twenty-four hours. The kind of nightmare thoughts that flash through your mind are: 'Have I built her too heavy so that she will turn turtle?', or, 'As she is lowered in will she keep going down to the bottom because I have left off a skin fitting?'

A week or two before the launch, you can at least draw up a final check-list of jobs to be completed and, more important, pre-launch checks so that you can have the confidence to enjoy launching day rather than it contributing to a heart attack!

## Launching Organisation

Wherever you are going to launch your boat you will need to inform some authority, be it waterway, river or harbour. Inland Waterways Board will immediately want to sell you a licence, while the harbour master will rub his hands as he prepares to take harbour dues off you. You will also have to arrange with these people, or the boatyard/marina owners, for a mooring or berth. With such crowded sailing areas, you would have done well to go on a waiting list right at the beginning, or even before you started building. It can sometimes take years to get a berth.

In tidal waters, look up the time of high water and time the launch when it is most convenient to launch without danger of grounding, running out of daylight or when officials and people helping you want to get off home at the end of their working day.

Your finished craft is likely to be higher and heavier than when the hull arrived.

Remembering this, check out and order crane hire, police escort, and insurances as already outlined in Chapter 1.

It is not a good idea to have the launching party on the actual launching day. There are bound to be hold-ups and your nerves will probably be in a taut condition. You will want to stay aboard to make sure you really have not left a valve out in the bottom of the boat.

## The Launching Party

In a couple of days, I was over the launching trauma and ready to crack a bottle over the stem head to name the boat. The local press and television may well be interested in your achievement but even if not, it is nice to share it with friends and those who have helped. I found that nearly forty people had helped build *Sea Hound of Dart,* rather scotching the myth of the DIY project.

## Trials

Once out on the mooring, it was a couple of days before I had the strength to start trials and for this I was fortunate to have two experts from the engine-makers with me. When you buy the engines it is worth enquiring if this kind of service is available as it can do a lot to ensure full warranty should you later have engine problems. It has been said that unless an installation conforms with the manufacturer's recommendations a warranty is null and void. If your installation passes the eye of the expert, then this is a great reassurance to maker and owner.

Although it was spring, I rowed my two engineers to the boat in a snow storm. We were white all over by the time we climbed aboard, and squalls of snow were hurtling down the harbour on a strong northerly wind that made conditions aboard distinctly uncomfortable — not exactly ideal conditions, but the engineers coped manfully, if pale about the gills.

First there was a visual inspection:

1  Fuel system. Look for leaks, check that appropriate fuel valves are opened or closed, fuel filters tight, visible filters full (primed by using the hand lever on the main fuel pump of the engine). Set ready to start.

2  Check all oil levels in engine and gearbox. Top up as necessary as levels change slightly when afloat.

3  Check cold-starting fuel supply on diesel engines.

4  Check the electrical installation starting side. Battery electrolyte levels, tightness of cable terminals at battery and engine. Batteries are best delivered fully charged just before the launch. A lastminute check on their charge and, if need be, a slow trickle charge to top them up is all that is needed before launching. Check wiring to instrumentation. Turn battery master switches on.

5  Inspect cooling system. Fill to correct levels, bleed air according to manufacturer's handbook, turn on sea-cocks, inspecting for any leaks and put ready to start.

6  Check exhaust system. Exhaust outlets cocks open. All hose and casting joints tight and ready for operation. Check wiring to instrumentation.

7  Bleed diesel fuel system of all air (manufacturer's handbook).

8  Check alignment of shafting now boat is afloat.

Item 7 was the beginning of our undoing. The northerly wind had strengthened, snow flurries covered the forward windows of the wheel-house and the smell of diesel knocked out my two engine men. The toilet system was inspected and speedily christened. It worked, and by this time I was the only one capable of sorting out the rest of the engine inspection and starting them. Distant voices gave me instructions and in no time I was able to turn the starter key to 'heater' and seconds later to 'start'. It seemed amazing that after almost three years from the engines being delivered to the moulder, they started almost immediately.

**Engine Running Checks**

With the engines started and checked for fuel, oil or cooling water leaks, instrumentation must now be checked.

The engine manufacturer's handbook should give you engine working temperature, oil pressure and possibly gear-box oil pressure. Perhaps it sounds obvious, but should there be anything abnormal showing on the instruments, switch the engines off immediately. It is less expensive to do this than persist in trying to find out what is wrong with the engines running. Sometimes, though you have bled the cooling water, there may still be small pockets of air which cause the engine temperature to soar. Always put a cloth over the pressure cap so that you do not get scalded with boiling coolant. When the engine runs up and maintains a steady temperature, look at all other parts of the installation:

1  That the generator warning light is now off and stays off. New drive belts need checking as they stretch.

2  Check shafting and stern-gear with the boat fully moored up. Put into gear and look and listen to shafting to see if it is running sweetly. Only engage gear for a very short time at low rpm so that nothing is at this stage strained.

If all is well, you are now ready to take her off the mooring for the first time.

New boat engines have to be run in just like a car. For the first few hours faying surfaces of piston on cylinder wall, crankshaft on big end and in fact all rotating surfaces literally scrape themselves to a decent mirrored finish and the scrap metal is carried off to the oil filter. The engine needs to work at a steady rpm and load, but not idling. Go out for gentle runs and wait until the engines are run in for speed trials.

**Sea or River Trials under Power**

Your new boat will have a character of her own when under way. You will have to get the feel of her steering. Well away from other craft, see how well she answers the helm. Twin rudders usually need some 'toe in' correction so that the boat runs straight. It is worth spending time getting this right. It will save on auto-pilot working and fuel consumption if you can get straight running with little or no pressure on the helm when under power.

When the engine or engines are run in the time has come for you to establish a repertoire of the yacht's behaviour.

From the beginning of trials it is a good idea to keep a log of what has been happening and any modifications needed to get everything working correctly. The repertoire consists of the skipper getting to know what the boat will do so that he can handle difficult situations with some confidence. A nice bright day with a bit of wind and a quiet area of sea are the main prerequisites. Near slack water is best for initial trials. A dan buoy with a suitable small anchor is the only other. Drop the buoy in the quiet area and see how the boat behaves in relation to it. Regard it as a reinforced-concrete harbour wall and try to avoid crashing into it at different speeds. See how the boat answers from going ahead to going astern and how long she takes to stop. Go alongside the buoy as though you were alongside a berth. How does she answer to the helm as you get under way? Try each manoeuvre with the wind in different directions. How does wind and current affect her at low speeds? Find out how the steering works when you put the engines into neutral and come up slowly to the buoy. Often outboards and outdrives behave badly and lose all steering when the propellers are not rotating.

After stopping and starting, turning the boat is the next manoeuvre to assess. Find the turning circle of the craft both to port and starboard. In twin-engined boats try turning on rudders and engines and then on engines alone. Discover the smallest space the boat will turn in. In all manoeuvres try different engine speeds to find the minimum speeds that allow you to keep full control. The lowest speeds can still inflict damage when a weight of several tons comes into contact with another boat or quay wall. With twin-screw boats try all manoeuvres on one engine, in case you lose one power unit and have to limp home and moor up or berth.

Going astern is never the same on any two boats. This important manoeuvre can get you out of a lot of trouble, but in marinas where finger berths are close together it is inevitable that you have to be very good indeed at this. With the bow up to the dan buoy, see how the boat reacts on going astern from different points of the compass with the wind in a different direction. Find out the minimum engine rpms needed to give you confident full control astern. Try steering astern on engines alone and on rudders alone with the engines out of gear.

You can play these games for days while the engines are being run in. Fifty hours' running-in time may seem to drag, but there are plenty of jobs to get on with before your boat is ready for sea.

**Instrument Calibration**
The depth-sounder must be calibrated so that you have accurate indication of depth. Depth shown might be at the transducer head, from the water-line or surface of the water, or from the lowest point of the keel. The maker's handbook will indicate whether there are adjustments to calibrate the instrument to your liking. If there is no calibration you can expect the depth shown to be that from the transducer head to the bottom. A comparison check with a weighted calibrated log line lowered over the side will give the exact picture. Measure the depth precisely and at the same time note the reading on the depth-sounder. Knowing how much below water the transducer head is you can work out any corrections needed by altering the instrument if it has a datum control or by adding the depth from water-line to transducer head to any given reading.

Deep-keeled sailing boats often carry gravity-operated transducer switches which operate two transducers. True soundings can then be obtained when the boat is sailing to windward on either tack. Obviously, you will need to be sailing like this to check out the gravity switch and to see that each head is operating correctly.

Similar checking must be carried out with forward-looking transducer heads. With voice-synthesised depth-sounders make sure you are not lulled completely to sleep by the tone of voice.

## Compass Errors

This subject would need a treatise to do it justice. It is not the province of the amateur navigator to adjust and correct a steering compass. You can, however, get some idea of expected errors so that when you engage the professional you can give some pointers. And you can make sure you are not causing errors by putting outboard engines or even sets of keys or tools close to the compass. I recommend that you try 'swinging' ship yourself to define the likely errors. You must be away from steel pontoons and preferably on a buoy where the boat can be swung with the yacht's tender to face all points of the compass. Do the first swing with the engines stopped and the second with engines running.

Another method, which I did with *Sea Hound*, is to get a number of transits worked out in the vicinity of a harbour. If you have a large-scale chart of a harbour where you can find enough room to manoeuvre without getting under the bow of any ships, take off notes of a number of transits. If you see two objects perfectly in line, then you are situated somewhere on a line produced from them (Fig 107). Transits give excellent results when and if the skipper can hold a steady helm while the crew take compass readings when the boat is in perfect alignment with the two transit points. The best lines are obtained when the distance between the observer and the nearest object does not exceed three times the distance between the objects in transit. Readings on reciprocals are taken. All readings are magnetic so that the bearings taken of transits must be read from the chart as magnetic. At this stage the professional should be called in and he will furnish you with a deviation chart after he has done any necessary work correcting your compass.

## Calibration of the Log

Since one of the basic necessities of naviga-

**Fig 107** Using transits for initial compass check

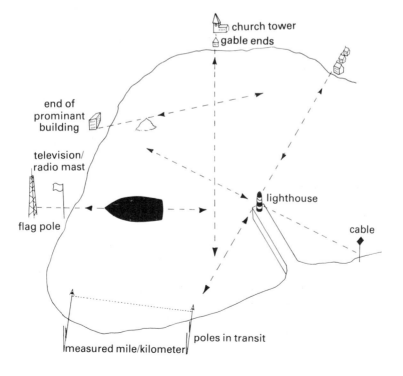

tion is to know the boat's speed and the distance it has run, calibration of the log is as important as swinging the compass.

Basically, you need a nautical almanac, such as Reed's, where a full explanation and tables will be found. Again, the system depends on the use of transits (bottom of Fig 107). The boat is run several times over the course, noting the precise time at the start of the run and again when the second set of transit marks is passed. Make allowance for tidal streams or currents in rivers. This means making several runs up- and down-stream and then calculating the true speed after allowance has been made for the effect of the current or stream. It is worth checking the facilities for correction before you buy the log. I have Brooks & Gatehouse equipment and their handbooks give instructions for calibration, which brings me to another important point.

## Manufacturers' Pamphlets

It is worth keeping all the pamphlets — engine-maker's, WC, log, echo-sounder, taps, filters, radio — in fact, all the information which could give you, or a future owner, details of how and where to get spares, how to lay up each item correctly, maintenance, etc. Manufacturers rightly complain that customers waste their time when information is given in detail in their handbooks but not read. Boat-builders may lose all this paper before a customer buys his boat. As you have built your own boat, keep all the leaflets and manuals for future reference.

**Fig 108** We have lift-off . . .

# 11  WATER UNDER THE KEEL

Much water has flowed under the keel of *Sea Hound of Dart* since she was built and, although much has changed in the boating world since 1975 when she was launched, I can truthfully say that the products and systems I chose first time round have, for the most part, withstood the test of time admirably.

However, in 17 years I have carried out certain modifications which are detailed here to bring readers right up to date for this edition. At the initial planning and construction stage, cash flow usually limits what one can actually spend. The priority list inevitably means that some things which one would like to have will be left off the final reckoning.

It is still important, though, that future needs are anticipated so that modifications are less costly and more quickly achieved. If, for example, you anticipate the future need of a radar set, then wiring in an extra MCB with cables to the wheelhouse is easily done when the initial wiring is taking place. Thinking ahead certainly pays dividends. Lots of removable panels fixed with screws may not be as smart as fixed lined panels without a fixing in sight, but I know which I prefer when modifications are to be put in hand.

**The fresh water system**
An earlier modification detailed in previous pages was the first modification undertaken to the fresh water system, but we later had persistent trouble when the foot valve lost the prime to the pump. At that stage it was decided to put in a complete new modern system.

While some parts of the original copper pipework could be retained, much of it was ripped out and an ITT Par CW84 pump with an CW70 accumulator tank was installed. The accumulator tank is a pressurised vessel which evens out the pulsations of a diaphragm pump. The water then flows evenly out of the faucets and, more importantly, actuates gas water heater diaphragms properly. When looking at the installation space it is important to note whether the accumulator tank is one that can be installed horizontally as well as vertically, as this varies from model to model.

Cleghorn Waring and Co advised on the systems specification since it is most important to ensure that pump pressure and capacity are matched to the length of pipe runs and to the pressures needed to supply water heaters, showers and a given number of faucets. Unfortunately I did not have room for a calorifier which heats the water indirectly from the engine's cooling system.

The company supplied 15mm Acorn plastic piping and push-fit plastic connectors. The plastic water pipe systems presently available are a boon to the amateur builder as they can be so easily and quickly put together, using only a small hacksaw to cut the pipe, and your fingers to tighten up the joint fittings. In fact, installing a complete new system and joining it into the pipework and the Vaillant heater took a mere five hours including time to take the pictures of the pump installation (Fig 109) sitting on the same site in the WC compartment. Basically the pipework run of the new system is the same as in Fig 83.

**Installation of electric anchor winch**
Sadly it is not only *Sea Hound* that is

**Fig 109** The ITT Par fresh water pump and accumulator tank sitting in the same place as the original electric pump (in the WC compartment)

seventeen years older as I write this chapter, and it has become necessary to relinquish some back strain and replace the manual Tiger winch with a Simpson-Lawrence electric 12v. Anchorman 700. The fitting instructions, wiring specification and diagram from S-L were first class, which made the job very straightforward.

The wiring (Fig 110) of any winch so far removed on the foredeck from the main battery needs care to ensure there is no voltage drop; hefty starter cable (quite expensive) is needed for the main run. However, switching is by solenoid operation and therefore the operation of the winch from both deck and wheelhouse only needs normal size electric cable. The 46 amp load from the battery through an MCB to the winch

motor was safe to be carried by 25mm square cross section cable. If the run is less than 13 metres total (+out and −return) then less costly 16mm sq cable will suffice. The draw on current is very heavy but lasts for only a short time. As the engines would always be running when the winch is in operation it was decided to link on to the starter batteries rather than the service ones. The Anchorman circuit is completely isolated from the starter circuit by the use of a micro circuit breaker (MCB) of 50A capacity installed on the main bulkhead where the other MCB's are fitted.

Running very stiff cables is not so easy in a completed boat, but it was a blessing that many parts of *Sea Hound's* panelling had originally been screwed into place for easy removal. Chafe protection to the cable was given where it passed through bulkheads. Silicone rubber sealant was used, and as this sets it provides excellent location and chafe protection.

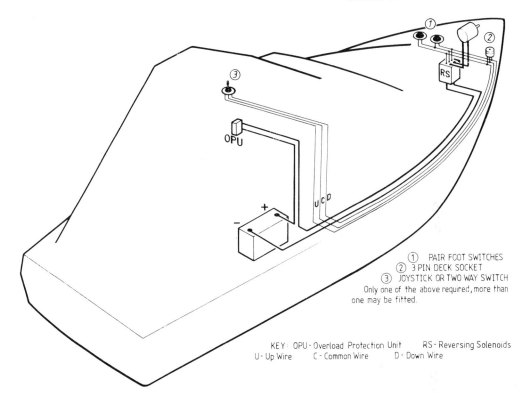

**Fig 110** Wiring of reversing installation

I was concerned to have no ugly holes in the deck where the Tiger had been located; fortunately the correct lead for the Anchorman used some of the old bolt holes (Fig 111) without modification. Only two new bolt holes and the shaft drive hole needed to be drilled, and the deck plug for the hand control managed to cover the other holes in the deck so the job looks very neat. I also needed new calibrated anchor chain to fit the new chain drum.

The chain hawse into the chain locker is still situated on the head of the substantial bollard (Fig 106) and therefore is not self feeding. However, as I do not favour any holes on the deck where green water could enter I do not mind feeding the chain by hand when it is laid out or recovered on deck. In fact, most anchoring these days is what I call 'picnic anchoring' for short stays, so a rope anchor warp is ideal.

Arbosil 1096 sealant was used to seal both winch and electric plug for the winch control to deck plates which I turned from inch (25mm) teak.

**Bilge pumping modifications**

Deterioration of electric bilge pumps, float switches and wiring is almost inevitable in the harsh corrosive environment where they are situated. *Sea Hound's* engine space was originally fitted with two electric pumps. The Stuart Turner fell victim to a disintegrated impeller (age hardened plastic) and the Rule to corroded circuit wiring near the pump itself.

In fact the Stuart was easily repaired but it was felt that it had been a mistake to have both pumps wired into the main distribution board MCB's. The reason for this was that I always isolate the batteries when the boat is left and in doing this, I left no bilge pump in operation to clear rain water that might enter the bilges.

It was therefore decided to rewire the Rule which was still in good order and

**Fig 111** The electric winch utilized the same
holes as the Tiger had done as far as possible

replace the Stuart with an ITT Par diaphragm bilge pump and Hydro-air pressure switch wired as in the sketch (Fig 112). The ITT Par is a diaphragm pump and this type is self-priming and can be situated well above bilge water levels.

The new bilge pump was to be wired directly to the service batteries so that it would remain working even when the rest of the electrical system was turned off. As the pump was to be on its own circuit it was essential for it to have its own fuse and switch so that the circuit could be isolated for servicing either the pump or the pressure switch. The junction/fuse box (fig 113) was made up in the workshop from items obtained from Tristate (Southern) Ltd.

The ITT Hydro-air pressure switch is interesting because, unlike a float switch, the electrical switching is totally remote from the bilge water. The actuation of the switch depends solely on pressure on a column of air which increases as the bilge water depth increases, and vice versa.

The modification was quickly effected as the pump used the same diameter pipe and skin fitting as the original one.

## Spurs rope cutters

After *Sea Hound* caught her first crabpot, sadly without any crabs in it, I decided that fitting rope cutters to the propeller shafts would be a wise addition. Spurs cutters (Fig 114) were chosen, which are the ones favoured by the RNLI and were supplied by Harold Hayles.

Fitting them was a fairly straightforward job. As cutless bearings on the P brackets were showing signs of wear it was decided that both propeller shafts would be removed and both bearings and cutters fitted at the same time. Normally it is not necessary to remove the bearings or shaft. Before any dismantling took place I took the dimensions shown in Fig 115a which Hayles required. In cases where there is insufficient space between the front face of the propeller hub and the bracket it is possible to fit a spacer at

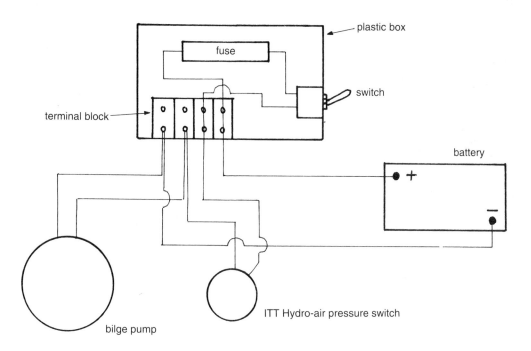

**Fig 112** Direct to service battery wiring diagram for the ITT bilge pump

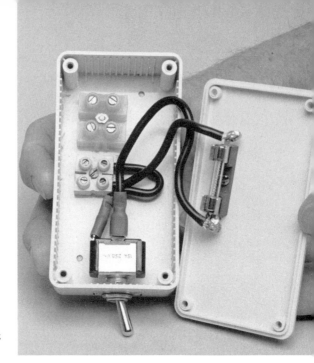

**Fig 113** Junction fuse box used to protect and switch the new ITT bilge pump

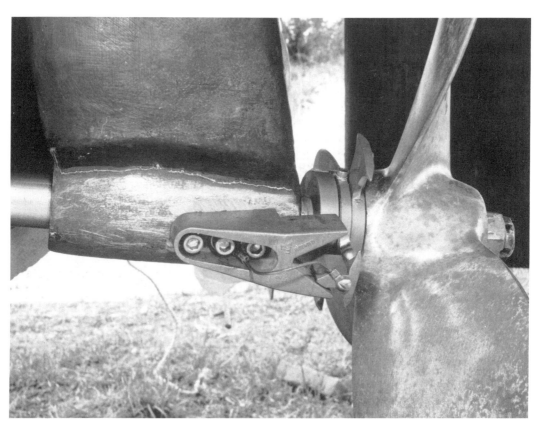

**Fig 114** Spurs cutter fitted on *Sea Hound of Dart*

the inboard end of the shaft to provide this necessity.

The actual engineering was very straightforward, and two cutters were fitted in one afternoon. The work consisted of correctly placing the holding block on the P bracket and marking three holes to be drilled and tapped. The hard aluminium bronze can only be drilled at low speed if you are to avoid burning the drill bit out. Check that the existing grub screws which hold the cutless bearing in the P bracket do not coincide with the new holes for the cutter. You can rotate the block slightly to avoid them.

A bottoming tap is needed if the cutless bearing is to be left in situ because there is a danger of drilling too far into the shaft bearing itself. However, with the bearing removed I did not have this problem. The cutters themselves only required a screwdriver to fasten them to the shafting. Since the rotating cutter moves on an isolating plastic bearing, it is necessary to use the bonding wire supplied in the kit to be certain that electrolytic corrosion is avoided. Both bearings and bonding wire require annual inspection and regular renewal.

It is worth mentioning that if you are removing cutlass bearings, make sure that you remove all the grub screws that retain them. These bearings always need a proper puller to get them out, but if you leave just one grub screw in it will strip the thread off the stoutest puller.

## Deck fitting modifications

As you will have gathered from the photographs (Fig 27), the deck fittings originally fitted to *Sea Hound of Dart* were of a stout nature but although it is traditional to have full length springs from bow and stern, the practice of using mid-ship springs has advantages. It still stops the boat moving forward or aft but the load is spread over more fittings and there is quicker access for the deck hand. Speed is of the essence when belaying a rope, and although many would disagree, I found the raked models inadequate to belay two or three $\frac{1}{2}$in(12mm) ropes despite them being $12\frac{1}{4}$ in (311mm) long

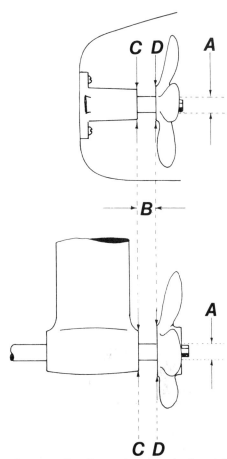

**Fig 115a** The dimensions required to order a Spurs Cutter:

    A –   the diameter of the prop shaft
    B –   the distance between the back of the bearing housing and the front face of the prop hub
    C –   the diameter of the bearing housing end face
    D –   the diameter of the propeller hub forward face

by $3\frac{1}{4}$ in (83mm) high. I therefore designed larger matched bar type bollards which used the same holes as the original raked bollards. Carisbrooke Marine Engineering made these specially for me as well as a matching pair of similar design but with a base that would fit neatly on the raised side-deck coaming for those to be fitted amidships. Incidentally, when you are

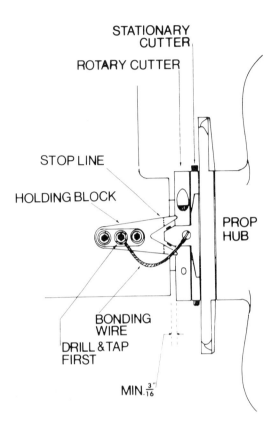

STATIONARY
CUTTER

ROTARY CUTTER

STOP LINE

HOLDING BLOCK

PROP
HUB

BONDING
WIRE

DRILL & TAP
FIRST

MIN. $\frac{3}{16}$"

**Fig 115b** The component parts of the Spurs Cutter. Note the 3/16in (1/2cm) clearance required between the after shaft and the front face of the cutter assembly

buying stainless steel deck fittings look for quality in the way that the welds are cleaned up. They should have invisible and smooth weld lines where any upstands join the base plate.

Just in case you imagine that the few modifications listed here have not been sufficient to keep me out of mischief over these many years I must say that in any boat, no matter how well built, there must be constant vigilance and maintenance to the whole of the fabric if an owner is to minimise the disappointment of breakdowns, failures, or worse. This will pay off when you come to sell, a well maintained craft keeps her price better than a poorly maintained one.

While many yachtsmen tend to put the boat away as quickly as possible at laying up time, I tend to take time not only to make her safe from the storms and frosts of winter but to get repairs well in hand before the really cold days set in. I keep a regular log to remind me of repairs and maintenance that need to be done immediately she is craned ashore, a list of spares and replacements needed, and a projected list of any new items for late installation.

I know that to lay up the engines properly takes me three solid days. After dosing the diesel fuel with a corrosion inhibiting oil, the engines are run up to working temperature before changing filters and oil in each engine, gearbox and reduction gear. At the same time the raw (sea-water) intake is changed over to fresh water from the shore so that the raw water side of the cooling system is thoroughly flushed. The fresh water side of the of the indirectly cooled Perkins engines are either left dry after the last flush with fresh water containing a rust inhibiting emulsifying oil, or are left 'wet' with a top quality anti-freeze in the system. In many engines which use light alloy extensively, manufacturers specify that they should be laid up wet, so it is worth reading the handbook to check.

Today anti-freeze based on propylene glycol already correctly diluted is available from a number of manufacturers such as Silkolene. The new products like Silkolene Pro-cool have superior cooling and anti-corrosion performance, as well as easier protection which lasts up to two years when topped up with the same product.

Once ashore, the last of the water in the inlet raw water strainers is drained down and the impellers from the raw water pumps removed. Bilges are cleaned out and left dry throughout the boat. Air cleaners are cleaned out and orifices sealed with plastic clingfilm and the exhaust lines are disconnected at the manifold if the system is to be left 'dry'. Owners seldom realise that if water is left in the exhaust system it will produce high humidity which will find its way through any open valves into the engine,

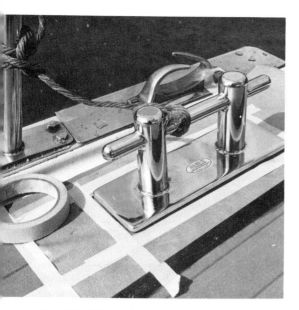

**Fig 116** When fitting the new Carisbrooke bollards brown paper masking and tape were used to keep the silicone sealant off the deck. The bollard is roughly tied on so that it is not lost overboard when bolting up from underneath.

where it will condense into water and set up cylinder and valve corrosion. It is no good putting a bung on the exhaust outlet in the hull if the pipe already contains water.

As far as the engines are concerned the last job is to spray them with a wax aerosol often used by the car trade to preserve new cars. Perkins produce a full range of laying up products and they can be safely used on any other makes of engine besides their own. The wax is easily removed with turps substitute at fitting out time.

The domestic side of the programme in-cludes disconnecting and removing the toilet so that the inlet and outlet valves can be completely dismantled and greased. In 17 years I have never had the Lavac fail, which is probably due to the annual cleansing of pipework and attention to the valves. In any case, all skin fittings – exhaust, water inlet, log

and WC – are left open to give ventilation to the hull.

It seems a waste of time to wash down and polish the hull and upper works when you are going to throw a cover over it. However, a winter cover resting on salt and grime will grind into surfaces, and those exposed to the weather will last longer if they are protected with a quality marine polish. I always expect to spend a whole day de-rigging the mast, putting up the ridge pole, tying chafe gear in place on the stanchions, and getting the winter covers on and adjusted.

*Sea Hound* always looks more of a wreck by the time all the dismantling has been done but I am sure that when the winter cover goes over her she really is proofed against the worst weather that might come along. Its good to sleep easy in ones's bed when the winter storms are raging, even if you are already thinking about fitting out in the spring.

The fitting out is simply a reverse of the laying up process. No, I do not enjoy anti-fouling, nor is any one anti-fouling product the answer to every owners prayer. There are so many variables in the water environment – temperature, salinity, light, pollution and chemical enrichment from land drainage – that what may suit one boat in one location will not necessarily suit another elsewhere and fresh water anti-foulings are obviously different in com-position. The best advice is to see what long standing yachtsmen in the area have used successfully on their own boats.

After all this hard work there is always a blissful feeling when everything is ready, the starter button is pressed and the engines roar into life again. I expect I will enjoy *Sea Hound* for many a year to come. By now we have both come to depend on each other, and I am sure that if you do start with a hull, you will find as much reward in the relationship as I have with *Sea Hound of Dart*.

# APPENDIX A

**Rough Costing List**
This list covers both motor and sailing boats. It is a rough
guide to the items you might want to incorporate into the
boat, and you will probably find a few more to add on.

|  |  | *Sea Hound Supplier* |
|---|---|---|
| Hull, bare | £ | Tylers |
| Hull, plus superstructure | £ |  |
| Jointing these two, plus bulkheads | £ |  |
| Wheel-house | £ |  |
| Fuel tank/s | £ | Tylers |
| Water tank | £ | Tylers |
| Sewage tank | £ | Tylers |
| Delivery cradle | £ | Tylers |
| Delivery charges from moulder | £ |  |
| Lifting-off crane hire | £ | British Crane |
| Ballast | £ |  |
| Fendering | £ | Wilks |
| Rudders | £ | Tylers |
| Steering gear plus wheel | £ | Mathway |
| Auto-pilot | £ | Sharp |
| Deck hardware (stanchions and cleats) | £ | GKN |
| Samson post | £ |  |
| Anchor winch | £ | Moyle |
| Pulpit/push-pit | £ |  |
| Navigation lights | £ |  |
| Basic engine/s plus instrumentation | £ | Perkins 4.108 |
| Propeller/s | £ | Teignbridge |
| Shafting | £ | Delta |
| Engine mountings | £ | Perkins |
| Fuel-tank hardware/fillers/piping/clips | £ | Delta |
| Fuel filtration | £ | Lucas/CAV |
| Ventilation fans (engine-room) | £ | AK Fans |
| Ventilation/accommodation space/toilet | £ | AK Fans |
| Ducting for ventilation | £ | Flexible Ducting |
| Cushioning for cabins | £ | Dunlopillo |
| Cabin/wheel-house windows | £ | Essex Aluminium |
| Jointing compounds/bedding compounds | £ | Adshead Ratcliffe |

| | | *Sea Hound Supplier* |
|---|---|---|
| Fasteners/screws/washers/nuts | £ | Mountford/GKN |
| Wood planks for interior furniture | £ | |
| Plywood BS 1088 for interior furniture | £ | Thames Plywood |
| Engine controls/stop controls and all cables | £ | Morse/Teleflex |
| Electrical wiring cables | £ | |
| Electrical distribution board/ circuit breakers | £ | |
| Electrical conduit (plastic) | £ | EGA Tube |
| Electrical Accessories | £ | HellaMarine |
| Mast/boom | £ | Sailspar |
| Standing rigging | £ | |
| Running rigging/blocks/winches | £ | Gibb |
| Sails/steadying sail | £ | |
| All ropes, running rigging/anchor warps mooring warps | £ | |
| Windscreen-wipers | £ | Wynn |
| Gas installation regulator/piping clips, joints/flexible sections | £ | Calor |
| Cooking stove | £ | |
| Refrigerator | £ | Aqua-Marine |
| Cabin hardware/hinges, hooks, etc | £ | Aqua-Marine |
| Ensign staff and ensign | £ | |
| Anchors (main and kedge) | £ | Aqua Marine |
| Depth-sounder | £ | Brooks & Gatehouse |
| Log | £ | Brooks & Gatehouse |
| Wood glue, 'Cascamite' | £ | Borden/Wessex Co |
| Wood glue, 'Cascophen' resorcinal glue | £ | Borden/Wessex Co |
| Laminating resins or epoxides | £ | Borden/Wessex Co |
| Laminating tools and brushes | £ | |
| Horn | £ | Klaxon |
| Electrical storage batteries | £ | Lucas |
| Heavy-duty cable for batteries | £ | |
| Battery terminals and isolating switch | £ | Albright |
| Legs to support craft | £ | |
| Hand fire-extinguishers | £ | Pyrene |
| Built-in fire extinguisher for engine | £ | Pyrene |
| Cathodic protection | £ | |
| Galley and toilet compartment sinks | £ | |
| Taps and plumbing for sinks | £ | Aqua-Marine |
| Laminates for galley, toilet compartment surfaces | £ | Formica |
| Brass panel-pins (½in (13mm), ¾in (19mm), 1in (25mm), 1¼in (32mm), 1½in (38mm)) | £ | |
| Life-jackets (at least one for each berth) | £ | Avon |
| Liferaft | £ | Avon |
| Safety harness | £ | |
| Pyrotechnic distress signals | £ | Pains Wessex/ Schermaly |
| Crockery (plastic) | £ | |
| Cookware (pans, etc) | £ | |
| Lifebelts | £ | |
| Cabin heater | £ | Remotron |
| Installation piping clips, etc for above | £ | Calor |
| Cost of lifting off and transporting finished boat to water | £ | |

# APPENDIX B

Any book out of print is usually obtainable through your local library

## Useful reading

Bobrow, Bill & Jinkins, Dana, *Classic Yacht Interiors* Concepts Publishing (USA) and Collectors Books (Cirencester, UK) 1983

Bowyer, Peter, *Boat Engines* (David & Charles)1979

Butler, Paul & Marya, *Fine Yacht Finishes for Wood and Fibreglass Boats* (Adlard Coles Nautical)

*Calor Gas Dealer Information* 3rd Avenue, Millbrook Trading Estate, Southampton, Hants. SO9 1WE

Collins, Mike *Fitting out a Fibreglass Hull* (Adlard Coles Nautical) 1991

Donat, Hans *Engine Monitoring on Yachts,* VDO Marine GmbH Frankfurt

Elbert & Malony, *Your Boat's Electrical System,* (Hearst Books, USA) 1988

Fox, Uffa, *Seamanlike Sense in Power Craft* (Peter Davies) 1968

French, John, *Electrical and Electronic Equipment for Yachts* (Adlard Coles Nautical) 1973

Goring, Loris, *Marine Inboard Engines: petrol and diesel* (Adlard Coles Nautical) 1990

Goring, Loris, *The Care and Repair of Marine Petrol Engines* (Adlard Coles Nautical) 1981

Henderson, Keith, *The Outboard Motor Manual* (Adlard Coles Nautical) 1992

*Marine Electrical Systems* (Lucas Marine, Camberley, Surrey) 1982

Mudie, R & C, *Power Yachts* (Adlard Coles Nautical) 1977

Nicholson, Ian, *Designers Notebook,* (Adlard Coles Nautical) 2nd ed. 1988

Nicholson, Ian, *Small Steel Craft* (Adlard Coles Nautical) 2nd ed. 1983

*Perkins Installation Manual* (Perkins of Peterborough)

Phillips-Birt, Douglas, *Motor Yacht and Boat Design* (Adlard Coles Nautical) 1966

Pike, Dag, *Boat Electrical Systems* (Adlard Coles Nautical) 1992

*Sell's Marine Market, Marine Trade Directory* (Benns Business Information Services) An annual publication and a gold mine of addresses when building your own boat.

Sleight, Steve, *Modern Boatbuilding: methods and materials* (Adlard Coles Nautical) 1985

Smith, Ben, *Design Your Own Yacht* (Adlard Coles Nautical) 1988

*River Thames Handbook* (NRA Thames Region, King's Meadow House, King's Meadow Road, Reading RG1 8DQ)

Verney, Michael, *Complete Amateur Boatbuilding* (Adlard Coles Nautical) 4th ed. 1990

*Volvo Penta Installation Handbook, Light Marine Inboard Engines* (Volvo Penta Agents)

Warren, Nigel, *Marine Conversions* (Adlard Coles Nautical) 1982

# APPENDIX C

The companies and agents who helped in the original project are still trading in specific products mentioned. Their products performed satisfactorily over seventeen years on *Sea Hound of Dart*, which is a tribute the their quality. Also listed are firms whose products I have used in later modifications to the boat, and hull moulders of sailing boats mentioned in text(*).

| | |
|---|---|
| Adshead Ratcliffe & Co Ltd, Belper, Derbyshire DE5 1WJ Agent EC Smith & Sons, Unit H & J, Kingsway Industrial Estate, Luton LU1 1LP; Tel 0582 29721 | *Marine sealants* |
| A K Fans Ltd, 32/34 Park Royal Rd, London NW10 7LN; Tel 081 961 6888 | *Electric fans* |
| Aqua-drive (GKN), Halyard Marine Ltd,(see below) | *Universal drive couplings* |
| Aqua-Marine Manufacturing, 216 Fair Oak Road, Bishopstoke, Eastleigh Hants SO5 6NJ; Tel 0703 694949 | *Hardware and Remotron heater* |
| Blakes Marine Paints Ltd, Harbour Road, Gosport, Hants; Tel 0705 510045 | *Marine paints* |
| Barbican Yacht Construction*, Sugar House, Coxside, Plymouth PL4 0HX; Tel 0752 266246 | *Halmatic 30* |
| Chillington Marine Ltd, Unit 3 Wessex Trade Centre, Ringwood Rd, Poole BH12 3PF; Tel 0202 747400 | *Blakes/Lavac; toilet /valves* |
| Calor Gas Ltd, Third Ave. Millbrook Trading Estate, Southampton SO9 1WE; Tel 0703 777244 | *Gas fittings/ cookers* |
| Carisbrooke Marine Engineering Ltd, 175 Gordon Rd, Fareham, Hants; Tel 0329 233324 | *Stainless steel deck fittings* |
| Cleghorn Waring & Co (Pumps) Ltd, 9/15 Hitchen St, Baldock, Herts SG7 6AH; Tel 0462 893838 | *Water system/ all pumps/plastic pipe and fittings; ITT pumps* |
| Shipmate Marine Electronics Ltd, Unit 5 Elm Court, Crystal Drive, Sandwell Business Pk, Smethwick B66 1RB; Tel 021 552 1718 | *VHF radios* |
| Ferodo Ltd, Chapel-en-le Frith, Stockport, Greater Manchester | *Deck tread* |
| Flexible Ducting, Milngavie, Glasgow; Tel 041 956 4551 | *Ventilation ducting; WC flexible pipe* |
| Gabriel Microwave Systems Ltd, Flexible Hose Division, Battle Road Heathfield, Newton Abbot TQ12 6XU; Tel 0626 834222 | *Armoured flexible fuel lines* |

| | |
|---|---|
| Halyard Marine Ltd, Whaddon Business Park, Southampton Rd, Whaddon, Nr Salisbury SP5 3HF; Tel 0722 710922 | *Acoustic cladding* |
| Hella Marine Equipment, Daventry Rd, Industrial Estate, Banbury, Oxon OX16 7JU; Tel 0295 272233 | *Lighting /cable; electrical accessories* |
| Honda UK Ltd, Power Road, Chiswick, London W4 5YT; Tel 081 747 1400 | *Portable power generators* |
| Harold Hayles Ltd, The Quay, Yarmouth, Isle of Wight, PO41 0RS; Tel 0983 760373 | *Propeller rope cutters* |
| International Paint Ltd, Yacht Division, 24/30 Canute Road, Southampton SO9 3AS; Tel 0703 226722 | *Paints and anti-foulings* |
| Key Terrain and Celuform, Larkfield, Maidstone, Kent; Tel 0622 717811 | *Plastic waste pipe and plastic sections / architrave* |
| Lucas Marine Ltd, Frimley Road, Camberley, Surrey GU15 2PL; Tel 0276 63252 | *Batteries, marine electrics* |
| Parsons Mathway Marine Ltd, Mercury Yacht Harbour, Satchell Lane, Hamble, Southampton SO3 5HR; Tel 0703 453765 | *Steering gear* |
| Simpson-Lawrence Ltd, 218/228 Edmiston Drive, Glasgow G51 2YT; Tel 041 427 53331/8 | *Electric anchor winch; chandlery* |
| TBA Industrial Products, PO Box 40, Rochdale OL12 7EQ; Tel 0706 47422 | *Duraform; Heatshield* |
| Teignbridge Propulsion Group, Forde Rd, Brunel Ind Estate, Newton Abbot, Devon TQ12 4AD | *All stern gear and valves* |
| Tristate (Southern) Ltd, PO Box 234, Southampton SO9 7RB; Tel 0703 234999 | *Electrical wiring accessories* |
| Tyler Boat Co Ltd, Tyler House, Morley Rd, Tonbridge, Kent TN9 1RP; Tel 0732 771101 | *Hull mouldings-Neptunian 35* |
| Norseman Gibb Ltd, Ollertonn Road, Ordsall, Retford, Notts DN22 7TG; Tel 0777 706465/7 | *Rigging terminals wire rope* |
| Sadler International*, 29/31 Dawkins Rd, Hamworthy, Poole, Dorset BH15 4JY; Tel 0202 679409 | *Sadler 26 and 29 hull mouldings* |
| 3M UK Plc (Marine Products Group), 3M House, PO Box 1, Bracknell, Berks RG12 1JU | *Abrasives and finishing systems* |
| VDO Instruments Ltd, Holford Way, Holford, Birmingham B6 7AX; Tel 021 356 2266 | *Engine instruments* |
| V-Tronix Ltd, Unit 29 Newtown Business Park,Ringwood Rd, Poole, Dorset BH12 3LL; Tel 0202 715517 | *Radio aerials* |
| Wessex Resins and Adhesives Ltd, 189/193 Spring Road, Sholing, Southampton SO2 7NY; Tel 0703 444744 | *All adhesives used on boat* |
| Wynstruments Ltd, Staverton Airport, Gloucester GL2 9QW; Tel 0452 713264 | *Window wipers* |

# APPENDIX D

**Starting and Service Battery Circuit Schematic for *Sea Hound of Dart***

The drawing below (Fig 117) is the original Lucas Marine schematic drawing used in my boat. The blocking diodes (d1, d2) were added so that either key switch would actuate the Albright relay rather than originally when only one key switch was wired to do this. It is not included in the main text as it has since been modified to include fully suppressed Lucas 17 ACRM alternators with Lucas Marine LM 119 screened radio interference suppression units. When the original engines were supplied these units were not available, the Perkins units

having the AC11 as standard equipment. The original system served its purpose well until it was decided that installing electronic gear justified the suppression modification.

Owing to limited staff availability, Lucas Marine are not able to provide a circuit design service but are able to offer advice on a design if submitted for scrutiny. I would certainly advise any builder to take advantage of this excellent service.

**Fig 117** Schematic of starting and service battery circuits initially used on *Sea Hound of Dart*

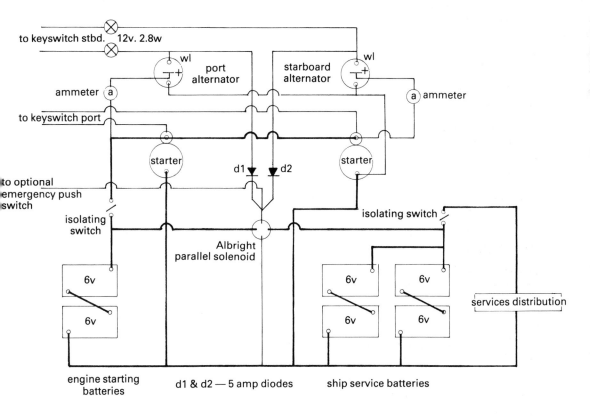

# ACKNOWLEDGEMENTS

Neither this book or my boat would have come into existence if it were not for the great encouragement and help given to me over many years by the yachting press, especially the past editors of *Motorboat & Yachting* – Erroll Bruce, John Lilley, Dick Hewitt and Alex McMullen – and, in recent years, Emrhys Barrell and Kim Hollamby of *Motorboats Monthly*. All have allowed me to share my boating experiences with their readers.

I would also like to thank the firms who have supplied me with the many reliable products which went into *Sea Hound of Dart* and which have contributed enormously to the pleasure my wife and I have had from cruising.

My thanks to John Tyler and Douglas Greenhead who supplied the Goring-Hardy hull and the many engineers at Perkins of Peterborough who have patiently taught me about their engines and suffered harassing sea conditions to ensure I had built the engines into the boat correctly.

I cannot name individually all the good folk who gave me help and information but I thank them here for their contribution to the enjoyment I have had and continue to have while building, modifying and cruising my boat.

Finally, my thanks to Eric Coltham who took many of the photographs which appear in the book.

**Fig 118** Sea trials — the proof of the pudding . . .

# INDEX

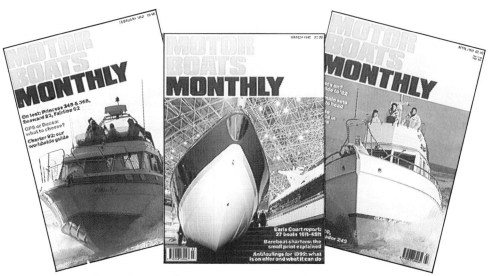